In this book, Manuel Vásquez shows how the contemporary interplay of religion and politics initially fostered a progressive Catholic theology in Brazil, and later, became an obstacle to its further development. In the 1970s, a dedicated core of bishops and pastoral agents drew from Catholic social thought, humanistic Marxism, and existentialism to forge a utopian vision of social emancipation. The "popular" church they constructed inspired a religious renewal and provided the moral and ideological impetus for the emerging democratization movement. By the mid-1980s, the advances made by progressive Catholicism were increasingly threatened by a host of economic, political, and ecclesial changes that reconfigured the role of the church in civil society. In this incisive study of a Catholic community near Rio de Janeiro, Vásquez argues that the plight of progressive Catholicism forms part of a more profound crisis of modernity and humanistic discourses in Brazil.

CAMBRIDGE STUDIES IN IDEOLOGY AND RELIGION 11

THE BRAZILIAN POPULAR CHURCH
AND THE CRISIS OF MODERNITY

CAMBRIDGE STUDIES IN IDEOLOGY AND RELIGION

Religion increasingly is seen as a renewed force, and is recognized as an important factor in the modern world in all aspects of life – cultural, economic, and political. It is no longer a matter of surprise to find religious factors at work in areas and situations of political tension. However, our information about these situations has tended to come from two main sources. The news-gathering agencies are well placed to convey information, but are hampered by the fact that their representatives are not equipped to provide analysis of the religious forces involved. Alternatively, the movements generate their own accounts, which understandably seem less than objective to outside observers. There is no lack of information or factual material, but a real need for sound academic analysis. Cambridge Studies in Ideology and Religion meets this need. It attempts to give an objective, balanced, and programmatic coverage to issues which – while of wide potential interest – have been largely neglected by analytical investigation, apart from the appearance of sporadic individual studies. Intended to enable debate to proceed at a higher level, the series should lead to a new phase in our understanding of the relationship between ideology and religion.

A list of titles already published in the series is given at the end of the book.

THE BRAZILIAN POPULAR CHURCH AND THE CRISIS OF MODERNITY

MANUEL A. VÁSQUEZ

University of Florida

CAMBRIDGE
UNIVERSITY PRESS

PUBLISHED BY THE PRESS SYNDICATE OF THE UNIVERSITY OF CAMBRIDGE
The Pitt Building, Trumpington Street, Cambridge CB2 1RP, United Kingdom

CAMBRIDGE UNIVERSITY PRESS
The Edinburgh Building, Cambridge CB2 2RU, United Kingdom
40 West 20th Street, New York, NY 10011–4211, USA
10 Stamford Road, Oakleigh, Melbourne 3166, Australia

First published 1998

Printed in the United Kingdom at the University Press, Cambridge

Typeset in Baskerville 11/12½ pt   [VN]

A catalogue record for this book is available from the British Library

Library of Congress cataloguing in publication data
Vásquez, Manuel A.
The Brazilian popular church and the crisis of modernity / by
Manuel A. Vásquez.
p.   cm. – (Cambridge studies in ideology and religion)
Includes bibliographical references.
ISBN 0 521 58508 2
1. Catholic Church – Brazil – History – 20th century.   2. Brazil –
Church history – 20th century.   3. Liberation theology – History.
I. Title.   II Series.
BX1467.2.V37   1997
282'.81'09045 – dc21   97-6078   CIP

ISBN 0 521 58508 2 hardback

Contents

General editors' preface

Only twenty years ago it was widely assumed that religion had lost its previous place in Western culture and that this pattern would spread throughout the world. Since then religion has become a renewed force, recognized as an important factor in the modern world in all aspects of life, cultural, economic and political. This is true not only of the Third World, but in Europe and North America. At this moment surprisingly and unpredictably it is the case in the UK. It is no longer unusual to find a religious dimension present in areas of political tension.

Religion and ideology form a mixture which can be of interest to the observer, but which is in practice dangerous and explosive. Our information about such matters comes for the most part from three types of sources. The first is the media which understandably tend to concentrate on newsworthy events, without taking the time to deal with the underlying issues of which they are but symptoms. The second source comprises studies by social scientists who often adopt a functionalist and reductionalist view of the faith and beliefs which motivate those directly involved in such situations. Finally, there are the statements and writings of those committed to the religious or ideological movements themselves. We seldom lack information but there is a need – often an urgent need – for sound objective analysis which can make use of the best contemporary approaches to both politics and religion. Cambridge Studies in Ideology and Religion is designed to meet this need.

The subject matter is global and this is reflected in the choice of both topics and authors. The initial volumes have been concerned primarily with movements involving the Christian religion, but it is intended that movements involving other world religions will be subjected to the same objective critical analysis. In all cases it is our intention that an accurate and sensitive account of religion should be informed by an objective and sophisticated application of perspectives from the social sciences.

Base communities are constantly referred to in any study of the popular church or liberation theology in Latin America, but it is notoriously difficult to get reliable information about the movement. Supporters tend to exaggerate the numbers involved and present it in idealized terms. Detractors feel free to mispresent behaviour, beliefs and objectives. Statistical surveys ignore its spiritual life. One of the aims of this series is to publish studies which arise from careful, local empirical research but which are sensitive to the religious life of communities. The present volume is an admirable example of just this balance. Manuel Vásquez had experience of base communities while a student in El Salvador in the 1970s. To investigate the crisis in the popular church he has recently spent time with base communities in Brazil. His findings undermine many current stereotypes. Liberation theology has failed to respond to the new reality in Latin America, preserving many utopian themes which now lack credibility. Its lay leaders are often isolated from the communities it intended to serve. The new reality is neo-liberalism in its ideological and economic forms. The rapid spread of Pentecostal churches may have been originally to compensate for a lack of attention in liberation theology to the emotional needs of the people, but now Pentecostals are better prepared to live and work within the new situation. This study is a valuable analysis of the actual situation of the popular church. Its findings may give food for thought to leaders of the traditional churches and of course the Catholic Church in particular.

DUNCAN FORRESTER AND ALISTAIR KEE
New College, University of Edinburgh

Preface

My first contact with progressive Catholicism came in El Salvador in 1974. Having just finished parochial school, I decided to enroll in the Externado de San José, a Jesuit-run high school in San Salvador. Just a year before, the Externado had been at the center of a firestorm. There were shrill accusations in the national media that Jesuits were indoctrinating students with atheist propaganda that incited social divisiveness and violence. Many wealthy parents reacted angrily, taking their children out of the Externado. They felt a deep sense of betrayal: a high school which they had built through their generous contributions and which had consistently provided an elite education to their children was implementing a curriculum that emphasized justice and equality and accepting working-class and lower-middle-class students.

The controversy over the Externado was one of the first skirmishes in a long, fierce battle to determine the proper role of the Catholic Church in Salvadoran politics during the 1970s, a period of growing popular mobilization and intensifying government repression. The Jesuits were at the forefront of pastoral innovation in the country, seeking to implement the conclusions of the Second Vatican Council (1962–1965) and the Second Conference of Latin American Bishops in Medellín, Colombia (1968). In addition to changing the academic curriculum at their high school and university to incorporate Catholic social teaching and socio-historical analyses of the Salvadoran reality, the Jesuits had, since the early 1970s, helped create small Christian communities in Aguilares, north of San Salvador. These communities, which came to be known as base ecclesial communities (*comunidades eclesiales de base* or CEBs), were a key pastoral initiative used by progressive Catholics in El Salvador and elsewhere in Latin America to build a "popular church" – a church that would at once serve and be "the people of God," focusing on the poorest sectors of the population.

In Aguilares and nearby villages, the Jesuits brought together impoverished peasants in CEBs where they read the Bible and reflected on the struggles of everyday life. Armed with a greater consciousness of their plight and of the possibilities of transforming it, the peasants formed a union. This increasing militancy alarmed local landowners, who reacted with an escalating campaign of intimidation and repression that led eventually to the assassination of Jesuit priest Rutilio Grande in 1977. Numerous attacks on progressive Catholics followed Grande's murder, claiming the lives of priests, nuns, pastoral agents, lay activists, and even an archbishop.

So it was in the polarized climate of the mid-1970s that I decided to attend the Externado. In retrospect, my years there represent without a doubt the single most important period in my intellectual formation. This is not all that surprising: to be confronted with the works of Adorno, Fromm, Frank, Cardoso, and others can be a turning point, especially at an age in which you are groping for answers to the question of who you are and at a time when the world around you is spiralling into violence.

But it was not so much the content of the curriculum as the underlying method and impetus that left an enduring mark on me. At the Externado, we drank from the tradition that Paul Ricoeur has characterized as "the hermeneutics of suspicion."[1] We developed an abiding passion for truth. We acquired an overwhelming drive to ask questions, to get behind the surface of things, to historicize and contextualize events, to demystify reality, uncovering the clever and the not so subtle deceptions that economic elites and the military government had fabricated to hide the many forms of oppression in Salvadoran society. We learned that the social order was neither a given nor a natural product. Rather, it was contingent, the result of an on-going history of domination and exclusion. This critical realization and the brutality of the

---

[1] P. Ricoeur, *The Conflict of Interpretations: Essays in Hermeneutics* (Evanston, IL: Northwestern University Press, 1974), 148.

situation compelled us to unmask the various forms in which power was being applied around us.

The concern for robust critical thinking continues to lie at the heart of my intellectual endeavors, even as I have distanced myself considerably from the religious roots of that "emancipatory interest," in Habermas's words.[2] Critical thinking need not be wedded to a particular institution or corpus of knowledge. It is grounded on and propelled by the human need and capacity to transcend, by what Foucault calls "our impatience for liberty," the principle of "permanent creation of ourselves in our autonomy . . . a principle that is at the heart of the historical consciousness that the Enlightenment has of itself."[3] Critical thinking is the cognitive expression of a larger, still "unfulfilled project," which found one of its most influential articulations in the Enlightenment, to recover, reflect on and advance humanity's "self-consciousness, self-determination and self-realization."[4] Progressive Catholicism, out of which my historico-critical attitude had emerged, represents but one specific deployment of that larger project.

In the late 1980s, as I embarked on graduate studies in religion, exaggerated reports in the media started to surface that liberation theology was dead and that Latin America was being overtaken by an unstoppable wave of politically conservative, pro-capitalist Pentecostalism. With the Reagan administration in power, it seemed in those years that liberal capitalism, in its supply-side version, was on the verge of conquering the world, even if it had to resort to violent, illegal means, as in the case of US policy toward Central America. That perception deepened as the Berlin Wall collapsed and the Soviet Union disintegrated. Those years also marked the height of the postmodernist controversy, when it became fashionable in US academia to proclaim the demise of modernity's emancipatory project.

In an attempt to go beyond facile readings of the apparent crisis of Latin American progressive Catholicism, I decided to examine

[2] J. Habermas, *Knowledge and Human Interests* (Boston: Beacon Press, 1971), 308.
[3] M. Foucault, "What is Enlightenment?" in *The Foucault Reader*, ed. Paul Rabinow (New York: Patheon Books, 1984), 44.
[4] J. Habermas, *The Philosophical Discourse of Modernity: Twelve Lectures* (Cambridge, MA: MIT Press, 1987), 338.

more closely the fate of liberation theology and the popular Catholic Church in Latin America as embodiments of modernity's emancipatory project. This decision was based on my own intellectual trajectory: I had witnessed too many progressive Catholics – including some of my classmates and teachers at the Externado – give up their lives in defense of the principles of human autonomy and truth to take the demise of modern utopias lightly and abandon myself to self-indulgent deconstructive games.

The decision to study progressive Catholicism in Latin America did not mean that I would take an apologetic, partisan approach. It meant, rather, that I would engage in an exercise in self-reflection, as it were, turning my critical lenses on the tradition that had first given them to me. Through this self-reflective distancing, I wanted to explore the possibility that the crisis of progressive Catholicism signaled the exhaustion of the underlying emancipatory impetus that inspires my critical thinking.

Therefore, my first acknowledgment must go to my peers and teachers at the Externado, for they are the ones who provided the intellectual inspiration for this project. Critical thinking by itself, however, can become impotent, prisoner to an endless exercise of theoretical "navel-gazing." To bear fruit, critical thinking must confront reality, as the people at the Externado well know. Thus, this study would not have been possible without the people of the Pedra Bonita base community in Brazil, whose experiences I was fortunate to share, however briefly. More than anything, it was their thirst for change and their perseverance in the face of contradictions and failures that inspired me to focus on the obstacles to transformative practices at the local level. Pedra Bonita's long, often inconclusive, everyday struggles to fashion a more democratic and just Brazil made concrete for me the implications of the crisis of modernity for men and women in Latin America.

Access to the places and people a researcher wants to study is not always easy. In my case, Marcello Azevedo and Francisco Ivern, both of the Instituto Brasileiro de Desenvolvimento (IBRADES), facilitated the process greatly, providing helpful connections with pastoral agents on the ground. Among these pastoral agents, I am most grateful to Janice Da Cunha, José Gatellier, Ivo Plunian, Mário Prigal and Lourdinha Dos Santos, for sharing with me their insights about the nature, potential, and limitations of the popular church in Rio de Janeiro and São Paulo. They also introduced me to many of the lay grassroots activists in the base communities, biblical circles, and the Ação Católica Operária (ACO), whose lives I have tried to document in this study.

In Brazil, I also received a great deal of assistance from the library staffs at Instituto Superior de Estudos da Religião (ISER) and the Centro Ecumênico de Documentação e Informação (CEDI), particularly from Christian Morais and José Atílio Silva Iulianelli. They were extremely helpful as I sorted through the vast bibliographical material that has been produced locally about the popular church.

In the US, I am indebted to my colleagues and friends at Temple University and the University of Florida. Kyriakos Kontopolous, Susan Lewis, Joseph Margolis, Azim Nanji, John Raines, Richard Schaull, Ofelia Schutte, Hal Stahmer, David Watt, Philip Williams, Howard Winant and Gibson Winter offered valuable observations and critiques that greatly enhanced the final product. I would also like to thank Ruth Parr of Cambridge University Press and the two anonymous readers for the Press.

I am especially indebted to my wife and colleague Anna Peterson for her patient and mindful readings of the manuscript and her incisive theoretical and methodological insights. More than anyone else, she has contributed to sharpening the arguments I advance in this study.

Finally, I want to thank my family: my parents, Manuel and Rosa Consuelo, and my sisters, María Evangelina and Carmen, for their abiding understanding and love. Together with my teachers and peers at the Externado de San José, they have shaped the emancipatory interest that informs my work. It is to them that I dedicate this study.

Introduction

Evangelical Protestantism has almost certainly replaced
Roman Catholicism as Brazil's most widely practiced faith.
The significance of this goes beyond theology: the old Brazilian order, based upon a rigid hierarchy and social immobility, has broken down. A new social atmosphere, one more
flexible and compatible with capitalism and democracy, is
emerging . . .
   A good case can be made that the local Catholic Church's
espousal of so-called liberation theology, with its Marxist,
class-struggle overtones, has weakened, not strengthened,
the Catholic Church among the poor. There is now a
widespread recognition that liberation theology overlooked
the emotional, personal message most people seek from
religion.[1]

SETTING UP THE PROJECT

In recent years, religion has been a major force in social change,
from the Middle East to Eastern Europe, from Latin America to
the US. One of the most dramatic cases of the powerful influence
of religion on political processes has been the Latin American
"popular church" (in Portuguese, *igreja popular*), a set of reformist
institutional and pastoral initiatives, among which liberation theology and base ecclesial communities (CEBs) are key components.
   The Latin American popular church arose out of the Second
Vatican Council's call for the Catholic church to enter into dialogue with the secular world. In this dialogue, "this-worldly"
Catholic doctrines such as the efficacy of works came to resonate

---

[1] J. Marcom Jr., "The Fire Down South," *Forbes* (October 15, 1990), 56 and 66.

I

with notions of intra-historical transcendence (the capacity to act effectively in history), self-realization, and social emancipation embodied in modernist ideologies such as humanistic Marxism and existentialism. The popular church became a prime example of the synthesis of secular and religious utopias, where divine history does not cancel human progress but rather represents its fulfillment.

During the repressive 1970s in Latin America, the popular church's modernist reading of the millenarian message of Christianity provided, in liberation theology, a mobilizing ideology to challenge social injustice and, in the CEBs, a model of a new, more egalitarian society. Indeed, CEBs – small, neighborhood-based groups in which poor people, inspired by their interpretations of biblical images of justice, solidarity, and liberation, seek to transform the world as both a precondition and a sign of the coming reign of God – represented to many Latin American Catholic intellectuals a unique mechanism for internal and external reform. Within the church, they increased the laity's participation and power; outside the church, they strengthened a beleaguered civil society.

Nowhere did CEBs attain greater prominence than in Brazil, where, with support from the bishops and an active core of liberation theologians, they became not only a source of church renewal but a major democratizing force as the country emerged from military dictatorship during the late 1970s. By the mid-1980s, however, CEB growth in Brazil had slowed down considerably while competing religions, especially Pentecostalism, continued to expand rapidly.

These two factors have triggered a sense of crisis among popular church activists, leading them to question the viability of pastoral strategies such as CEBs in reaching and serving the poor. Why are the poor apparently betraying their own emancipatory interests, refusing to participate in a church that is actively working to transform unjust social conditions? Why are many poor people instead joining Pentecostal groups which seem to advocate a conservative or at best quietist stance *vis-à-vis* the status quo? Is it a case of alienation and false consciousness, or is it that the popular church's pastoral methods do not respond to the felt needs of the poor?

This study explores the crisis of the popular church's religio-political utopian project. More specifically, it reconstructs the economic, socio-political, cultural, and religious conditions that have hindered the production and reception of the popular church's message of intra-historical transcendence. These conditions have also created a favorable climate for the acceptance of alternative readings of the Christian soteriological message such as those advocated by certain brands of Pentecostalism.

As I will argue throughout the book, the crisis of the popular church's project and the ascendence of Pentecostalism in Latin America point toward a deeper crisis: that of modernist conceptions of human action, history, resistance, and utopia. Thus, understanding the crisis of the popular church, particularly in one of its most mature embodiments in Brazil, might shed light on modernity's plight.

I contend that the roots of the problems facing the *igreja popular* lie in a widening gap between the goals, demands, and internal logic of its pastoral-pedagogical method and worldview, on the one hand, and, on the other, the emergence of a social configuration that blends elements of a transnational capitalism with local patterns of economic and political activity more typical of pre-modern, patrimonial societies. This hybridization results from the uneven penetration of capitalism in Brazil.

Brazilians have experienced radical changes in their life conditions, especially during the late 1980s when the country's economy underwent a period of crisis and restructuring to reposition itself more competitively in the world market. For the vast majority of the population, and particularly for the poorest sectors, these changes have meant a drastic deterioration of their material conditions of existence. The pressures and needs generated by this deterioration have in turn forced poor people to react defensively, resorting to the pragmatic use of short-term, individualistic, and patrimonial survival strategies drawn from the national political culture.

Poverty is not new to Brazil. In fact, during the 1960s and '70s the struggle to eliminate poverty was one of the key motivating forces behind the popular church's politico-religious activism. In the 1980s, however, the narrow margin of stability that allowed poor people to dream of improvement and to engage in transformative social action was dramatically reduced. The worsening socio-economic situation has redrawn the limits of the possible for poor Brazilians, redefining notions of agency, history, and social change. Faced with a continuous decline in life conditions, with an unresponsive, impotent, and corrupt political system, and with an increasingly unpredictable and baffling economic world-system, many poor Brazilians are experiencing a severe crisis of belief. In the face of this chaotic situation, it has become less and less plausible to claim, as do liberation theology and the popular church, that Brazilians can become the "artisans of their own destiny," that they can, by their own efforts, make their society more rational, just, and egalitarian.

The popular church's eschatological reading of the modernist project of self-consciousness, self-determination, and self-realiz-ation, and its pastoral-pedagogical methods to advance this project stand in stark contradiction to the loss of plausibility of the notion of intra-historical transcendence brought on by the economic and socio-political crisis of Brazilian society. More concretely, the *igreja popular*'s reading of social change conflicts with most poor people's pragmatic reliance on short-term, individualistic, and patrimonial survival strategies. The popular church's emphasis on long-term, structural transformation undertaken by collective emancipatory agents acting from below has become increasingly difficult to carry out, given the constraints facing people, particularly the poor, and given the increasing fragmentation of everyday life. This fragmen-tation has disqualified appeals to and reliance upon a unified, collective emancipatory subject such as "the poor."

The contradiction between the popular church's *Weltanschauung* and praxis and evolving life conditions on the ground may explain not only the loss of appeal of the liberationist message but also the expansion of alternative religious traditions which offer more flexible strategies to negotiate the demands of the economic and political crisis. I hypothesize that the growth of Pentecostalism coincides with the emergence of new conceptions of utopia and transcendence at the grassroots, some of which pose serious chal-lenges to the process of democratization, while others have the potential for strengthening it.

To ground my argument empirically, I focus on a particular

case study: a base ecclesial community on the periphery of the diocese of Nova Iguaçu, a working-class city at the outskirts of Rio de Janeiro. The diocese is known for its vigorous implementation of post-Medellín pastoral and ecclesiological reforms.[2] Drawing from fieldwork in the diocese between November 1990 and June 1991, I trace the evolution of the community from its inception to its present state of decline, showing how changes in the international, national, and local economies interact with pastoral and ecclesial variables to condition this decline. I reconstruct the base community's trajectory through informal conversations, focus groups and in-depth interviews with members located at various levels in the organization, community documents (such as the logbooks of the base community, the neighborhood association, and of the local chapter of Catholic Action), and my own observations of social, religious and political events.

I first map out at the micro- (community) level the obstacles and contradictions that have hindered the pastoral-pedagogical activists of progressive Catholics in the evolving (macro) economic context. Then I turn to the ways in which the case study may help us understand the overall crisis of the popular church in Brazil, of progressive Catholicism, and of modernity's emancipatory project.

SOME THEORETICAL CONSIDERATIONS

As characterized above, this study seeks to link macro- and micro-levels of social analysis.[3] I believe that only by elucidating the relations of reciprocal determination between local and global processes can one apprehend the complexity of social phenomena.

Recent readings of the crisis of the *igreja popular* range from detailed ethnographic studies of particular religious communities,

---

[2] On the popular church in Nova Iguaçu, see S. Mainwaring, *The Catholic Church and Politics in Brazil: 1916–1985* (Stanford, CA: Stanford University Press, 1986). Mainwaring stops at the mid-80s, a time when the full effects and complex dynamics of the crisis were not completely apparent.

[3] Micro-dynamics and macro-processes are linked by interconnected, intermediate levels of social activity. An example of these "meso-levels" in my study is the diocese of Nova Iguaçu, which connects global institutional forces (i.e., the Vatican conservative offensive) and local practices and organizations (Pedra Bonita's CEB).

that neglect larger social and cultural dynamics,[4] to institutional approaches which, concentrating on intra-ecclesial politics at the elite level, do not consider the impact of the crisis at the grassroots.[5] This study seeks to avoid the shortcomings of these partial readings. On the one hand, I examine how the crisis affects the life and work of grassroots Catholic activists and pastoral agents. I am interested especially in capturing the local actors' interpretations of the crisis and of their pastoral strategies to negotiate it. On the other hand, I place these interpretations and strategies in the context of power dynamics that take place at the institutional (church), national, and international levels.

My interest on the local actors' perceptions and reactions arises, first, from the need to ground empirically my speculations about the fate of progressive Catholicism in Brazil and other modernist emancipatory grassroots projects in Latin America as capitalism enters a new phase of globalization and deepening, as it penetrates into regions and spheres of life hitherto unexploited. This phase is characterized by "flexible forms of accumulation" that permit capital to flow across existing geographical and temporal boundaries, not only transforming the configuration of the working-class worldwide but also generating new challenges for local communities. According to David Harvey, flexible accumulation has "allowed capital to shed its social responsibilities not only in the workplace . . . but also toward the communities in which it operates."[6] He elaborates his argument: "Multinational corporations [have] ransacked the globe for new profit opportunities and [have been] prepared to abandon their home bases to take advantage of them, taking capital and employment to wherever they judged conditions to be most advantageous." This approach has had "radical implications for the functioning of labor markets, for work

[4] See for example J. Burdick, *Looking for God in Brazil: The Progressive Catholic Church in Urban Brazil's Religious Arena* (Berkeley: University of California Press, 1993).

[5] See for example R. Della Cava, "The 'People's Church,' the Vatican and the Abertura," in *Democratizing Brazil*, ed. A. Stepan (New York: Oxford University Press, 1989), and "Vatican Policy, 1978–1990: An Updated Overview," *Social Research* 59, no. 1 (1992), 171–199; J. Daudelin and W. E. Hewitt, "Latin American Politics: Exit the Catholic Church?" Paper delivered at the conference on "Church, State, and Society in Latin America: Sociopolitical and Economic Restructuring Since 1960," Villanova University, Villanova, PA, March 18–19, 1993.

[6] D. Harvey, "Flexibility: Threat or Opportunity?" *Socialist Review* 21, no. 1 (1991), 72.

styles and labor skills, for the quality of life, and for patterns of consumption."[7]

The second reason for the focus on local perspectives is that, since the popular church's stated goal is to serve the (poor) people, it is necessary to identify the specific ways in which it is fulfilling and/or failing to fulfill the concrete expectations and needs of the people. Only then can we evaluate its success in implementing its emancipatory project. Such an evaluation may help sociologists of religion and those interested in the interaction between economic and cultural change to construct comparative studies of the differential appeal various religious traditions have on the ground in the emerging socio-economic context.

Finally, and most importantly, since it is the local actors who experience the effects of global and structural economic changes, it is crucial to gather their perceptions and reactions in order to understand the specific transformations of the everyday world upon which and within which they act.

Although local actors bear the brunt of macro-structural changes in their daily struggle for survival, they do not always perceive the multiplicity of determining factors that accompany these transformations. Even when they can name the needs and constraints they face, local actors are often not able to trace the historical roots of these needs and constraints, or the links the latter have with systemic processes. This is because the actors are immersed in these processes in ways which demand immediate attention to often life-threatening effects and which limit access to socio-analytical tools.

Intellectuals, on the other hand, possess, as Bourdieu notes, a relative "distance from necessity," that is, a capacity awarded by their privileged position to "neutralize ordinary urgencies and bracket practical ends."[8] Taking advantage of this capacity, I introduce my own interpretation of the crisis of the popular church in Brazil. This interpretation historicizes and contextualizes the crisis, elucidating its local, national, and global components. The theoretical framework that informs this interpretation is the world-

---

[7] Ibid., 67.
[8] P. Bourdieu, *Distinction: A Social Critique of the Judgement of Taste* (Cambridge, MA: Harvard University Press, 1984), 54.

systems paradigm, which in my view provides the most synthetic and coherent critical approach to global economic transformations to date.[9]

There have been already some attempts to apply the world-systems perspective to the study of religious phenomena.[10] Nevertheless, these efforts have tended to remain at the abstract and macro-level, focusing on general notions such as the "new world order" and "globalization" and failing to indicate how analyses of the transformation in the capitalist system may help us understand the nature of religious choices, beliefs, and practices in particular historical settings. Sociology of religion's persistent concern with developing grand models of secularization together with the emergence of overly mechanical game-theoretical approaches to religious behavior has exacerbated this ahistoricism further. Moreover, analyses informed by the world-system paradigm have tended to ignore cultural and ideological elements or to present them as mere reflections of material processes. My study of the obstacles faced at the local level by the popular church's utopian ideology and emancipatory pastoral practices in the context of contemporary capitalism and changes in world Catholicism seeks to address these weaknesses.

The tension between the macro and the micro and between local and outside knowledge is not new to sociology. Ever since Weber proposed a methodological individualism to counter-balance Marxist holism, sociological theory and research has been disabled by what George Ritzer calls a "micro-macro extremism."[11] The first extreme includes scholars who count as social facts only the observable behavior of individuals and small groups. For these micro-sociological empiricists, including approaches such as exchange theory, symbolic interactionist, and ethno-

[9] See I. Wallerstein, *The Modern World System*, vols. 1–3 (New York: Academic Books, 1974–1989); and J. Smith, I. Wallerstein, et al., *Creating and Transforming Households: The Constraints of the World Economy* (Cambridge: Cambridge University Press, 1992).

[10] See among others W. C. Roof, ed., *World Order and Religion* (Albany, NY: State University of New York Press, 1991); and R. Robertson, "The Globalization Paradigm: Thinking Globally," in *Religion and the Social Order: New Developments in Theory and Research*, ed. D. Bromley (Greenwich, CT: Jai Press Inc., 1991).

[11] G. Ritzer, "Micro-Macro Linkage in Sociological Theory: Applying a Metatheoretical Tool," in *Frontiers of Social Theory: New Syntheses*, ed. G. Ritzer (New York: Columbia University Press, 1990).

methodology, larger collective mechanisms do not exist. The social space is constituted by the aggregation of individual behavior across time and in different micro-situations. "Structures" are, at best, heuristic devices which the researcher introduces to order the world. At worst, they are unfounded abstractions that divert attention from real social facts, leading to erroneous analyses of social reality.

For the other sociological camp, which includes structuralism, structural functionalism, systems theory approaches, conflict theory, and certain forms of Marxism, the behavior of particular individuals, though appearing spontaneous and erratic, results from underlying symbolic and material arrangements which transcend the will of any given individual. It is in this sense that, as Durkheim argued, these arrangements are "collective social facts."[12] Macro-theorists believe that institutional, structural and/or systemic arrangements determine individual behavior, compelling the actor to behave in specific ways given her/his position in those arrangements.

Often the dispute between micro and macro approaches is accompanied by other disabling dichotomies such as those between subjectivism and objectivism, agency and structure, and the mental and the material. In this book I have sought to avoid getting caught in these unproductive dichotomies, attempting to bring into play macro and micro levels of analysis, as well as subjective and objective visions and cultural and economic realms of activity. However, I have not merely juxtaposed the various terms. Rather, I have tried throughout the essay to establish relations of mutual determination between micro and macro levels of analysis, moments of interpretation, and fields of praxis. Like Giddens and Bourdieu, I believe that social facts are best characterized not in terms of dichotomies (which one must then somehow bridge inductively or deductively), but in dialectical terms.[13] A social fact has both micro and macro-referents, it is at the same

---

[12] E. Durkheim, *The Rules of Sociological Method* (Glencoe, IL: Free Press, 1938).

[13] On the epistemological basis of a dialectical approach to social practice see A. Giddens, *The Constitution of Society: Outline of the Theory of Structuration* (Berkeley: University of California Press, 1984); and P. Bourdieu, *Outline of a Theory of Practice* (Cambridge: Cambridge University Press, 1977).

time structuring and structured, it both produces and reproduces micro–macro social reality, and it contains "mental" as well as material elements.

In unraveling the crisis of Brazilian popular church's utopian project, I explore the ways in which larger structural processes express themselves at the local, everyday level, shaping, constraining, and enabling the interactions, perceptions, and strategies, particularly religious ones, of situated social actors. I examine the ways in which systemic processes that transcend local dynamics and knowledge generate material and cultural pressures and needs for historically located, embodied individuals. As Giddens correctly notes, "All social systems, no matter how grand or far-flung, both express and are expressed in the routines of daily social life, mediating the physical and sensory properties of the human body."[14]

Needs, interpretations, resources, and practices at the personal, household, and community levels that are conditioned by systemic processes, in turn, set the limits of intra-historical transcendence, that is, of the extent to which actors may engage in practices that challenge the effects and causes of larger structural processes. In other words, micro-environments provide the horizons within which social actors construct, maintain, and transform the social order. Micro and macro dynamics are, thus, constitutive of each other. In Giddens's words, "the structural properties of social systems are both medium and outcome of the practices they recursively organize."[15]

On the question of structure versus agency, I steer a middle course between those who see social action as generated from disembodied structures and those who picture it as issuing from the individual conceived abstractly, either as a totally sovereign subjectivity or as a purely rational consciousness always guided by a means–ends, calculative rationality. I focus on the actions of situated individuals who must work strategically with the resources at hand, which often include a limited knowledge and control of all the factors involved, in order to construct viable micro-environments of existence within the constraints of macro-social processes.

This view corresponds with sociologist Ann Swidler's concep-

---

[14] Giddens, *The Constitution of Society*, 36.   [15] Ibid., 25.

tion of culture as a "'tool kit' of symbols, stories, rituals, and world-views which people may use in varying configurations to solve different kinds of problems."[16] Culture, with religion as one of its central components, offers a repertoire of discursive and non-discursive resources from which individuals may draw to articulate identities and to construct alternative "strategies of action" to deal with the particular existential predicaments they confront. Not all social actors have the same access to these resources or face the same problems. Both the problems at hand and the resources to deal with them depend greatly on the actors' social position. Although power configurations are sustained and/ or challenged only through the activities of the social actors, they transcend their control and full understanding.

This reading of social action may help us to understand the logic behind the ethos and strategies of Brazil's urban poor. Poor people are subjected to the pressures of deteriorating material life conditions which they do not have the power to control because of their disadvantaged position in the social configuration. Thus they must devise micro-strategies to adapt and survive, drawing from a surrounding "settled culture," in Swidler's words, which is often characterized by authoritarian, clientelist and exclusionary patterns of activity and intersubjectivity. As a result, although poor people's micro-strategies may be an effort to navigate, and even to resist, the perils of hazardous macro-social processes, they often end up reproducing the power structures. Counter-hegemonic strategies, such as those articulated by the popular church, which seek structural transformation through long-term, grassroots political engagement may not be viable for the Brazilian urban poor given the pressing existential demands and constraints for social mobilization they face. This fact may explain in part the Brazilian popular church's present crisis of participation and mobilization.

A conception of culture as a tool kit of resources presupposes an understanding of strategies of action as "cultural products": "The symbolic experiences, mythic lore, and ritual practices of a group or society create moods and motivations, ways of organizing experience and evaluating reality, modes of regulating conduct,

---

[16] A. Swidler, "Culture in Action: Symbols and Strategies," *American Sociological Review* 51 (1986), 273.

and ways of forming social bonds, which provide the resources for constructing strategies of action."[17] If this is true, then, we can begin to examine the interaction between macro-social (structural and systemic) and micro-cultural (identity formation and everyday activity) processes, developing analyses of "how culture is used by actors," as Swidler notes, "how cultural elements constrain and facilitate patterns of action, what aspects of a cultural heritage have enduring effects on action, and what specific historical changes undermine the vitality of some cultural patterns and give rise to others."[18] In other words, we can begin to ask why liberationist Catholicism seems less attractive to many poor Latin Americans than Pentecostalism in the context of contemporary capitalism.

This brings us to our last dichotomous pair: the mental versus the material. To transcend this dichotomy, I work with a non-reductive type of materialism that recognizes the density and determining force of all forms of human practice. All forms of human practice, even those considered symbolic and cultural, have a decisive effect in defining the configuration of everyday life; they all shape the individual's field of experience, giving rise to meaningful transformative or reproductive action. A non-reductive materialism allows us to have a fuller understanding of poor people's "lived experience":[19] the different economic, political, and cultural forces that constrain and enable their "being-in-the-world."

Non-reductive materialism does not imply that social practice is ultimately "undecidable" or indeterminable. Obviously there are different fields of human practice, each with its particular institutions, rituals, locales, and its own logic for the production, circulation, and consumption of such artifacts. The task for critical social science is not to trace determination in the last instance to the deepest social stratum (i.e., the mode of production) as a "geological conception of materialism"[20] would have it. Rather, it is to identify in a particular historical setting the main force that defines a social configuration, taking care to show how these dynamics intersect with others.

---

[17] Ibid., 284.   [18] Ibid.

[19] I borrow this term from Marxist historian E.P. Thompson. See "The Poverty of Theory, or an Orrery of Errors," in *The Poverty of Theory and Other Essays* (New York: Monthly Review Press, 1978).

[20] A. Touraine, *The Return of the Actor: Social Theory in the Postindustrial Society* (Minneapolis: University of Minnesota Press, 1988), 31.

THE STRUCTURE OF THE BOOK

This study of the crisis of the Brazilian popular church begins by introducing the latter's ideological and theological bases in chapter 1. This chapter explains what the Brazilian popular church is, presenting the key elements of its utopian worldview and pastoral-pedagogical methodology. It also identifies the ways in which this worldview and methodology appropriate conceptions of human agency and history that are fundamental to modernity's emancipatory project, particularly in its Hegelian-Marxist version. Obviously, such an effort requires that I offer a definition of modernity.

I should add here that I understand ideology in a non-normative fashion. I do not associate it with false consciousness, fetishism, and/or alienation. As we shall see later on, such an association is the product of a form of totalitarian Enlightenment-based rationality that is now in crisis. I define ideology not as opposed to right consciousness, but as a more or less coherent ideational framework, a worldview, formulated in support of a particular set of interests. It is possible for a worldview to lead to oppression if it reinforces the power effects of other social dynamics in the political and economic fields, such that it "naturalizes" a given social configuration, making it appear as a normal and necessary order of things. Nevertheless, one should not define ideology as being necessarily negative or oppressive. In my view, liberation theology and the popular church's worldview represent a utopian ideology born of an interest in fulfilling the preferential option for the poor.[21] This book, as such, is an effort to evaluate the effectiveness of the popular church's utopian ideology in fulfilling this interest.

I supplement the background to the crisis with a brief discussion of the institutional bases of the popular church and its impact on Brazilian society in chapter 2. Having laid the back-

[21] It would seem contradictory to speak of "utopian ideology," given the influential distinction that Karl Mannheim makes between these two terms. Mannheim defines ideologies as "fictions" which reproduce the status quo and utopias as "revolutionary wish-images" that transcend present reality. K. Mannheim, *Ideology and Utopia: An Introduction to the Sociology of Knowledge* (New York: Harcourt, Brace & World, 1936). Mannheim's distinction is, as he himself readily admits, difficult to establish for a concrete worldview. Furthermore, it also based on the same problematic notion of correct consciousness which shapes pejorative readings of the concept of ideology.

ground, I characterize in chapter 3 the different intra- and extra-ecclesial, international and national components of the crisis, establishing those aspects I consider more central. The key question here is the following: what evidence is there to warrant the affirmation that the popular church is in crisis? As we shall see, the crisis has two dimensions: an internal one that relates to the failure of the popular church to fulfill the expectation of Catholic grassroots activists to become a true mass movement, and an external one connected to the increasing fragmentation of the religious field and the rapid growth of Protestantism, especially Pentecostalism, among the urban poor, one of the popular church's main intended audiences. Although the external dimension, which I take up in chapter 4, is important, it represents a background condition to the internal dynamics of the crisis. Thus, the remainder of the book focuses on the internal dimension of the crisis, seeking to identify through a case study some of the economic, political, cultural, and religious factors that have combined to produce a crisis of mobilization and participation for the *igreja popular*.

Once the nature of crisis has been defined, I present in chapter 5 two competing intra-institutional readings of the causes behind this crisis. These readings reflect the views of the two opposing camps struggling for hegemony within the Brazilian Catholic church: the conservatives and the so-called liberals or progressives. Although both the conservative and progressive Catholic readings are flawed, they give us an idea of the stakes of the crisis for institutional actors. The confrontation of these readings helps us understand the issues and struggles involved as the Catholic church seeks to redefine its role in Brazilian society.

In chapters 6, 7, and 8 I offer my reading of the crisis. First, I trace the development of a base community I shall call Pedra Bonita, highlighting intra- and extra-ecclesial changes that conditioned its birth, expansion, and crisis. Chapter 7 places those changes in the context of macro-logical transformations at the international, national, and regional level, focusing more specifically on the socio-economic changes that have hindered the production, circulation, and reception of the popular church's liberationist message in Pedra Bonita.

In chapter 8, I use the case study to illuminate the crisis of the Brazilian popular church as a whole, and secondarily, the expansion of Pentecostalism. Contrary to excessively reductive and micrological readings of the crisis, I contend that the root of the popular church's plight is closely connected to the crisis of modernity, particularly of modern utopian projects. To support this contention, I explore key elements of the modernity–post-modernity debate as they bear on the situation of the poor in Latin America.

In recent years, debates on post-modernity and post-Marxism have come to occupy center stage in discussions about the fate of the precarious process of democratization in Latin America.[22] While these discussions have both redefined the terms of the post-modernist controversy and helped to highlight some of the overarching political and cultural implications of our present age in Latin America, they have not dealt adequately with the specific impact of the crisis of modernity on everyday life. This is a gap that I hope to begin to fill with this study.

The book concludes with a discussion of the lessons the crisis of modernity leaves not only for the popular church in Latin America but also for this-worldly religious utopias. I present these lessons through a critique of the popular church's methodology and social epistemology against the background of debate of post-modernism and post-Marxism. At a deeper level, this critique represents an attempt to reformulate the modernist notion of intra-historical transcendence that has shaped the liberationist understanding of collective identity, social change, and utopia. To formulate my critique, I build on the contrasting perspectives of two Catholic activists, both with extensive grassroots experience in Nova Iguaçu, who take a critical view of popular church's pastoral-pedagogical methods.

In the end, I see this study of the Brazilian popular church as an attempt to rethink the role of utopian ideologies, particularly those that find their inspiration in modernity, in the face of the challenges posed by contemporary capitalism and post-modernity.

---

[22] See for instance the collection of essays published in special issues of *Boundary 2* (1993), *The South Atlantic Quarterly* (1993), and *Nuevo Texto Crítico* (1991).

PART I

Background to the crisis

The popular church's utopian project: ideological and theological bases

In this chapter I map out the sources and nature of the popular church's theology, pastoral method, and social epistemology (i.e., its conceptions of human agency, history, and social change). I pay special attention to the continuities and ruptures between modern emancipatory discourses and the popular church's methods and worldview. This will help locate the crisis of the *igreja popular* within the larger crisis of modernity.

The first part of the chapter traces the popular church's ideological bases to the rise of Catholic modernism. Section II explores the ideological development of progressive Catholicism in Latin America in the 1960s and 1970s.

THE CATHOLIC CHURCH AND MODERNITY

The Second Vatican Council (1962–1965) marked a turning point in the Catholic Church's relation to modernity. Until that point the church had maintained a defensive attitude to social and cultural changes ushered in by modernity, seeing in them only the potential erosion of the overarching Catholic moral order. More specifically, the church viewed modernity as synonymous with secularization, understood most immediately as the rise of secular philosophies and the decline of religious ways of understanding the world and guiding action in it.

More generally, however, the secularization linked to modernity symbolized the loss of legitimacy of a unified cosmos centered around Catholic values and forms of organization. In this sense, modernity represented a threat to the church's hegemony over all spheres of life. This hegemony was often characterized by the term

"Christendom,"[1] seen as a society centered on a hierarchical church ordering and giving meaning to politics, the economy, education, family relations, and cultural and intellectual life, in addition to religion. Christendom reached its peak during the Middle Ages, when the feudal agrarian structure resonated with the organic and hierarchical Thomistic system. By shattering the feudal world through the rapid change and severe social dislocation brought about by the Industrial Revolution and urbanization, modernity posed a direct challenge to the Christendom model. The church's approach to modernity thus reflected a rejection of these social changes and an attempt to return the church to its "rightful" place at the center of all dimensions of social and intellectual life.

The Syllabus of Errors, a document issued by Pius IX a century before Vatican II, provides a clear example of the church's prevailing attitude towards modernity even up to the twentieth century. The aim of the document was to defend the Catholic *Weltanschauung* against a whole host of secular "ideologies" which had begun to offer alternative ways of life to the growing urban masses. Among the modern ideologies condemned in the document are not only (and predictably) communism, Marxism, and atheism, but also democracy, rationalism, and ecumenism. Moreover, attempts within the church to adapt its teachings to the modern age were, like Catholic modernism,[2] severely censured in papal encyclicals, such as *Pacendi gregis* (1907).

The church's defensive position, which built on the reaction to the this-worldliness generated by the Protestant Reformation, had dire consequences insofar as it widened the gulf between the laity's experiences of social change and the church's teachings and methods. Faced with an increasing isolation and the growth of right- and left-wing political parties and mass movements, the church took some tentative steps in the encyclicals *Rerum novarum* (1891) and *Quadragesimo anno* (1931). Both documents addressed

---

[1] See P. Richard, *Death of Christendom, Birth of the Church* (Maryknoll, NY: Orbis Books, 1987).

[2] Catholic modernism was an intellectual movement within the Church which took place roughly from 1890 to 1910. Led by Alfred Loisy and George Tyrrell among others, it sought to defend and re-interpret Catholic doctrine in the light of post-Enlightenment scientific rationality.

social questions raised by industrialization, liberalism, and socialism. The church, however, responded to these questions with a
mixture of accommodation and self-assertion. For example, while
the church recognized the right of the workers to organize in trade
unions, it insisted that they should do so only through Catholic
unions. Despite the church's effort to deal with some aspects of the
modern predicament, the documents still presented Catholicism as
the only viable and legitimate ideological and cultural framework.
These documents still embraced the view that the church's worldview and internal organization represented an alternative to modernity, which was still conceived in purely negative terms, as a
source of secularization, rationalization, and atheism. The church
saw itself as the "third way" between liberalism and socialism, both
of which it rejected. *Rerum novarum* and *Quadragesimo anno* constituted, in the end, a re-assertion of the Christendom model. Both
documents still held – or at least hoped – that an all-encompassing
social order under the church's tutelage was possible and desirable.[3]

Only with Vatican II did the church stop defining itself against
modernity and placing itself in opposition to a secular world
perceived as decadent. At Vatican II, rather than presenting itself
as the way, the church defined itself as a "pilgrim" in the world,
open to what secular ideologies and institutions might have to say
about the modern predicament. According to *Gaudium et spes*,
Vatican II's final document, the church

goes forward together with humanity and experiences the same earthly lot
which the world does . . . In addition the Catholic Church gladly holds in
high esteem the things which other Christian Churches or ecclesial
communities have done or are doing cooperatively by the way of achieving the same goal. At the same time, she [the church] is firmly convinced
that she can be abundantly and variously helped by the world in the matter
of preparing the ground for the gospel. This help she gains from the talents
and industry of individuals and from human society as a whole.[4]

[3] I do not wish to imply that there are no significant differences between *Rerum novarum* and
Quadragesimo anno; the former, for instance, seems to accept the triumph of liberal
capitalism, while the latter reflects the perceived instability of liberalism in 1931. For a
survey of contemporary Catholic social thought, see D. J. O'Brien, "A Century of
Catholic Social Teaching," in *100 Years of Catholic Social Thought: Celebration and Challenge*,
ed. J. A. Coleman (Maryknoll, NY: Orbis Books, 1991).
[4] *Gaudium et spes*, Section IV, no. 40. In *The Gospel of Peace and Justice: Catholic Social Teachings
since Pope John*, ed. J. Gremillion (Maryknoll, NY: Orbis Books, 1976).

With Vatican II, the church recognized the deeper impulse that drives modernity. Its focus expanded beyond the potentially pathological symptoms of modernity (secularization and the rationalization of everyday life) to reflect on the character of modernity itself.

But what is the essence of this character? Defining modernity is not a simple task. Different authors have tied its emergence to historical events such as the Enlightenment, the Industrial Revolution, the Copernican scientific revolution, the Protestant Reformation, or Europe's violent encounter with the peoples of the Americas.[5] I contend that all these partial definitions, like the church's initial focus on secularization, point to a more general impulse.

Rather than characterizing modernity as an event that can be readily identified and isolated, I define it as a long, complex, and arduous struggle through which humanity seeks to free itself from the bondage of arbitrary rule. Modernity represents humanity's quest to assert its radical historical openness and to express its creative potential. Put in other words, modernity expresses humanity's impulse to bring itself constantly up to date (in Latin *modo* means "of today"), that is, to live in a present that is always subject to transgression. Conceived thus, the modern impulse precedes the Industrial Revolution, the Enlightenment, or even the Renaissance, as the original Christian vision of a god taking human form or the Athenian attempts at democracy show.

Nevertheless, prior to the end of the eighteenth century this impulse remained implicit, surfacing only sporadically. The confluence of developments in the areas of science (physics building on Newton), politics (the French Revolution), society (the decline of the feudal order), and culture (the Enlightenment) at the close of the eighteenth century qualitatively changed the nature of the modern impulse. At that juncture the impulse gained ascendence, becoming the conscious project of the emerging cultural and social

---

[5] See for example, J. Habermas, "Modernity – An Incomplete Project," in *Postmodern Culture*, ed. H. Foster (London: Pluto Press, 1985), 3–15; A. Giddens, *The Consequences of Modernity* (Cambridge: Polity Press, 1990); H. Blumenberg, *The Legitimacy of the Modern Age* (Cambridge, MA: MIT Press, 1983); and E. Dussel, "Eurocentrism and Modernity (Introduction to the Frankfurt Lectures)," *Boundary 2* 20, no. 3 (Fall 1993), 65–76.

elites. These elites took it upon themselves to disseminate this project in the expanding public space of cultural salons and the printed press.

The newly found consciousness of the modern impulse expressed itself in Kant's famous assertion that with the Enlightenment humanity had "come of age," that it had reached "maturity."[6] For Kant, this maturity meant that humanity was on the threshold of achieving independence *vis-à-vis* forms of external, "self-incurred tutelage" such as tradition, religion, and superstition, which had held back expression of its full potential. The term "self-incurred tutelage" suggests that the bondage is of humanity's own creation, that the yoke issues from distorted perceptions of its own potential or from sheer cowardice to actualize its essence. This is why Kant asserted that Enlightenment's motto was "*Sapere aude!* Have the courage to exercise your own understanding."

Thus, the rise of the Enlightenment's version of the modern impulse is connected to use of critical faculties to apprehend the world and to unmask ideologies that enslave humanity. Humanity's adulthood means that there is no longer any need to rely naively on supernatural and suprasocial forces to give meaning and orientation to actions. History then becomes an open field where humanity, drawing from its own resources, especially from its rational and critical faculties, can construct its own fate. This is the true meaning of autonomy: human beings can be governed only by the laws they create.

For all its emancipatory drive, post-Enlightenment modernity carried some serious *aporias* that would distort, and even contradict the original aims of the modern impulse. Accompanying post-Enlightenment modernity's affirmations of human autonomy are a triumphalist optimism and a fervent belief in progress, especially in the human capacity to shape and control fully the future. This confidence led to an absolutist reading of the modern impulse, i.e., the idea that the pursuit of human self-realization can take only one form. Buoyed by scientific and technological advances, which had begun to "uncover" the general laws governing nature, post-Enlightenment modernity came to conceive of society as an organ-

---

[6] I. Kant, "An Answer to the Question: What is Enlightenment?" in *Postmodernism: A Reader*, ed. P. Waugh, (London: Edward Arnold, 1992).

ism with a single *telos* and an inner logic readily available to rational apprehension. Human emancipation then became synonymous with the scientific and technological mastery of reality.

The possibility of discovering society's lawful behavior, in turn, led post-Enlightenment thinking to posit the "utopia" of a totally rationalized society – one fully transparent and pliable to human will. As Alain Touraine rightly states, the post-Enlightenment appropriation of the modern impulse is "closely associated with the idea of rationalization": the increasing expansion of a means–ends rationality that now "commands not only scientific and technical activities, but the management [*gouvernement*] of men [*sic*] as well as the administration of things."[7] Under this conception of utopia, modernity as transgressive history gives way to a predetermined movement towards a single goal. This flattened, teleological reading of history is most evident in Hegel's reconstruction of the Spirit's journey to full self-identity. The transformation of the modern impulse towards human emancipation into a drive to construct a totalized vision of nature, society, history, and the self in order to exert full control over reality is the deleterious side of post-Enlightenment thinking.

The dream of a fully rationalized society, engineered according to scientific principles, served as the ideological underpinning for the industrial revolution and capitalism. Both appeared as necessary steps in a teleological process of human progress from the perspective of modernization theories, which came to dominate the nascent field of sociology. Modernization theories construed the modern impulse as the drive to dominate the "Other," that which stands against the sovereign rational subject. The Other represented not only nature but those at the margin of society, i.e., women and people in the colonies. These were perceived as primitive entities still under the yoke of prejudice and superstition and thus in need of illumination. This is how the Enlightenment's "prejudice against prejudice,"[8] as Gadamer terms it, became tied to normative ideas of evolution and progress.

The defensive stance of Pre-Vatican II Catholicism *vis-à-vis* modernity can be construed as a conservative reaction against the

[7] A. Touraine, *Critique de la modernité* (Paris: Fayard, 1991), 24.
[8] H. G. Gadamer, *Truth and Method* (New York: Seabury Press, 1975), 240.

post-Enlightenment distortions of the modern impulse. Since the church was interested in bolstering its own *modus operandi* against modernity, it found a focus on the negative aspects of modernity convenient. Church proclamations concentrated in particular on the elements of modernity – atheism and secularization – which posed the most direct and obvious threat to Catholicism. In this way the church could dismiss the modern impulse *tout court* without coming to terms with its original essence, which, as previously defined, was connected to the precarious struggle for human freedom.

Not until Vatican II did the Catholic Church confront this original essence head on. While reiterating its rejection of the excessive rationalism of post-Enlightenment modernity, in Vatican II the church relinquished its static vision of history and hierarchical understanding of authority, affirming instead the creativity and effectiveness of human action. Rather than seeing divine will and providence as standing against and above human projects in history, Vatican II posited humanity's free and creative praxis as fulfilling God's plan. *Gaudium et spes*, for instance, stated that "To believers, this point is settled: considered in itself . . . human activity accords with God's will. For man [*sic*], created to God's image, received a mandate to subject to himself the earth and all it contains, and to govern the world with justice and holiness." Thus, it concludes that

far from thinking that works produced by man's own talent and energy are in opposition to God's power, and that the rational creature exists as a kind of rival to the Creator, Christians are convinced that the triumphs of the human race are a sign of God's greatness and the flowering of his own mysterious design. For the greater man's power becomes, the farther his individual and community responsibility extends. Hence it is clear that men are not deterred by the Christian message from building up the world, or impelled to neglect the welfare of their fellows.[9]

It is important to note here that Vatican II's valuation of human action is not entirely foreign to the Catholic tradition, but builds upon the Thomistic conception of natural law. The council's formulation represents not a reversal of Catholic tradition but

---

[9] *Gaudium et Spes*, Section III, no. 34.

rather a radical, modernist re-reading of the doctrine of the holiness of works. This doctrine asserts that salvation is not simply a
gratuitous divine act over which we have no control. Rather,
salvation is affected by one's merits and good works in this world.
Prior to Vatican II, such potentially radical and humanistic
soteriological ideas had remained stifled by the dominant principle
that the church constituted the only sanctioned guardian of tradition, the sole arbiter of what constituted good works and thus the
legitimate means of salvation. This monopoly, which underlay the
medieval model of Christendom, led to abuses and distortions that
the Protestant Reformation, with its emphasis on God's sover-
eignty and humanity's fallenness, challenged.

Vatican II recovered the doctrine of the holiness of works and
corrected some of the distortions that had characterized earlier
versions. Vatican II's renewed valuation of human works and
openness to the secular world opened up the possibility for new
approaches to pastoral action, including most significantly the
appropriation of the "see-judge-act" method in the second meeting of the Latin American bishops in Medellín in 1968.

The see-judge-act method was introduced in the late 1940s by
Joseph Cardijn, one of the central figures in the development of
Catholic Action.[10] Intent on reaching the laity in their homes and
workplaces, Cardijn developed the see-judge-act method to
understand the particular life conditions of the various segments of
the emerging working class. The method is in essence a dynamic
process of reflection and action. It departs from a specific social
fact, seeking to identify the economic, social, political and ideological conditions that lie behind that fact. It then moves to a second
moment in which the fact is analyzed and evaluated to ascertain
whether it violates ideals of justice and solidarity. If it does, then
the question arises: what courses of action can be taken to change
the situation so that it would be more compatible with the Christian vision of the world? On the basis of this reflection the individuals engaged in this pedagogical exercise can undertake an in-

---

[10] On the origins of Catholic Action, see G. Poggi, *Catholic Action in Italy: The Sociology of a
Sponsored Organization* (Stanford: Stanford University Press, 1967). On the life of Joseph
Cardijn, see M. de la Bedoyere, *The Cardijn Story* (London: Longman, Green and Co.,
1958).

formed emancipatory praxis. Praxis, in turn, leads to new problems and questions that can be taken up in a new "see" moment,
thereby initiating another cycle of reflection and action.

The affinity of the see-judge-act method with the Enlightenment's critical attitude is readily discernible. Implicit in the
method is the view that human beings can understand and change
the world around them through their own rational efforts. Like the
Enlightenment's critique of ideology and prejudice, the see-judge-
act method is an approach to social reality that historicizes and
contextualizes it, showing its contingent human origins. In fact,
the Catholic *aggiornamento* – the church's coming up to date –
recovered and embraced the underlying impulse of modernity
through the distortions of post-Enlightenment thinking. By this I
mean that together with the appropriation of the notion of human
freedom, the church sometimes accepted a quasi-teleological reading of history. For example, the notion of the church as the
"pilgrim people of God," so central to Vatican II reforms, suggests
a progressive, even inevitable movement towards the fulfillment of
history. As I contend later, this teleological reading receives perhaps its most elaborate articulation in liberation theology and the
ideology of the popular church.

The acceptance and use of the see-judge-act method had a
dramatic effect on Latin American Catholic thinking, performing
a role similar to that which Feuerbach's materialist inversion of
Hegelian idealism played for Marx. The method represented the
overturning of scholastic Catholicism. Rather than deducing
Christian activity in the world from abstract, universal theological
and doctrinal premises, Catholic activists and pastoral agents
began with historical conditions, interrogating church teachings to
see how they responded to that particular human situation. Once
this inversion was in place, progressive Catholic theologians in
Latin America began to draw out the full ethical, christological,
eschatological, soteriological and anthropological implications of
this upending of traditional theology, gradually constructing what
we now know as liberation theology.

It would be wrong to claim Catholic Action's methodology gave
rise single-handedly to liberation theology and the Brazilian popular church. As we shall see later, other important experiences also

contributed to the process more directly. Nevertheless, it is clear that the see-judge-act methodology bears close affinity with liberation theology's epistemological and praxical core – what Juan Luis Segundo calls the "hermeneutic circle." According to Segundo, the hermeneutic circle "is the continuing change in our interpretation of the Bible which is dictated by the continuing changes in our present-day reality, both individual and societal" such that "each new reality obliges us to interpret the word of God afresh, to change reality accordingly, and then to go back and reinterpret the word of God again, and so on."[11]

Moreover, Catholic Action's see-judge-act method, particularly in its later variant, the *revisão de vida* (reflection on a fact of life), has influenced pastoral-pedagogical approaches in CEBs. Rather than choosing any social fact and analyzing it, in the *revisão de vida*, grassroots Catholic activists who share work and life experiences, come together in small groups (*equipes*) to discuss concrete events in their own everyday existence. Focusing on a particular problem at the factory, in the neighborhood or in the household, the activists seek to grasp underlying causes in order to be able to act effectively. The small group setting and the focus on members' everyday lives in the *revisão de vida* are constitutive elements of the base ecclesial communities' attempts to link everyday life and faith.

Finally, the fact that prominent liberation theologians such as Gustavo Gutiérrez and progressive bishops such as Helder Câmara, Luis Fernandes, Antonio Fragoso, Waldir Calheiros and José Maria Pires, who have been vocal supporters of the popular church, were involved early in their careers with Catholic Action attests to the movement's significance.[12]

Despite the importance of Catholic Action's approach to the world in the development of the popular church in Latin America, I argue that the *igreja popular's* link to the modern emancipatory project is deeper, having to do not only with a critical methodology but with the content of the religious message itself. To trace the true extent of the popular church's implication with modernity we

[11] J. L. Segundo, *The Liberation of Theology* (Maryknoll, NY: Orbis Books, 1976), 8.
[12] On the influence of Catholic Action on Gustavo Gutiérrez, see D. J. Molineaux, "Gustavo Gutiérrez: Historical Origins," *The Ecumenist* 25, no. 5 (1987), 65–69. On the bishops, see Mainwaring, *The Catholic Church and Politics in Brazil*, 73.

need to look more carefully at its more immediate roots. Of these I have chosen three that I consider the most important: the second meeting of the Latin American Episcopal Conference (CELAM) in Medellín in 1968, Paulo Freire's grassroots pedagogical experiences in the 1950s and 1960s, and Gutiérrez's formulation of liberation theology in 1971.

MODERNITY AND THE POPULAR CHURCH'S EMANCIPATORY PROJECT

Although the popular church did not begin with the episcopal meeting in Medellín, it is fair to say that the conference represented a turning point for progressive Catholic forces in Latin America. The conclusions of the conference provided the ideological framework and the institutional recognition for innovative pastoral initiatives already operative, though in a haphazard fashion, at the grassroots. These initiatives, in fact, shaped the nature of the discussions at Medellín. In Brazil, the pioneering experiences in Barra do Piraí in the State of Rio de Janeiro during the late 1950s and in Nízia Floresta in the diocese of Natal at the beginning of the 1960s deserve special mention.[13] Barra do Piraí introduced the possibility of training lay pastoral and evangelizing agents recruited from the poor, a strategy that paved the way for what CEB advisor Faustino Teixeira calls the "declericalization of pastoral work among the poor."[14] This declericalization found its most mature form in the various lay ministries within CEBs. Nízia Floresta, on the other hand, made it possible for nuns to come into contact with the poor masses. More than priests, whose work continues even to this day to be constrained by the rigid, impersonal parish structure, sisters played a key role in the emergence of grassroots organization at the base. This is because nuns have entered the everyday world of the poor more often and more deeply.[15]

[13] On Barra do Piraí, see A. Rossi, "Uma experiência de catequese popular," *Revista Eclesiástica Brasileira* 17, no. 3 (1957), 731–737. On Nízia Floresta, see I. V. Bastos, "Experiência de Nízia Floresta," *Revista Eclesiástica Brasileira* 24, no. 2 (1964), 497–498.
[14] F. Teixeira, *A gênese das CEBs no Brasil: Elementos explicativos* (São Paulo: Paulinas, 1988), 72.
[15] M. Adriance, "Agents of Change: The Role of Priests, Sisters and Lay Workers in the Grassroots Catholic Church in Brazil," *Journal for the Scientific Study of Religion* 30, no. 3 (1991), 299.

In its underlying thrust, Medellín represented an attempt to work out the implications for Latin America of the Vatican II dialogue with modernity, as the title of the meeting indicates.[16] Medellín took up Vatican II's humanism and new spirit of openness. For the Latin American bishops at Medellín, "Historical events and authentic human striving are an indispensable part of the content of catechesis."[17] This is because the bishops "recognize all the value and legitimate autonomy of temporal works."[18] To ground this approach the bishops drew from Paul VI's closing address to the Second Vatican Council: "The Latin American Church ... has chosen as the central theme of its deliberation Latin American man [*sic*] who is living a decisive moment of his historical process. In making this choice she [the church] has not 'detoured from,' but has actually 'returned to' man, aware that 'in order to know God, it is necessary to know man.'"[19]

In order "to understand this historical moment in the life of Latin American man," the bishops at Medellín considered that it was "indispensable to form a social conscience and a realistic perception of the problems of the community and of social structures."[20] To achieve this aim, the bishops relied on social scientific analyses of Latin American societies, and with these they opened the Catholic church to the critical impetus of modernity. Using these critical tools, the bishops discovered "the misery that besets large masses of human beings" in the region. This misery, they declared, resulted from a situation of "institutionalized violence" rather than individual sin.[21]

To deal with this condition, the bishops at Medellín pledged "to encourage and favor efforts of the people to create and develop their own grass-roots organizations for the redress and consolidation of their rights and the search for true justice."[22] Medellín, therefore, officially endorsed the grassroots experiments already in place, sanctioning them as an essential way of fulfilling the church's "duty of solidarity with poor." The Latin American

---

[16] CELAM (Conference of Latin American Bishops), *The Church in the Present-Day Transformation of Latin America in the Light of the Council: Medellín Conclusions* (Washington, DC: National Conference of Catholic Bishops, Secretariat for Latin America, 1979).
[17] Ibid., 110.   [18] Ibid., 178.   [19] Ibid., 26.   [20] Ibid., 40.   [21] Ibid., 53.
[22] Ibid., 56.

bishops encouraged "those who feel themselves called to form from among their members small communities, truly incarnated in the poor environment [because] they will be a continual call to evangelical poverty for all the people of God" (p. 177).

Medellín's call to serve the poor in community provided the institutional justification for the creation of base ecclesial communities. On the issue of the renovation of pastoral structures, for example, the bishops declared that "the Christian base community is the first and fundamental ecclesiastical nucleus, which on its own level must make itself responsible for the richness and the expansion of faith, as well as of the cult which is its expression. This community becomes then the initial cell of the ecclesiastical structures and the focus of evangelization, and it currently serves as the most important source of human advancement and development."[23] The call to serve and be in solidarity with those at the margins of society also foreshadowed the church's "preferential option for the poor," adopted by the Latin American bishops in the third meeting in Puebla in 1979. The preferential option for the poor is the unifying principle and *raison d'etre* of the popular church. The adjective "popular" here refers to "the people," in Portuguese "*o povo*," a term that designates mainly the poor majority of Brazilians.

Over against the injustice and "inhuman wretchedness" they found, the bishops quoted from *Gaudium et spes* to proclaim a message of "authentic liberation":

The very God who created men in his image and likeness, created the "earth and all that is in it for the use of all men [*sic*] and all nations, in such a way that created goods can reach all in a more just manner," and gives them power to transform and perfect the world in solidarity. It is the same God, who in the fullness of time, sends his Son in the flesh, so that he might come to liberate all men from the slavery to which sin has subjected them: hunger, misery, oppression and ignorance . . .[24]

Besides reflecting a bit of the post-Enlightenment instrumental approach to nature, this paragraph points towards the gradual intertwining of historical teleology with Christian eschatology. Struggles for human promotion begin to be construed as necessary

---

[23] Ibid., 185.   [24] Ibid., 33.

steps in God's salvific scheme. The merging of the eternal and the temporal, the sacred and the profane became central to the popular church's vision of history and salvation. Here we begin to see the influence of the modern emancipatory project on the popular church at the level of message.

At Medellín, the bishops came to the realization that the historical conditions they were confronting in Latin America were "intimately linked to the history of salvation," that the "aspirations and clamors of Latin America [were] signs that reveal[ed] the direction of the divine plan."[25] Such a realization made it possible for popular church activists to establish a link between faith and life, religion and politics, and the human and sacred realms in their quest for intra-historical transcendence with the history of salvation.

The full implications of the convergence of human transcendence and eschatology in Latin American progressive Catholicism would be drawn more fully in the work of educator Paulo Freire and theologian Gustavo Gutiérrez. Freire's contribution to this convergence was a pedagogical method based on an anthropology that blended elements of historicist Marxism, existentialism, phenomenology, and Catholic personalism. During the early 1960s, working with support from the reformist government of Jânio Quadros and the National Conference of Brazilian Bishops (CNBB), Freire helped to create educational programs administered by and targeted to local rural communities. These programs eventually led to the articulation of a nation-wide Movimento de Educação de Base (Movement for Grassroots Education, or MEB).[26]

Within the MEB, Freire sought to formulate an alternative to what he called the "banking concept of education." According to Freire, the traditional model of Western education works with a banking conception: the teacher is seen as the only active agent in the pedagogical exchange, as the only holder of legitimate knowl-

[25] Ibid., 19.
[26] On the history of MEB, see L.E. Wanderley, *Educar para transformar, educação popular, Igreja católica e política no movimento de educação de base* (Petrópolis: Vozes, 1984). For a critical assessment of Freire's work, see V. Paiva, *Paulo Freire e o nacionalismo-desenvolvimentista* (Rio de Janeiro: Ed. Civilização Brasileira, 1980); and D. Collins, *Paulo Freire: His Life, Work and Thought* (New York: Paulist Press, 1978).

edge which s/he deposits in the student's head. Students, in this model, are defined as empty "receptacles," passive "depositories" of external information, which they later must recite by rote to show progress. Against this method, Freire proposed a dialogical approach that draws from the students' experiences and culture, making them co-participants in their own growth. According to Freire,

In the banking concept of education, knowledge is a gift bestowed by those who consider themselves knowledgeable upon those whom they considered to know nothing. Projecting an absolute ignorance onto others, a characteristic of the ideology of oppression, negates education and knowledge as a process of inquiry. The teacher presents himself [*sic*] to his students as their necessary opposite; by considering their ignorance absolute, he justifies his own existence.[27]

In contrast to the banking approach to education, Freire sought to develop a method that awakens the students' critical consciousness, enabling them to "name" their reality, that is, to become aware of the socio-political forces that shape such a reality. Knowledge of the contingent, changing nature of social reality is, in turn, a necessary step to restoring the individual's capacity to exert his/her creative powers by transforming the world. This is what Freire meant by the celebrated term *conscientização* (consciousness-raising).

Conscientização is an exercise in intra-historical transcendence, or in "revolutionary futurity," as Freire puts it, whereby the individual breaks the shackles of fatalism and reclaims his/her ontological essence, which is pure becoming. Freire sees humans as "beings in the process of becoming ... unfinished, uncompleted beings in and with a likewise unfinished reality."[28] In contrast to animals, Freire claims, "only men [*sic*] are *praxis* – the praxis which, as the reflection and action which truly transforms reality, is the source of knowledge and creation." And "it is as transforming and creative beings that men, in their permanent relations with reality, produce not only material goods – tangible objects – but also social institutions, ideas, and concepts. Through their continuing praxis, men

[27] P. Freire, *Pedagogy of the Oppressed* (New York: Herder and Herder, 1972), 58–59.
[28] Ibid., 72.

simultaneously create history and become historical-social beings."[29]

Thus, for Freire, a true pedagogy must take as its point of departure humanity's radical historicity: human beings are "beings who transcend themselves, who move forward and look ahead, for whom immobility represents a fatal threat."[30] In this sense, Freire's anthropology and vision of history and change partake of post-Enlightenment modernity's emancipatory impulse. Freire appears to be saying, like Kant, that rational, critical knowledge is the key to liberation from all forms of bondage. However, we must be careful not to equate the notion of *conscientização* with Kantian critical thinking. Unlike Kant and his predecessor Descartes, Freire does not start with an isolated, abstract subjectivity deploying its critical capacities. Rather, Freire starts with historical individuals located in a particular socio-cultural setting, engaged in a web of social relations. This is because the modern emancipatory impulse enters Freire's anthropology through the mediation of Hegelian Marxism and Catholic organicism.

Freire posits as the protagonist of the struggle for human promotion not the detached, rational individual who lies at the core of Cartesian-Kantian thinking, bourgeois liberalism and capitalism, but, in a way reminiscent of Marx, a collective, sensuous agent acting from below.[31] The aim remains the same: to restore our "vocation to become more fully human." However, the main actor in this quest changes: it is the "oppressed" as a collective subject. Freire sees in the oppressed "the restorers" of humanity. Since the oppressed, more than anyone, have experienced the horrors of dehumanization, their rise from bondage will guarantee that those horrors are not repeated. In Freire's eyes,

the great humanistic and historical task of the oppressed . . . [is] to liberate themselves and their oppressors as well. The oppressors, who

---

[29] Ibid., 91. Here Freire echoes Marx's arguments in *Economic and Philosophical Manuscripts of 1844* and in "Theses on Feuerbach" in *The Marx-Engels Reader*, ed. R. Tucker (New York: Norton, 1978)."

[30] Freire, *The Pedagogy of the Oppressed*, 91.

[31] Marx uses the term "sensuous" to counter Hegelian idealism. Human beings are embodied beings who not only think but labor – for Marx the most important expression of praxis – in order to fashion the material world in which they find themselves. See "Theses on Feuerbach."

oppress, exploit, and rape by virtue of their power, cannot find in this power the strength to liberate either the oppressed or themselves. Only power that springs from the weakness of the oppressed will be sufficiently strong to free both.[32]

This vision of history derives from Marx's reading of the master–slave dialectic in Hegel.[33] Whereas for Hegel the central actor in humanity's inexorable march towards independence is the Spirit going through a process of formative development in search of full self-consciousness; for Marx it is the proletariat as collective agent struggling to break the bonds of estrangement. The proletariat does this, first, by moving from a class in itself to a class for itself, that is, a class that is conscious of its status and interest as oppressed. On the basis of this consciousness the proletariat struggles to achieve a social order that actualizes humanity's essence.

Freire, however, adds a Gramscian twist to the dominant readings of Marx's teleology of emancipation from the 1920s to the 1940s. The movement from class in itself to a class for itself is neither the result of a mechanical, subjectless process, as the economism of the Second International would have it; nor is it a spontaneous spiritual reaction to capitalism's deepening economic crisis. Rather, the transformation is operated at the level of consciousness, where the oppressed gradually develop, along with a sense of collective identity, a critical approach and a counter-hegemonic ideology that allow them to de-mystify the ideas of the ruling classes.

Unlike Lenin, who regards the intelligentsia (as represented by the party) as the source of this counter-hegemonic ideology, Freire, borrowing from Gramsci's idea of the "organic intellectual," sees the oppressed as the protagonists of their own collective conscience. Thus, for Freire "the conviction of the oppressed that they must fight for their liberation is not a gift bestowed by the revolutionary leadership, but the result of their own *conscientizaço*."[34] According to Gramsci, "Every social group, coming into existence on the original terrain of an essential function in the world of

---

[32] Freire, *Pedagogy of the Oppressed*, 28–29.
[33] See the discussion on lordship and bondage in G. W. F. Hegel, *The Phenomenology of Mind* (New York: Harper and Row, 1967), 229–240.
[34] Freire, *Pedagogy of the Oppressed*, 54.

economic production, created with itself, organically, one or more strata of intellectuals which give it homogeneity and an awareness of its own function not only in the economic but also in the social and political fields."[35] These organic intellectuals are "for the most part 'specialisations' of partial aspects of the primitive activity of the new social type which the new class has brought into prominence."[36] Applying this vision to the Latin American setting, Freire came to see those among the oppressed group who are able to sharpen their critical consciousness in the dialogical encounter with the committed intellectual/teacher as teachers themselves. They would bring social awareness among those around them, unleashing a massive process of grassroots consciousness-raising. The poor would teach the poor using their own cultural resources, with outside intellectuals only as facilitators.

Freire's approach to education had an enormous influence in the Catholic church's formulation of grassroots pastoral and educational initiatives in Brazil and elsewhere in Latin America. Grassroots pastoral initiatives such as *grupos de evangelização* (grassroots evangelization teams), *círculos bíblicos* (Bible circle), and CEBs, which form the pastoral heart of the *igreja popular*, were developed by the church during the 1960s and 1970s precisely to train lay leaders who, given the scarcity of priests, would be able to minister to the poor. In the context of Medellín's call for the church to be in solidarity with the poor and the generalized climate of repression in Latin America in the 1970s, these leaders became not only pastoral workers but also agents of political change. As we shall see later in the case of Brazil, their training allowed them to play a crucial role organizing the masses, in the absence of political parties and trade unions. Borrowing an expression that enjoys wide usage among popular church activists, these lay leaders became a *fermento de massa*, the leaven that would make the masses rise and reclaim their rights. They came to be seen as the *sementes* [seeds], or the "heralds" of a new, more egalitarian society.

Freire's method of working with "generative themes" (i.e.,

[35] A. Gramsci, *Selections from the Prison Notebooks* (New York: International Publishers, 1971), 5.
[36] Ibid., 6.

themes the poor identify as central in their everyday life), became particularly important for CEBs and other grassroots initiatives. The work of Dutch biblical scholar Carlos Mesters among *círculos bíblicos* is a case in point. Mesters adopted Freire's insight that the teacher needs to acknowledge the superior wisdom of the oppressed in matters of life, death and spirituality, a recognition that forces the teacher to depart from and always refer to the poor's worldviews and culture.[37] Rather than imposing church dogma from above, Mesters allowed the poor to confront the Bible directly, encouraging them to work in small groups to select those stories, images, and figures that resonated with their experiences. He argued that interpreting their dreams, anxieties, and needs in terms of biblical events, the poor gain a better understanding of their situation and a new sense of self-esteem.

In their biblical reflections poor people discover, for instance, that Jesus was poor like them, that rather than carrying out his ministry among the rich and powerful, he chose the humble and marginalized. Or they may encounter a God who intervenes in history on behalf of enslaved people to liberate them and lead them to the promised land. They may read Hebrew prophets such as Amos, Micah, or Jeremiah condemning political and religious authorities for failing to abide by the Covenant or for engaging in an idolatrous behavior that places their own self-interest over the well-being of the people. In all of these examples, the poor come to recognize themselves and their situation in the biblical stories, placing themselves within the framework of the arduous but hopeful march of the people of God toward the reign of God. In *círculos bíblicos* and CEBs the Bible becomes, in Mesters' words, "a critical mirror of life":

In the people's eyes the Bible and life are connected. When they open the Bible they want to find in it things directly related to their lives, and in their lives they want to find events and meanings that parallel those in the Bible. Spontaneously they use the Bible as an image, symbol, or mirror of what is happening to them here and now. Sometimes they even confuse the two and say, "Our Bible is our life."[38]

[37] C. Mesters, *Defenseless Flower: A New Reading of the Bible* (Maryknoll, NY: Orbis Books, 1989).
[38] Ibid., 70.

We see in this citation once again the intersection of divine and human planes, or rather what I would call the sacralization and "cosmization"[39] of present human history, whereby the idea of progress and liberation comes to be inextricably connected with God's work to usher in the divine reign.

This connection and Freire's humanism, especially his notions of *praxis, conscientização*, empowerment, intra-historical transcendence and the revolutionary role of the oppressed found a fuller elaboration in the works of liberation theologians, especially Gustavo Gutiérrez.[40] Gutiérrez outlined the central issues and themes of liberation theology as early as 1968 in a meeting with progressive priests in Chimbote, Perú.[41] The discussions at the meeting led to the publication of a working paper entitled "Notes for a Theology for Liberation." The essay argues that "Theology . . . [is] a critical reflection on the Church's presence and action in the world" and that the world in Latin America is characterized by "a process of liberation." Once these methodological points are established, the crucial issue is "the connection between salvation and the process of man's emancipation in the course of history."[42] Jesuit theologian Ignacio Ellacuría puts this key question clearly: "How are the human efforts to seek a historical, or even sociopolitical, liberation related to the coming of the kingdom of God that Jesus preached? How is the proclamation and realization of the kingdom of God related to the historical liberation of the oppressed majorities?"[43]

By the time of the publication of his book *Teología de la liberación* in 1971, Gutiérrez had responded to this question with formula:

[39] Sociologist Peter Berger uses the term "cosmization" to refer to the process by which events, activities and institutions in the human realm "are projected into the universe as such." See *The Sacred Canopy: Elements of a Sociological Theory of Religion* (New York: Anchor Books, 1967).

[40] Liberation theology is not a monolith. Particularly, its most recent manifestations encompass a wide range of concerns and approaches. However, at least in Latin America, liberation theology is distinguished by certain key assumptions, which I highlight in the present discussion. I focus this discussion on the writings of Gustavo Gutiérrez because his work is so foundational and so influential on liberation theology as a whole.

[41] See Molineaux, "Gustavo Gutiérrez," and also R. M. Brown, *Gustavo Gutiérrez: An Introduction to Liberation Theology* (Maryknoll, NY: Orbis Books, 1990).

[42] G. Gutiérrez, "Notes for a Theology of Liberation," *Theological Studies* 31, no. 2 (1970), 255.

[43] I. Ellacuría, "Historicidad de la salvación cristiana," in *Mysterium liberationis: Conceptos fundamentales de la teología de la liberación*, vol. 1, eds. I. Ellacuría and J. Sobrino (San Salvador: UCA Editores, 1991), 326.

"there is only one history – a 'Christo-finalized' history."[44] By this Gutiérrez means that "we do not have two juxtaposed histories, one sacred and one profane." Rather, "there is only one single process of human development, definitively and irreversibly assumed by Christ, the Lord of history." According to Gutiérrez, then, salvation "is an intrahistorical reality."[45] It is a process that "embraces the whole of man [*sic*] and human history" because it signifies the "communion of men with God and the communion of men among themselves." As such, "the struggle for a just society fits fully and rightfully into salvation history."[46] Instead of conceiving the *eschaton* as the radical suspension of human history, salvation becomes the fulfillment of a utopian promise embodied (in the figure of Jesus Christ) in human time. In fact, it is this utopian promise, which finds "partial fulfillment through liberating historical events, [producing] new promises marking the road towards total fulfillment," that drives history to its anticipated completion.

Through this conception of history and eschatology, Gutiérrez and other liberation theologians reclaimed "the human power embedded in the messianic promises," which had been buried under what he calls "a benighted spiritualization."[47] "To work for a just world where there is no servitude, oppression, and alienation is to work for the advent of the Messiah." Thus, when liberation theologians "say that men and women fulfill themselves by carrying out the work of creation through their own labors, [they] are asserting that [human beings] are operating within the framework of God's salvific work."[48] In the words of Brazilian liberation theologian Leonardo Boff, "History is the ongoing process leading toward [total liberation as the essence of the reign of God], and it is up to humans to help the process along." Although the reign of God cannot be reduced to a particular historical event, "it is a present reality that finds concrete embodiments in history. It must be viewed as a process that begins in this world and reaches its culmination in the eschatological future."[49]

[44] G. Gutiérrez, *A Theology of Liberation: History, Politics and Salvation* (Maryknoll, NY: Orbis Books, 1973), 153.   [45] Ibid., 152.

[46] Gutiérrez, "Notes for a Theology of Liberation," 256.

[47] G. Gutiérrez, *The Power of the Poor in History* (Maryknoll, NY: Orbis, 1983), 32.

[48] Ibid.

[49] L. Boff, *Jesus Christ Liberator: A Critical Christology for Our Times* (Maryknoll, NY: Orbis Books, 1978), 281.

The basis for the affirmation that "history is one" is the realization that God is constantly acting in history. The God of Genesis inaugurates history by creating humanity. This God also fashions a people from Abraham's seed, then liberates them from the Pharaoh, making a covenant with them to defend them against all forms of bondage. The unity of history, however, finds no greater expression than in the figure of Jesus Christ, at once a "true God" and a "true human being" in the words of liberation theologian Jon Sobrino.[50] God's incarnation, the fact that God assumes fully the human form, with all the limitations and suffering entailed, being faithful even unto death, demonstrates the depth of God's involvement in human history and love for humanity, especially for the downtrodden.

The foregoing discussion of liberation theology's eschatology allows us to see its connection at the level of content with the Hegelian-Marxist reading of modernity's emancipatory project. Both share the view that history is a meaningful process grounded on a single driving force. This force is _intrinsic_ to the historical process; it is a _telos_, a potential seeking actualization. The crucial link that makes possible the connection between liberation theology's eschatology and the Hegelian-Marxist view of history is the Aristotelian doctrine of natural law. Aristotelian teleology is a key philosophical foundation for both Catholic thinking, as shaped by Thomas Aquinas, and Hegelian-Marxist thinking.

The connection between Christian eschatology and secular theories of history has been explored by philosopher and historian Karl Löwith. He argues that the modern idea of progress "originates with the Hebrew and Christian faith in fulfillment and that it ends with the secularization of its eschatological pattern."[51] This is why, instead of a philosophy of history, Löwith calls for a "theology of history" to understand "history as the history of fulfillment and salvation." Löwith's position has been subjected to strong criticism.[52] However, the influence of Christianity's linear conception of history on Hegel's reconstruction of the Spirit's journey to the full self-consciousness supports his reading.

Whatever the intrinsic merits of Löwith's theory, I want to

---

[50] J. Sobrino, _Jesus in Latin America_ (Maryknoll, NY: Orbis Books, 1987).
[51] K. Löwith, _Meaning in History_ (Chicago: University of Chicago Press, 1949), 2.
[52] See Blumenberg, _The Legitimacy of the Modern Age_.

suggest that the relation between modernity and Christian eschatology is perhaps more complex and dialectical, so that Christianity
too becomes influenced by ideas and methods of modern discourses. I believe that liberation theology and the popular church's
project represent an appropriation or, to mirror Lowith's terminol-
ogy, a sacralization of certain aspects of one of modernity's emancipatory patterns, more specifically the Hegelian-Marxist one.

I do not contend that liberation theology and the popular
church's project are reducible to Marxism. Further, I am not
interested in showing whether liberation theology is "Marxist" or
not. As I said earlier, the relationship between Latin American
progressive Catholicism and Marxism is a complex one: at times
there is clear cross-fertilization, while at other times there are
tensions, especially around the issue of economic determinism and
mechanicism, which Gutiérrez calls "metaphysical materialism."[53] I shall discuss the specifics of this relationship in the next
chapter, when I present the responses of the popular church's
intellectuals to the crisis of existing socialist models.

I am interested, rather, in tracing the aspects of post-Enlightenment thinking that are constitutive of both Marxism and liberation
theology in their various forms. I want to focus on liberation
theology's religious appropriation of the post-Enlightenment version of the modern emancipatory project through a dialogue with
historicist/culturalist currents of Marxism. The liberationist vision
of the popular church, I contend, appropriates from Marxism
more than a set of analytical tools to interrogate reality. The
influence of Marxism, especially read through Hegelian lenses, on
liberation theology is deeper. At the epistemological level, Marxist
conceptions of the nature of human praxis, social change, and
history are incorporated and given a Catholic interpretation.
What liberation theology and the Marxist-Hegelian vision share is
a strong version of "metaphysical holism," a philosophical position that conceives of society as a totality and of history as a unity
susceptible to closure.[54]

---

[53] G. Gutiérrez, *The Truth Shall Make You Free: Confrontations* (Maryknoll, NY: Orbis Books,
1990), 62.
[54] Metaphysical holism holds that there are collective entities and dynamics that are
irreducible to the actions of single actors. For a discussion of holism and individualism in
the social sciences, see K. Kontopoulos, *The Logics of Social Structure* (Cambridge: Cambridge University Press, 1994).

A clear example of this shared holism is liberation theology's appropriation and transformation of the Marxian concept of class, as the privileged subject of history, into the biblical poor [*anawim*]. Clarifying his view of social conflict, Gutiérrez points out that the "economically based deterministic view of class struggle is completely alien to liberation theology."[55] This contention seems to me correct. The use of the terms "poor" and "oppressed" allows Gutiérrez and other liberation theologians to "take into account the non-economic factors present in situations of conflict between social groups." This is why Gutiérrez "continually refer[s] to races discriminated against, despised cultures, exploited classes, and the conditions of women."[56] However, despite the rejection of class determinism in Marxism, Gutiérrez shares with Marx the idea of a unified, collective subject engaged in a cosmic battle to bring history to fulfillment. Echoing Freire, Gutiérrez conceives of the poor as the main protagonists of the process of liberation: "The future of history lies with the poor and the exploited. Authentic liberation will be the deed of the oppressed themselves: in them, the Lord will save history. The spirituality of liberation will have its point of departure in the spirituality of the *anawim*."[57]

In Gutiérrez's version of holism, the poor/oppressed become a kind of supra-individual subjectivity with its own intentionality, with a single set of desires and goals. Despite Gutiérrez's recognition that the poor/oppressed contain a myriad of life experiences and power dynamics, the term becomes a catch-all category that refers in the last instance to a corporate agent *in potentia*. It is as if the poor had occupied the role of the *Geist*, or more properly of the proletariat conceived spiritually as by the young Marx, in the journey towards humanity's self-realization. The ultimate goal of the poor is the recovery of humanity's essence, which is distorted by a process of alienation with roots in class exploitation. Liberation theology interprets this alienation religiously as sin, which separates human beings from God, from each other, and from their essential being. This sin is committed by the powerful against the weak, not only individually, but most importantly through

---

[55] Gutiérrez, *The Truth Shall Make You Free*, 71.   [56] Ibid., 70–71.
[57] Gutiérrez, *The Power of the Poor in History*, 53.

social and economic structures. Thus for Gutiérrez, the poor are

the oppressed, exploited proletariat, robbed of the fruit of their labor and despoiled of their humanity. The poor, the oppressed, are members of *one* social class that is being subtly (or not so subtly) exploited by another social class. This exploited class, especially in its most clear-sighted segment, the proletariat, is an active one. Hence, an option for the poor is an option for one social class against another. It means entering into the world of the exploited social class, with its values, its cultural categories. It means entering into solidarity with its interests and its struggles.[58]

Thus, for both Marxism and liberation theology, even when history is rife with conflict, it is possible to gain a total vision of social reality by following the actions of the proletariat and the poor, both conceived as totalities *in potentia*. Despite his rejection of "a totalitarian version of history that denies the freedom of the human person,"[59] Gutiérrez still engages in a different kind of totalization. In his vision, history and society derive their meaning through the struggles of the poor (construed as the universal emancipatory/salvific subject) against the forces that oppress them. Furthermore, the claim that these struggles are the partial fulfillment of a "Christo-finalized history" turn historical processes into a cosmic unity whose meaning and trajectory have been already laid out by God.[60]

I stated above that liberation theology sacralizes and cosmicizes the Hegelian-Marxist reading of social conflict. Whereas for Marx the activities of the proletariat are embedded in the internal contradictions of the capitalist mode of production, in liberation theology the struggles of the poor are interpreted in terms of a divine plan, in connection with the unfolding of the eschatological promise. This is why the Latin American poor come to be represented in liberation theology by the people of Israel in bondage in Egypt. The God of the Exodus, thus, becomes the God of the

---

[58] Ibid., 44–45. Emphasis added.

[59] Gutiérrez, *The Truth Shall Make You Free*, 61.

[60] In this sense, liberation theology's totalization of history is far more absolute than Marx's. Whereas for Marx history's *telos* is solely the product of human praxis, for Gutiérrez it is ultimately of divine origin, connected with notion of revelation and providence. In other words, despite Gutiérrez's drive to historicize the Christian utopian message, the foundational ground for his totalization is supra-historical, a fact makes the latter more compelling than a law of either history or nature.

poor, a God of life, committed to bringing total liberation. As Leonardo and Clodovis Boff characterize it, the God of life

is especially close to those who are oppressed; [a] God who hears their cry and resolves to set them free. God is father of all, but most particularly father and defender of those who are oppressed and treated unjustly. Out of love for them, God takes sides, takes their side against the repressive measures of all pharaohs.[61]

The privileged place of the poor in this march toward salvation, as the main carriers of prophetic inspiration and knowledge for renewal is most poignantly expressed in the figure of Jesus Christ. According to Sobrino, although the "New Testament universalizes the humanity of Christ, and presents Jesus as sharing the condition of every human being," the Gospels present Jesus as a poor human being, in his birth, in the unfolding of the events of his life, and in his death. They present him as a human being in solidarity with the poor and with sinners, whose cause he defends, to whom he proclaims the coming of the kingdom, and whose lot he assumes. This is the partisan presentation of Jesus' humanity.[62]

Jesus Christ is partisan because "The true human being appears as the poor and the impoverished human being," s/he who is subjected most radically to the tribulations of the flesh. Jesus Christ's crucifixion is the most radical indication of God's "absolute nearness" not only to human beings but to the poor. In Sobrino's words, God's impotence in the cross expresses "God's absolute nearness to the poor, sharing their lot to the end. God was on Jesus' cross. God shared the horrors of history. Therefore God's action in the resurrection is credible, at least for the one who has been crucified."[63]

Liberation theology presents a Christ whose ministry, death and resurrection, aims to free humanity from the bondage of sin, the underlying cause of injustice and exploitation, two conditions that distort our essence, producing self-estrangement and separating us for each other and from God. Christ in liberation theology is "Christ the liberator."

---

[61] L. Boff and C. Boff, *Introducing Liberation Theology* (Maryknoll, NY: Orbis Books, 1987), 50–51.
[62] Sobrino, *Jesus in Latin America*, 33.   [63] Ibid., 153.

Liberationist christology thus highlights the ways in which the popular church's worldview appropriates and resonates with some of the key themes of modernity's emancipatory project, especially in its Hegelian-Marxist version. While the popular church rejects post-Enlightenment instrumental rationalism and bourgeois individualism, it shares with the Hegelian-Marxist reading of modernity the notion that self-reflexive human action plays a central role in the struggle for liberation. More importantly, the popular church shares an optimistic and ultimately totalizing reading of history: history has a *telos*, an emancipatory drive – embodied in the actions of a collective emancipatory subject – that is pushing it, at least *in potentia*, towards completion.

Now that I have traced the ideological bases of the *igreja popular*, showing its connections with modernity, we can ask how well this worldview stands against the challenges of contemporary capitalism in Brazil. I shall argue later that the popular church's totalizing reading of history (i.e., history conceived as the progressive movement towards the reign of God), which it derived from a modernist reworking of Christian eschatology, causes it to lose sight of the precariousness of the struggles for liberation at the grassroots. In the context of a deepening and widening capitalism, these struggles do not evince a clear movement toward the *eschaton*, but rather demonstrate the haphazardness, fragility, and sometimes even futility of local gains. Furthermore, through the "ontologizing" of the poor (i.e., understanding the poor as unified collective agent with a single set of interests and goals, as a kind of supra-individual subjectivity) the popular church misses the poor's increasingly heterogeneous life conditions, and especially the structural obstacles to organization and mobilization which they face. This misperception, in turn, has led the popular church to place the whole pastoral-pedagogical burden on small groups like base communities, which are more effective in training grassroots lay leaders than in evangelizing the masses. The masses, as a result, may be finding other religious options that respond to their felt needs.

Before exploring the nature and causes of the crisis of the popular church's project, I will characterize more fully the particular history and institutional configuration of the *igreja popular*.

CHAPTER 2

The consolidation of the igreja popular and its impact on Brazilian society

As the 1960s came to a close, pastoral innovations, experimental forms of ecclesial life, and new theological approaches began, under the auspicious climate inaugurated by Vatican II and Medellín, to coalesce into the popular church, a church "born of the poor." As we saw earlier in Medellín, the Latin American bishops provided the social-analytical framework, pastoral principles, and institutional basis for the eventual formation of the *igreja popular*. The bishops' denunciations of the region's economic dependence as the root cause of poverty, their solidarity with the poor, and their pledge to work for an integral liberation gave impetus to pastoral initiatives already operative on the ground.

By the mid-1970s the Brazilian popular church had consolidated, becoming the highly differentiated organization it is today. Today, the *igreja popular* is an interlocking set of institutions, scholarly activities, and pastoral programs operating at the national, diocesan, and local levels. Although these elements together form a coherent whole built around the preferential option for the poor and the ideological themes described above, each of them has its own agents, audience, religious products, and range of action.

At the local level, the popular church consists of members of the base ecclesial communities and biblical circles and activists involved in various pastoral outreach initiatives. Among these, the *Pastoral Operária* (Workers' Pastoral), the *Comissão Pastoral da Terra* (Commission for the Land Pastoral, or CPT), and the *Conselho Indigenista Missionário* (Missionary Council for Indigenous Populations, CIMI) became the most visible. Joining them are *militantes* (activists) of internationally-based Catholic lay movements (such as the Workers' Catholic Action or ACO, and the Youth Catholic

Action or JOC), and a large contingent of pastoral agents and *assessores* (advisors such as sociologists, theologians and popular educators) who accompany and often guide work at the base.

At middle level, the *igreja popular* is constituted by a cadre of theologians and intellectuals, most with ties to universities, research institutes and non-governmental organizations, whose main task is to systematize and reflect on experiences at the base. Efforts at this level produce liberation theology proper, as an internationally-recognized corpus of knowledge. Although there is a high degree of interaction between pastoral activities on the ground and the work of theologians, it is incorrect to reduce the popular church to liberation theology, as critics and sympathizers alike sometimes do. It is true that CEBs and *círculos bíblicos* often work closely with liberation theologians. However, we should not confuse a grassroots theology constructed by poor, often uneducated people seeking to deal with concrete situations in their everyday lives, with a system of ideas produced by professional theologians at some distance from the pressures of economic hardship. Conflation of these two levels of theological and pastoral action can lead to misguided accusations of elitism against the popular church, as I will argue in chapter 8.

The relationship between the base and liberation theology is more often one of reciprocal influence in which the levels interact without losing their specificity and relative autonomy. Biblical readings, personal growth and communal life at the base inspire new christological, soteriological, philosophical, and anthropological insights at the level of professional liberation theology. These insights, in turn, help orient and design better pastoral approaches to fulfill the preferential option for the poor. The key link in this relation of mutual determination is the pastoral agent, who very often plays the dual role of professional theologian and active participant in community life.

Finally, at the institutional level, the Brazilian popular church is institutionally anchored through the support of "liberal" prelates, including cardinals such as Paulo Evaristo Arns of São Paulo and Aloísio Lorscheider of Fortaleza, and bishops like Pedro Casaldáliga of São Félix de Araguaia, Tomás Balduíno of Goiás, Antonio Fragoso of Crateús, Mauro Morelli of Duque de Caxias, and Adriano Hipólito, who headed the diocese of Nova Iguaçu during the period I conducted field work.

Since in this study I am interested in examining the crisis of the *igreja popular* at the local level, it is necessary to document more fully the development of initiatives there. As base ecclesial communities represent the most visible and influential local pastoral initiative, I will concentrate on their emergence, evolution, and impact on the Brazilian church and society. In some parts of Latin America, especially in El Salvador and Nicaragua, base communities formed "parallel" churches independent of the hierarchy, in the context of deep divisions in their episcopal bodies and broader societies. In contrast, CEBs in Brazil thrived in close connection with the official church, receiving substantial episcopal support.[1] Together with other outreach pastoral initiatives to serve the marginalized, CEBs represented a viable option for the CNBB to respond effectively to the challenges of the Brazilian economic model, the rise of a repressive military regime, and the erosion of the church's influence among the poor.[2]

Between 1968 and 1985, CEBs provided a guiding pastoral model for the Brazilian Catholic Church. As early as 1974, after a sociological and theological study of the first ten years of CEB work in Brazil, the CNBB declared base communities one of the pastoral priorities for the national church. Earlier references to base communities had been made in the CNBB's *Plano Pastoral Conjunto* (Joint Pastoral Plan) of 1965, which sought to establish some guidelines for parish renewal. Nevertheless, this document conceived of base communities as politically centrist groups under the strict control of the clergy, cast in the mold of the Christian communities organized and ministered by lay catechists that had been functioning since the late 1950s in Barra do Piraí.

[1] For a comparison of the Brazilian and Nicaraguan experiences, see T. Bamat, "Political Change and the Catholic Church in Brazil and Nicaragua," in *New Perspectives on Social Class and Socioeconomic Development in the Periphery*, ed. N. W. Keith and N. Z. Keith (New York: Greenwood Press, 1988).

[2] Bruneau, *The Political Transformation of the Brazilian Church*. Bruneau sees CEBs as the result of a strategic move by the Brazilian hierarchy to revitalize the old, impersonal, and static parish model and implement the conclusions of Vatican II. While these considerations may explain the adoption of CEBs as an overarching pastoral model by CNBB, they do not exhaust the extra and intra-ecclesial forces and events that shaped the development of base communities in Brazil. For a more balanced reading, see Teixeira, *A gênese das CEBs*.

By the third and fourth biennial pastoral plans (1975–1976 and 1977–1978 respectively), the CNBB had designed a dozen specific projects involving base communities, including one to

analyze the local experiences of CEBs, reflect on their evangelizing function, liturgy, their relationship with pastoral structures and local ecclesial forms: diocese, parish, pastoral coordination, zone and vicariates, [and] their influence on the behavior of Christians concerning [the latter's] commitment to the world.[3]

In the general pastoral guidelines for 1983–1986, the CNBB highlights the work performed by CEBs and calls for an emphasis on base communities that "clearly shows the interest and love the Brazilian church has for 'this new way of being church.'"[4] Quoting from an earlier CNBB study of CEBs, the document goes on to declare that "'It is around base communities that the evangelizing work of the church is being and will be developed more and more.'"[5]

The originality of CEB practices and organizational forms led theologians, pastoral agents, and later bishops to recognize in base communities "a new experience of church, of communion of persons within the more legitimate . . . ancient tradition" of the early Christian church.[6] According to Leonardo Boff, CEBs seemed to offer an alternative to modernity's "wild atomization of existence and [the] general anonymity of persons lost in the cogs of the mechanisms of the macro-organization and bureaucracies" and also to a hierarchical church that had institutionalized "mechanical, reified inequalities and inequities."[7] In Boff's words,

Christian life in the basic communities is characterized by the absence of alienating structures, by direct relationships, by reciprocity, by a deep communion, by mutual assistance, by communality of gospel ideas, by equality among members. The specific characteristics of society are absent here: rigid rules; hierarchies; prescribed relations in a framework of distinction of functions, qualities and titles.[8]

---

[3] CNBB, *Comunidades eclesiais de base no Brasil: Experiências e perspectivas*, CNBB Studies no. 23 (São Paulo: Paulinas, 1979), 5–6.

[4] CNBB, *Diretrizes gerais da ação pastoral, 1983–1986* (São Paulo: Paulinas, 1983), 92.

[5] Ibid.

[6] L. Boff, *Ecclesiogenesis: The Base Communities Reinvent the Church* (Maryknoll, NY: Orbis Books, 1986), 1.

[7] Ibid.   [8] Ibid., 4.

The enthusiasm generated by uniqueness of base community life contributed to the CEBs' rapid acceptance among progressive Catholics. In their eyes, CEBs became the main "artisans" of a new church and a new society. Progressive Catholics came to see base communities as, on the one hand, "a church revolution to the extent that they correspond to a gigantic restructuring of the Catholic community on the Latin American continent."[9] On the other hand, many also came to understand CEBs "not simply as the means to attain something else – a liberated society. They are already an end – an end in the process, insofar as they are the seeds of such a society."[10] I shall argue later on that this idealization of CEB life and its elevation to the model for a new church and society have opened base communities to challenges from conservative ecclesial forces and produced vanguardist readings of pastoral work that run the risk of missing the poor's felt needs.

It should be noted, however, that for all their initial enthusiasm, theologians and pastoral agents such as Leonardo Boff were careful to warn against naive, triumphalistic stances *vis-à-vis* CEBs. In response to Toennies' society-community dichotomy,[11] Boff writes:

Community does not constitute a typical phase of human-group formation. Nor is it possible for community to exist in a pure state. Concretely, there is always a power structure, in either the dominative or the solidarity version. There are always inequalities and stratified roles, in function of some particular scale of values. There are conflicts and particular interests. Historically, social formations are mixed: they have some societal and some communitarian characteristics.[12]

The task of base communities is, thus, not to replace society altogether but to inject their communitarian drive into it in order to renew it. Since societal and the communitarian poles are constitutive of all human institutions, including the CEBs, base communities' work is more modest: to assert the "supremacy of the communitarian over the societal." At the ecclesial level, base

[9] D. Barbé, *Grace and Power: Base Communities and Nonviolence in Brazil* (Maryknoll, NY: Orbis Books, 1987), 89.
[10] C. Boff, "CEBs e práticas de libertação," *Revista Eclesiástica Brasileira* 40, no. 160 (1980), 611.
[11] See F. Toennies, *Community and Society* (New York: Harper and Row, 1963).
[12] Boff, *Ecclesiogenesis*, 5.

communities "cannot pretend to constitute a global alternative to the church as institution. They can only be its ferment for renewal."

Despite Leonardo Boff's attempts to offer a more dialectical reading of the process of institution-building, he continues to view CEBs as *sementes* (seeds) of the new church and society. Boff continues to identify CEBs with the communitarian force that will "re-invent the church," but he does not give enough attention to the "societal" elements they contain or the intra and extra-institutional obstacles that confront them as they work for renewal. The use of the images of *fermento* (leaven) and *semente* to describe CEBs paves the way for vanguardist interpretations of their ecclesial and social role. At the CEBs' fifth national meeting in 1983, for instance, base communities become "the people united, seed of a new society." CEBs become the seeds of a "new tree," "because the present society has reached its limits. It does not work anymore. It does not bear fruits. It is against life. It is old and rotten; it cannot be repaired or recovered."[13]

The adoption of this triumphalistic view of CEBs was bolstered by the protracted years of repression during the military regime (1964–1985) and by the popular church's success in offering a viable strategy to support grassroots resistance. With the 1964 coup that overthrew a reformist, populist civilian government, all forms of mass mobilization, beginning with trade unions and opposition parties, were violently disassembled by a highly bureaucratic-authoritarian state apparatus.[14] To suppress resistance to authoritarian regime, the *de facto* government decreed a series of "Institutional Acts," one of which set the basis for the creation of the National Information Service (Serviço Nacional de Informações, SNI), a powerful intelligence gathering bureaucracy with the role of coordinating a vast network of spies which penetrated all aspects of national life. The SNI passed the information it collected on to various security forces which arrested, intimidated, tortured, and "disappeared" thousands of dissenters.

In 1968, the same year that the Latin American bishops

---

[13] "V encontro interecclesial das comunidades de base do Brasil," *SEDOC* 16 (1983), 275.
[14] A. Stepan, ed., *Authoritarian Brazil* (New Haven: Yale University Press, 1976).

gathered in Medellín, the military regime passed the Fifth Institutional Act, also known as AI-5, which inaugurated the most repressive period in post-1964 Brazil (1968–1973). AI-5 suspended constitutional civil rights, such as *habeas corpus*, closed down the congress, and established a strict censorship of the press, further restricting a drastically curtailed public sphere. All these moves were justified by a "doctrine of national security" that sought to safeguard the nation against the threat of world communism and to foster conditions (i.e., internal stability and a disciplined work force) for an economic development driven by international capital and coordinated from above by state technocrats.[15]

Against the intricate web of informants, repressive laws, and tactics deployed with the bureaucratic-authoritarian state, the popular church provided a two-pronged approach that made it the single most powerful opposition voice in the country. On the one hand, their decentralized mode of organization and locally-based focus of action enabled CEBs to escape the severe repression that struck oppositional groups like trade unions, political parties, and student movements.[16] Working close to the ground, on the basis of residence, and relying on tightly-knit bonds of solidarity, CEBs provided capillary spaces to keep the dialogue about a different, more egalitarian Brazil alive.

Foucault's work on the "micro-physics of power" can help illuminate the role CEBs played during the years of military repression. Base communities functioned as "zones of darkness" in a "panopticized" society.[17] They were "shadowy areas" beyond the inspecting and overseeing gaze of the authoritarian regime in which religion and politics mixed in non-traditional ways. In these zones of darkness, CEBs offered a proven consciousness-raising methodology and a participatory form of education to train local informed citizens, many of whom later became grassroots activists.

---

[15] For an analysis of the doctrine of national security from a liberationist viewpoint, see J. Comblin, *The Church and the National Security State* (Maryknoll, NY: Orbis Books, 1979).

[16] T. Bruneau, "Brazil: The Catholic Church and Basic Christian Communities," in *Religion and Political Conflict in Latin America*, ed. D. Levine (Chapel Hill: University of North Carolina Press, 1986).

[17] Foucault offers a study of the power effects of surveillance in *Discipline and Punish: Birth of the Prison* (New York: Vintage Books, 1977).

CEBs' location at the interstices of the repressive system allowed them to avoid the fate of dominant forms of Catholic mobilization during the 1960s, such as the specialized forms of Catholic action (i.e., the Catholic Youth Workers Movement and the Catholic University Youth), which worked on the basis of occupation and class and became highly politicized, vanguard movements. These two conditions made them a visible target of military repression to the extent that they virtually disappeared.

Activists nurtured in the free spaces provide by CEBs would play a key role in the *abertura* (1974–1985), a transitional period of political liberalization that eventually led to the naming of a civilian to the presidency. Local leaders trained by CEBs, for example, took part in the huge 1978–79 metalworkers' strikes in São Paulo, the industrial heart of the country. These strikes led to the creation of the Workers' Party (Partido dos Trabalhadores, or PT) which came very close to winning the 1989 presidential elections.

The second element behind the church's central oppositional role *vis-à-vis* the state was located at the elite level. The severity of repression under the military and the fact that it touched Catholic workers led the official, hierarchical church to build a unified front against state brutality. The Brazilian bishops not only became vocal critics of the government but also promoted institutional initiatives to advance the cause of justice and truth and to defend the rights and lives of dissenters.[18] The church thus became an institutional umbrella under which the opposition could survive the harsh years of repression.

Historian Ralph Della Cava characterizes the dual role of the popular church during the military regime thus:

in the absence of viable voluntary associations and political parties, the Churches in general and the Catholic in particular had . . . become the single largest opposition force to military rule. In the case of the Catholic [church], no other institution except the military, enjoyed a nation-wide

---

[18] One well-known initiative was taken by the archdiocese of São Paulo under progressive Paulo Evaristo Arns. Arns authorized the gathering of testimonies and reports about human rights violations and political crimes in Brazil. The information collected was published under the title *Brasil nunca mais* (Petrópolis: Vozes, 1985). Another initiative was the creation of diocesan chapters of the Justice and Peace Commission, which offered legal services in cases involving human rights violations. See Mainwaring, *The Catholic Church and Politics in Brazil.*

network of cadres, a system of communications (even if only door-to-door) that functioned despite censorship and, unlike the military, a world-wide organization on which it could draw for support and bank on for an international "hearing."[19]

Since the legalization of opposition parties in 1979, the Roman Catholic church has gradually gone from being the main oppositional force to being a player among others in the expanding civil society. However, its role in the transition to an elected civilian government has also been extremely important. The church's decisive support for the 1985 national campaign in favor of direct presidential elections attests to this fact. The massiveness of this movement so threatened the hegemony of the governing military–capitalist elite alliance that a civilian was named president to defuse the explosive situation. The church also had an active role in the formulation of the new constitution promulgated in 1988, introducing and lobbying for specific initiatives. This constitution represented the last step towards the direct elections of 1989.[20]

The Catholic church's involvement in civil society reflects the coherence and high level of legitimacy of the popular church's project. How is it then that, given the successes and optimism of the 1970s, by the end of the 1980s some data began to indicate that there was "a rather weak link between the progressive Catholic Church and the Brazilian population generally"?[21] Simultaneously, an increasing number of activists began to voice serious concerns about the future of the popular church. What had changed so radically to induce, in the words of N. Peritore, "a dominant tone of pessimism among church activists"?[22] What events had challenged the optimism behind the utopian project of the popular church and liberation theology? I turn to these questions in the next two chapters.

---

[19] Ralph Della Cava, "The 'People's Church,'" 147.
[20] T. Bruneau and W.E. Hewitt, "Catholicism and Political Action in Brazil: Limitations and Prospects," in *Conflict and Competition: The Latin American Church in a Changing Environment*, ed. E. Cleary and H. Stewart-Gambino, (Boulder, CO: Lynne Rienner Publishers, 1992), 55.
[21] T. Bruneau and W. E. Hewitt, "Patterns of Church Influence in Brazil's Political Transition," *Comparative Politics* 22, no. 1 (October 1989), 60.
[22] N. P. Peritore, *Socialism, Communism and Liberation Theology in Brazil: An Opinion Survey Using Q-Methodology* (Athens, OH: Ohio University Center for International Studies, 1990).

PART II

The nature of the crisis

CHAPTER 3

The internal dimension: a crisis of participation

INTRODUCTION: A PHENOMENOLOGICAL APPROACH TO THE CRISIS

Before exploring the causes behind the crisis of the *igreja popular*, it is necessary to address the following questions: What do I mean by the crisis of the popular church in Brazil? What kind of "empirical" evidence do we have to ascertain that the Brazilian popular church is in crisis? These questions are especially relevant given the relative paucity of reliable statistical data on the levels of participation in and political influence of base communities and Catholic outreach programs for the poor.

The first nation-wide studies of base communities were conducted in the 1970s by the National Conference of Brazilian Bishops (CNBB). These studies place the number of base communities throughout Brazil somewhere between 80,000 to 100,000.[1] Estimating that the typical CEB has 50–100 members, membership in base communities would stand in the range of 4 to 10 million, that is, between 3 and 8 percent of the national Catholic population.

CNBB figures have been widely cited in the academic literature on the popular church.[2] Nevertheless, some observers have dis-

---

[1] CNBB, *Comunidades eclesiais de base no Brasil*; and *Comunidades eclesiais de base na base na igreja no Brasil* (São Paulo: Paulinas, 1982).

[2] See, for example, Della Cava, "The 'People's Church;'" S. Mainwaring, "Brazil: The Catholic Church and the Popular Movement in Nova Iguaçu, 1974–1985," in *Religion and Political Conflict in Latin America* ed. Levine; and R. Ireland, "Catholic Base Communities, Spiritist Groups, and the Deepening of Democracy in Brazil," in *The Progressive Church in Latin America*, ed. S. Mainwaring and A. Wilde (Notre Dame: University of Notre Dame Press, 1989).

puted these figures.[3] At the low end, political scientist Jean Daudelin estimates that membership in base communities reached, at most, 250,000 (less than 0.5 percent of the national Catholic population).[4] Daudelin's figure contradicts more recent estimates by sectors sympathetic to the popular church that CEBs make up about 5 percent of the Catholic population.[5]

A recent, rigorous nation-wide study conducted by the Center for Religious Statistics and Social Investigations (CERIS) and the Superior Institute of Studies in Religion (ISER) appears to confirm the higher estimates.[6] Drawing from surveys obtained in 2965 parishes throughout the country (40 percent of the total number nationally), researchers concluded with a good degree of certainty that there are approximately 100,000 communities in Brazil. Nevertheless, the study relies only on reports provided by the parish priests and vicars rather than on actual field work. It is quite possible that priests might have given an overly optimistic picture of communities in their parishes. More importantly, the numbers reported in the study refer to Catholic ecclesial communities, a broad definition that includes not only base communities but also other groups, such as the *Vicentinos*, which have a more spiritual, assistential, and local character.

Given the fact that complete, reliable data on CEBs nation-wide is hard to obtain, it is very difficult to assess whether or not base communities are in crisis. Long-term observers of the Brazilian Catholic church seem to think that CEB fortunes are declining. Bruneau and Hewitt, for instance, state that:

Much was expected of the CEBs, and indeed their importance in the late 1970s and early 1980s in providing alternate form of organization and mobilization cannot be denied. Nevertheless, they have not matched expectations, despite inflated figures on their numbers. An independent lay leadership has not emerged from the CEBs, and they still rely very

---

[3] C. A. Drogus, "Popular Movements and the Limits of Political Mobilization at the Grassroots in Brazil"; and Bruneau and Hewitt, "Catholicism and Political Action in Brazil," in *Conflict Competition*, ed. Cleary and Stewart-Gambino.

[4] J. Daudelin. "L'Église progressiste brésilienne: la fin d'un mythe?" in *L'Amérique et les Amériques*, ed. J. Zylberberg and F. Damers (Sainte Foy, Quebec: Les Presses de l'Université de Laval, 1992), 678.

[5] A. Antoniazzi, "O catolicismo no Brasil," in *Sinais dos tempos: Tradições religiosas no Brasil*, ed. L. Landim et al., (Rio de Janeiro: ISER, 1989).

[6] R. Valle and M. Pitta, *Comunidades eclesiais católicas* (Petrópolis: Vozes, 1994).

much on clergy and bishops. They have not been unified in socio-political matters, and their general impact is weak.[7]

At a more micro level, Hewitt, who has mapped the trajectories of a group of CEBs in São Paulo since the mid-1980s, could not find almost a fourth of his original sample communities in a recent attempt to update his work. In the communities he could find, he noticed a transformation of their *modus operandi*. According to Hewitt, many of the CEBs under study have become de-politicized: progressive members have all but disappeared because the communities have either shunned them or pushed them out. Moderates with a stronger concern for traditional, devotional practices, in the meantime, have steadily taken control of vital resources. Concurrent with these shifts there has been an increase in priestly control over the communities. All these changes lead Hewitt to hypothesize that CEBs, as they existed in the 1980s, are bound to disappear. They will give way to communities modeled after and connected to the charismatic movement.[8]

To avoid getting bogged down in an unproductive numerical dispute about the strength of Brazilian CEBs, I have chosen a different approach. I take at face value the perceptions of popular church members, who time after time expressed their sense that the *igreja popular* was in crisis. The task then becomes to understand what progressive Catholics mean by the assertion that the Brazilian popular church is in crisis. This "subjective" approach is justified by the insights of social phenomenology, which states that an event becomes a crisis only when it is grasped as such by the individuals who suffer its direct impact. Unless the phenomenon becomes problematic for the actors, unless it breaks with what sociologist Alfred Schutz's terms their "natural attitude," which grasps things as they appear, it will continue to be part of the taken-for-granted world of ordinary experience.[9]

In privileging the "subjective" dimension of the crisis, I do not want to claim that the condition does not have measurable "objec-

---

[7] Bruneau and Hewitt, "Catholicism and Political Action in Brazil," 58.

[8] W. E. Hewitt, "CEBs and the Progressive Church in Brazil: What Comes Next?" paper presented at the XVIII International Congress of the Latin American Studies Association, Atlanta, Georgia, March 10–12, 1994.

[9] On Schutz's social phenomenology, see H. Wagner, ed., *Alfred Schutz on Phenomenology and Social Relations* (Chicago: University of Chicago Press, 1970).

tive" components. Rather, the focus on the actors' experience will help us identify precisely those "objective" pressures and contradictions that the actors themselves consider central to the crisis. This is so because actors construct their interpretations in response to objective processes and changes at the local, national, and international levels. These processes and transformations shape the actors' perceptions of the challenges the popular church is facing and define the activists' field of experience. Thus, it is also necessary to characterize the dynamics of such processes in themselves, as they transcend the actors' perception. I do this by introducing the viewpoints of outsiders, among which I include my own. The interaction and dialectic of reciprocal critique between the actors' perceptions and outside perspectives will allow us to understand the nature of the crisis.

The crisis contains two closely interrelated but analytically distinct components: an internal one that points to the limits of grassroots mobilization for the popular church and an external one that refers to the competition Catholicism is facing in the Brazilian religious field. In this chapter I will concentrate on the internal component of the crisis, which given my intra-Catholic focus is the most important one. I will deal with the external dimension in the next chapter.

THE POPULAR CHURCH AND THE LIMITS OF GRASSROOTS MOBILIZATION

As the 1980s drew to a close, a generalized sense of crisis befell progressive Catholic activists in Brazil. More and more, they came to the consensus that, after the trying but heady years following Medellín and Puebla, the *igreja popular* was entering a perplexing period of "pastoral transition" in the midst of a "highly diversified reality" that defied any recourse to old conceptual schemes and strategies.[10] Popular church advisor Júlio de Santa Ana offers a poignant expression and a clear assessment of the depth of this sense of crisis. In a lecture delivered to a team of Brazilian pastoral agents at the end of 1990, he characterized the crisis thus:

---

[10] F. Teixeira, "CEBs: Recriação evangelizadora," *Tempo e Presença*, no. 234 (1988), 30.

We are at a crossroads ... in a country where we don't know the language. We can ask the classic question: "Quo vadis?" "Quo vadis ecclesia?" "Quo vadis each one of us?" It is the image of the traveler, the passenger, who had the certainty of treading the right path, but who begins to doubt, gets to the crossroad and waits in the transit hall. For about a period of 20, 25 years we knew where to go, but then the landscape began to change and the compass that gave us directions began to not correspond with experience. Questions and perplexities emerged.[11]

If Santa Ana is correct, the crisis stems from a widening gap between reality and the models the popular church has developed to organize, apprehend and act upon this reality. The gap emerges from a changing landscape that has rendered obsolete traditional, taken-for-granted pastoral-pedagogical modes of apperception and action, leading to bafflement and despair among grassroots Catholic activists. But what is the new landscape to which Santa Ana refers?

Beginning in the mid-1980s, many changes have radically alter-ed the socio-political terrain in which the popular church is situ-ated. Internationally, the most dramatic change has been the collapse of existing socialist societies in Eastern Europe and the disintegration of the Soviet Union. Although popular church theo-logians and intellectuals did not specifically uphold those societies as models for a new, more egalitarian Brazil, this collapse has forced them to revise their socio-analytical apparatus and to re-define the socialist utopian horizon that framed their struggles for justice and equality. According to theologian Clodovis Boff,

theoreticians of liberation, like any other group active in society, are feeling the powerful impact of the present crisis brought about primarily by the crisis of socialism and by the vigorous expansion of neo-liberal capitalism. All these changes led us to a revision of the categories we used to interpret society, especially those linked to Marxism.[12]

The need to revise methodological tools and utopian horizons has taken on added urgency particularly because in the West the breakdown of existing socialist societies has been taken to signify the definitive failure of the Marxist-socialist emancipatory "grand

[11] J. de Santa Ana, *Lecture to the National Team of Advisors to the Popular Pastoral Program* (Rio de Janeiro: CEDI, 1991), 22.
[12] 'Entrevista com Clodovis Boff," *Politicas Governamentais* 7, no. 68 (1991), 15.

narrative" and the triumph of capitalism.[13] In the words of CEB advisor Frei Betto, one of the main protagonists of the Marxist-Christian dialogue in Latin America,

For critics of liberation theology the fall of the Berlin Wall also meant the end of that theology which had sprung up in Latin America some 25 years earlier. They claim that in using Marxist theory to analyze society – which put socialism on a utopian par with the cause of liberation – that theology "ideologized" itself to such a degree that, when socialism collapsed in Eastern Europe, it lost all credibility as a symbol of hope for the poor – and hence as a legitimate reflection on the divine mystery within Catholic doctrine.[14]

Some critics have gone as far as proclaiming that the collapse of Marxism marks the "end of history." Political analyst Francis Fukuyama, for instance, affirms that, with the fall of the Berlin Wall and the "universalization" of liberal democracy and free markets, humanity has reached the end of its ideological evolution.[15] In the eyes of these critics the birth of democracy is tied to industrialization, the rise of market economies, the values of individualism, and the utilitarian interests that accompany these economic transformations. Thus we can expect a worldwide upsurge of democracy, now that the market has "proven" to be the only viable model to order not only production but social life in general. Market forces reign supreme while communitarian, managed economic models of the type suggested by liberation theologians and the popular church have become delegitimized, seen as prone to excessive bureaucratic centralization and technocratic control by elites. According to Fukuyama, "With the collapse of communism worldwide, we are now in a remarkable situation where left-wing critics of liberal societies are singularly lacking in *radical*

---

[13] French philosopher Jean-François Lyotard uses the term "grand narratives" to characterize forms of knowledge that purport to offer a unified, total reading of history and society. According to Lyotard, Marxism is part of modernity's "emancipatory master-narrative," the origins of which can be traced back to the French Revolution and the Enlightenment. See *The Postmodern Condition: A Report on Knowledge* (Minneapolis: University of Minnesota Press, 1984). On the crisis of Marxist master-narrative, see R. J. Antonio, "The Decline of the Grand Narrative of Emancipatory Modernity: Crisis or Renewal in Neo-Marxist Theory," in *Frontiers of Social Theory*, ed. Ritzer, 88–116.

[14] F. Betto, "Did Liberation Theology Collapse with the Berlin Wall?" *Religion, State and Society* 21, no. 1 (1993), 33.

[15] F. Fukuyama, "The End of History and the Last Man," *National Interest* 16 (1989), 4.

solutions to overcoming the more intractable forms of inequality."[16]

The elevation of the market model as the single social ordering principle has provided ideological support for the spread of neo-liberalism and the rise of a populist right wing throughout Latin America. Despite the deleterious effects of neo-liberal policies on the region's poor, the Latin American left has not yet been able to articulate a coherent political strategy and a viable alternative utopian vision to counter neo-liberalism. Thus far the left has remained trapped in abstract debates about the nature of "post-Marxism" which do not address the specific problems that Latin American people face every day.

At a regional level, the decline of the Marxist-socialist emancipatory master-narratives has been aggravated by the unexpected electoral defeat of the Sandinistas in 1990 and by the increasing isolation of Cuba. For the Latin American left, Nicaragua's and Cuba's successes in fighting imperialism and setting alternative economic models represented the possibility of attaining a revolutionary utopia that would spell the end of the status quo once and for all. As Mexican political scientist Jorge Castañeda argues, in view of Nicaragua's and Cuba's precarious situation, this revolutionary utopia now appears "unarmed," unable to provide a desirable and viable social order.[17]

Closer to home, the Brazilian left, and more generally the country's politically progressive forces, suffered a severe setback with the Workers' Party's (PT) loss in the 1989 presidential elections. A great deal of work and hope went into trade-union activist Luis Inácio "Lula" da Silva's candidacy, but in the end, conservative Fernando Collor and his "phantom" party won the day, bolstered by Brazil's powerful media conglomerates.[18] Lula's loss deflated expectations among activists, a natural effect in a country with an oppositional political culture defined more by spontaneous and ultimately unfulfilled messianic episodes than by long-term

---

[16] F. Fukuyama, *The End of History and the Last Man* (New York: Free Press, 1992), 293.

[17] J. G. Castañeda, *Utopia Unarmed: The Latin American Left After the Cold War* (New York: Alfred A. Knopf, 1993).

[18] The election of social democrat Fernando Cardoso in 1994 has also proven to be a disappointment for the Brazilian left, given his espousal of many of the neo-liberal reforms initiated by Collor.

projects and strategies. More importantly, it showed the limits of popular mobilization in Brazil: in a country where the majority are poor and working-class, a worker, who presumably has the interests of that majority at heart, could not win the elections. Commenting on Lula's defeat, pastoral agent Cláudio Perani writes:

Collor's victory had a real basis in Brazilian society: the business, political and military elites were successful in coopting the poorest and most marginalized strata of the Brazilian population. It is important to recognize that a great majority of the Brazilian population stands at the margins of the organized sectors of the popular movement, and is thus not reached by them. The left's popular base has grown in the recent years, but it is still limited. Even the *pastoral popular*, whose presence has contributed to enlarging the limits of many political channels, has to recognize that it does not have a wide base and that it is encountering difficulties when it wants to dialogue with the majority of the Brazilian people.[19]

Reacting to these international and national events, intellectuals within the *igreja popular* have insisted that although liberation theology borrows some analytical tools from historical materialism, it is not wedded to the Marxist "metaphysical materialism."[20] Thus liberation theology is not in danger of adopting reductive, atheist stances. Sociologist of religion Otto Maduro, for instance, turns the tables on liberation theology's critics. According to Maduro, for liberation theology "Marxism is just a tool and not an untouchable worldview." Moreover, in selectively appropriating on those elements of historical materialism that help to make sense of Latin America's reality and to advance the cause of emancipation, liberation theology is undertaking "a deconstruction of Marxism as a unified whole that must be accepted (or rejected) in its totality, as if it were a sacred or satanic [doctrine]."[21] Liberation theology's

---

[19] C. Perani, "Notas para uma pastoral missionária," *Cadernos do CEAS*, no. 127 (1990), 74.

[20] This argument is based on the observations of Gramsci and Latin American social philosopher José Carlos Mariátegui that Marxism is not an indivisible whole defined by dialectical materialism. Quoting Mariátegui, Gutiérrez asserts that "Marxism is not a 'body of principles which can be rigidly applied the same way in all historical climates and all social latitudes . . .' For Mariátegui as for many today in Latin America, historical materialism is above all 'a method for the historical interpretation of society'" *A Theology of Liberation*, 90.

[21] O. Maduro, "A desmistificação do Marxismo na teologia da libertação," *Comunicações do ISER* 9, no. 39 (1990), 63.

search for the humanist and historicist aspects of historical materialism unleashes a process of "on-going critique and rejection of those aspects in Marxism that the majority of texts, leaders and Marxist parties in Latin America consider fundamental."[22] Therefore, liberation theology is, in effect, "demystifying and desacralizing Marxism."[23]

This reading, as I argued in the previous chapter, is only partially correct. While it is true that Marxism is not of a single piece and that liberation theology borrows selectively from the Marxist analytical apparatus (i.e., at the methodological level), at a deeper epistemological level liberation theology and the various forms of Marxism share a post-Enlightenment understanding of agency, history, and social change. The link between liberation theology and Marxism does not have to do with the materialist method, which is indeed appropriated in different fashion by various Marxist currents, but with the underlying social epistemology that informs post-Enlightenment modernity.

If, as I hypothesize, the crisis of the Marxist metanarrative is connected to a crisis of that post-Enlightenment modernity, then attempts to defend liberation theology by distancing it from the Marxist analytical method miss the mark. The crisis of liberation theology's emancipatory project goes beyond the decline of Marxism. The crisis has to do with the loss of plausibility of post-Enlightenment modernity's social epistemology, particularly its teleological and holistic understanding of history, which both Marxism and liberation theology share. This is why the postmodernist debates are relevant to this study of the Brazilian popular church.

Popular church intellectuals reject the notion that the collapse of existing socialist societies means the eclipse of liberation theology, Leonardo Boff writes:

Liberation theology does not feel itself affected, in its original intuition, by the implosion of socialism and by the crisis of Marxist rationality. Its option never was for Marxism or for socialism, but for the poor. Socialism is a vehicle to achieve a better life and justice for the oppressed. Liberation theology thrives on its original intuition: to have discovered the intimate connection among a God of life, the poor and liberation.

[22] Ibid., 56.   [23] Ibid., 57.

From that intuition it has constructed a spirituality, a pastoral practice and a theology.[24]

Along the same lines, Frei Betto argues that liberation theology would have reached its endpoint only if "the social conditions which engendered it were well and truly over. But it has to state its theme again and again without there being any solution" to these conditions.[25]

Although liberation theologians appear to be moving towards a new phase of reflection that draws its emancipatory inspiration from within Christianity, especially from Catholic social teaching, the crisis of socialism and of the Latin American left has forced them to revise the tools they have used to understand and act upon social reality. This comes at a time when conservative forces within the Vatican have launched an offensive to rein in progressive pastoral and ecclesial initiatives. I shall discuss the implications of this offensive for the Brazilian popular church in the next chapter when I deal with intra-institutional readings of the crisis. It suffices to say that the changes in the socio-political landscape I have described above have contributed to a sense of confusion and pessimism among liberation theologians and popular church intellectuals.

The *igreja popular*, however, consists not just of liberation theologians and intellectual elites. As we saw in chapter 2, it also includes pastoral agents and, in even greater numbers, grassroots activists for whom the collapse of the Berlin Wall is, if anything, only a distant event that takes an ancillary place to the local struggles to transform precarious life conditions in their communities. When asked how the crisis of socialism and liberation theology is affecting the bases, Clodovis Boff responds:

People at the base speak very little of liberation theology. Faith for them is more linked to primary survival needs. But one cannot deny that there has been a de-acceleration in the development [*caminhada*] of base communities, of pastoral outreach programs dealing with land, indigenous populations, marginalized women and blacks.[26]

---

[24] L. Boff, "Implosão do socialismo e teologia da libertação," *Tempo e Presença*, no. 252 (1991), 36.
[25] Betto, "Did Liberation Theology Collapse?" 34.
[26] "Entrevista com Clodovis Boff," 17.

In other words, for pastoral agents and community activists the crisis of the popular church has an altogether different referent than for ecclesial and intellectual elites. For the former, the core of the crisis lies in the apparent failure of the progressive Catholic pastoral effort to extend its reach within its intended audience – the poor. That is, the popular church appears unable to increase participation at the base, precisely among those for whom it has made a preferential option.

As we have seen in the previous chapter, the violent closure of civil society with the 1964 military coup transformed the Catholic church into the only viable space to engage in agonistic political action. This situation, besides bolstering the church's position *vis-à-vis* the state, provided the clergy most sympathetic with the spirit of Medellín a privileged access to the poor. Yet, the highly authoritarian nature of the regime thwarted full-scale engagement with the poor, as any mass movement met swift repression. This is why CEBs thrived during those years: their strategic capacity to mobilize people at the micro level, beyond the spying gaze of the state apparatuses, placed the popular church at the center of political resistance. The small group setting, which entailed meetings in the relative security of the members' homes and brought together people who could be more readily trusted because they were neighbors, proved very effective in the context of the state of national security. As the only relatively safe space to organize, the popular church tended to attract those who had already some involvement in politics.

The political opening (*abertura*) and the expansion of the public space from 1974 to 1985 offered, for the first time, the real possibility for the *igreja popular* to go beyond pastoral action among political and community activists and to expand its evangelizing activities to the vast majority of unorganized poor, thereby truly fulfilling its "preferential option for the poor." To make this transition the church would have to rely on local leaders who had reached their theological and political maturity in the CEBs. Community leaders trained in the small groups that had proven so effective in the years of the military regime would function as *fermento de massa* (leaven) – a kind of lay vanguard – evangelizing, energizing, and mobilizing those around them. As I argued in the previous chapter, here the *igreja popular* operated with a model of consciousness-raising and popular education based on the Gramscian concept of the "organic intellectual" and on Paulo Freire's emphasis on co-responsibility in the pedagogic process. From the popular church's perspective, local leaders trained in base communities were organic intellectuals. Their "organicity" lay in their social location, in the fact that they themselves suffered political repression and economic exploitation. This made them keenly sensitive to the needs, interests, and aspirations of other poor people. CEB activists were also intellectuals; their experience with consciousness-raising techniques gave them tools to articulate in a more systematic fashion the incipient class-consciousness of the oppressed and the fragmentary forms of critique and resistance to domination already present on the ground. Base community activists' direct contact with the Bible, a theology that sought to link faith and life, and with the analytical tools of social science made it possible for them to gradually construct a coherent worldview capable of guiding pastoral and political action.

The transition from a *pastoral de grupos pequenos* (a pastoral approach that serves small groups) to a *pastoral de massa* (pastoral approach for the poor masses), nevertheless, has been fraught with difficulties and contradictions. Rather than being able to broaden the popular church's presence among the poor, serving as the seeds for more base communities and the vehicles of evangelization, local leaders trained by CEBs appear to have become an isolated minority not only in Brazil's complex religious field but within Catholicism. In CEB advisor Pedro Ribeiro de Oliveira's words, although "CEBs are a form of popular Catholicism . . . they are very far from representing the majority of the Catholic population of Brazil."[27]

Since the late 1980s, after more than a decade of growth, "CEBs appear to be increasingly in a period of stagnation."[28] Pastoral agents working with base communities began to voice fears that CEBs could

---

[27] P. R. de Oliveira, "Religiões populares," in *Curso de Verão II*, ed. M. Schwantes et al. (São Paulo: Paulinas, 1988), 125.
[28] Bruneau and Hewitt, "Catholicism and Political Action in Brazil," 58.

become a small Christian vanguard dominated by enlightened pastoral agents (the "activists" of the popular church) unable to have any impact on the *povão*, the great Catholic mass, in an unfavorable ecclesial and political context. Even when the CEBs are a popular expression of Catholicism, they neither represent nor reach the majority of the country's Catholics. Through a very optimistic appraisal we can argue that the CEBs assemble, in the countryside, 5–10 percent of the population, and in the big cities 1–2 percent. There is also the impression that these numbers are not growing, that work at the base level has stagnated, while the Pentecostal churches multiply and expand full speed.[29]

The concern for CEB stagnation is present in all sectors of the *igreja popular*. A CEB member in Nova Iguaçu complained about the crisis of his base community in the following terms:

I feel that the community stopped growing four, five years ago ... it stopped growing and it is hard, tough to make it advance. I think that the financial condition of the people ... unemployment, violence ... so many things that I believe impede very much the growth of the community. So I don't know what's happening, especially within the church itself ... that I don't know the strategy, the system, it uses that limits its own growth. We see those other religions there growing day-by-day, right? And we see that the community has stagnated; it stopped.

A consensus is emerging among pastoral agents and community activists that the *pastoral de grupos pequenos* has reached primarily a "popular elite": those among the poor who are better educated, enjoy a relative level of economic stability, and have a history of activism in grassroots organization and workers' unions. This segment of the poor population is definitely in the minority, and as I shall later argue, shrinking further as a result of recent socio-economic transformations. In Perani's words,

Even acknowledging the church's advance in [entering] into the poor's [world], we can see that the *pastoral popular* is still not very influential, particularly *vis-à-vis* certain popular class fractions. In the large urban peripheries, parishes and CEBs often disappear. They are very limited groups; sometimes they have a greater range of action when they succeed in opening themselves to the fundamental problems of the neighborhood. At other times they are insular groups, with little inspiring presence. In relation to the various categories of laborers ... there is a

---

[29] R. Van Der Ploeg, "As CEBs no nordeste," *CECA* 2, no. 2 (1990), 57.

separation from the world of factory, construction, and domestic workers, [from that of] vendors and day laborers.[30]

Thus, the crisis hinges on the gap that has emerged between the popular church's stated goal to become a church for and of the poor and the limited success of the pastoral-pedagogical strategy used to achieve that aim. It is a gap "between the intentions of social agents linked to the so called 'progressive' sector of the Catholic Church (advisors and pastoral agents) and the real effects of their intervention in the midst of the popular classes, their target audience."[31] More concretely, a church "that wants to be expressive of 'an entire people' [has instead] produce[d] a pastoral of small groups (the CEBs), incapable of resulting in a mass pastoral."[32]

The gap between the popular church's expectations and desires and its modest achievements prompts Van Der Ploeg to ask "whether work at the base level to form CEBs . . . would expand if there were not some internal factors in the popular church that limit the missionary impulse," or whether "work at the base level has reached its saturation point and should evolve into a *pastoral de massa.*"[33] Clodovis Boff, for his part, wonders about the challenge of reaching the poor masses.

Yes, we discovered the people [*o povo*] – that part of the masses which became conscientized [*se conscientizou*] and organized, now struggles in the base ecclesial communities and in the party. But what of the people itself [*o povão*], the great mass [*massona*], which continues with its popular religiosity, which goes into the Protestant sects [*seitas*], which votes for the current administration, which is messianic and keeps waiting for the "savior," be it religious . . . or political . . .? And they are the true majority.[34]

From the perspective of local actors, the crux of the crisis, therefore, resides not in the collapse of the Berlin Wall, or even in the

[30] Perani, "Notas para uma pastoral," 76.
[31] R. Novaes, "Nada será como antes, entre urubus e papagaios," unpublished manuscript, 1991, 1.
[32] R. C. Fernandes, "Santos e agentes – das dificuldades e da possibilidade de uma comunicação entre eles," paper presented in the Colóquio Franco-Brasileiro em Ciências Sociais, CNRs/CNPq, Paris, April 27–30, 1989, 32.
[33] R. Van der Ploeg, "A Igreja dos pobres no nordeste," *Cadernos do CEAS*, no. 132 (1991), 69.
[34] C. Boff, "Desafios atuais da pastoral popular," *Tempo e Presença*, no. 232 (1988), 31.

decline of the Marxist-socialist emancipatory narrative. Rather, it lies primarily in the perceived inability of the popular church to move beyond the limited scope of its 1970s work, to transcend the small group setting and become a true church of the people, i.e., of the poor. Thus, close to the ground, the crisis appears to be essentially one of participation and mobilization, and only secondarily one of ideology.

So how is the crisis of participation at the local level connected to the crisis of post-Enlightenment modernity? I contend that one of the key factors contributing to the crisis at the local level resides in contradictions and limitations in the popular church's pastoral-pedagogical approach and this-worldly utopian vision. Both the method and worldview of the *igreja popular* are grounded in a post-Enlightenment social epistemology that is showing itself unable to deal with the restructuring of everyday life generated by current trends in capitalism. The transformation of everyday life, especially for the urban poor, is what links macro to micro dynamics and participation/mobilization to ideological crisis.

The crisis of mobilization at the grassroots thus forces us to look at the larger socio-cultural context, in which economic (neo-liberal capitalism), political (the crisis of Marxism and rise of neo-liberalism), and religious (the conservative Vatican offensive and the expansion of Protestantism in Latin America) dynamics are at play. In fact, this is what progressive Catholic activists and intellectuals have begun to do, embarking first on a revision of the popular church's pastoral-pedagogical methodology and utopian horizons. This revision raises troubling questions for the popular church: Why are the poor betraying their "own emancipatory interests," failing to participate in a church that is actively working to transform the social conditions that disenfranchise them? Is this failure a case of false consciousness and alienation, or is it that the popular church has erred in identifying the felt needs of the poor and as a result has adopted a mistaken pastoral approach? Could it be that the crisis is due to the limitations and contradictions of pastoral-pedagogical method (i.e., *pastoral de grupos pequenos*) that was useful during the years of the military regime, but now has become an obstacle to a fulfillment of the preferential option for the poor? If this is so, is it a matter of disposing of this method altogether or can it be reformulated to respond better to the new challenges on the ground? How? These questions will occupy our attention in the succeeding chapters, as I seek to explore the "internal" (i.e., intra-Catholic) dimensions of the crisis: the structural obstacles to effective Catholic grassroots work on the ground and the contradictions within the popular church that create a gap between the *pastoral de grupos pequenos* and the situation of the poor.

Despite my focus on intra-Catholic dynamics, there is one important "external" aspect of the crisis at the grassroots that deserves consideration before we move into the book's main section. This factor has lent urgency to the popular church's drive to revise its *modus operandi* and to design alternative pastoral strategies. Parallel to the stagnation of CEB growth there has been an explosive spread of Protestantism among the poor, as part of a more global process of fragmentation of the country's religious field. Indeed, the last two decades have witnessed a significant expansion of African-based religions such as Umbanda and a proliferation of new religious movements. Accompanying this religious fragmentation has been a decrease in the number of practicing Catholics. According to statistics furnished by the IBGE (Brazilian Institute of Geography and Statistics), in 1940 95 percent of the population declared themselves to be Catholics. By 1980 that number was down to 89.1 percent. Preliminary figures of the 1991 national census indicate a further decline to 82.9 percent.[35] In cities the situation might be more critical for the Catholic church. In a survey conducted in the country's most populous urban centers, only 76.2 percent of those interviewed considered themselves Catholics.[36]

The spread of Protestantism is particularly disturbing for the *igreja popular* because the fastest growing Protestant group is constituted by Pentecostals, who are perceived by progressives to advocate a conservative or at best quietist stance *vis-à-vis* the unjust status quo. One Latin American political scientist, for example, argues that

[35] Electronic communication, Biblioteca Central do IBGE, 07/17/96.
[36] See J. Hortal, "Panorama e estatisticas do fenômeno religioso no Brasil," unpublished manuscript, 1990.

The expansion of Pentecostal sects represents a tendency opposed to the Popular Church, because Pentecostal sects impart to their faithful an attitude totally opposed to any form of social struggle or demands. They submerge them in conformism, in a scale of values which prevents them from perceiving exploitation and makes them accept existing social relations as a sacrifice.[37]

If this is true, then, the poor should not be converting to Pentecostalism. Rather they should be joining the Catholic popular church, which actively seeks to transform the society in their benefit. Yet, precisely the opposite seems to be happening. As a Brazilian journalist noted during his interview of Bishop Luciano Mendes de Almeida, former president of the CNBB, while the Catholic Church has made a preferential option for the poor, "the poor seem to be making a preferential option for the Pentecostal sects [*seitas*]."[38]

In the next chapter I examine the most relevant literature on Pentecostalism in Latin America, and more specifically in Brazil, in an effort to shed light on this paradox. We shall see that, contrary to what some progressive ecclesial and lay sectors suppose, Pentecostalism contains multiple and often contradictory dimensions. Field research suggests that Pentecostalism is far from being a monolithic conservative force, a fact that may explain its attraction to the urban poor.

[37] D. Camacho, "A Society in Motion," in *New Social Movements in the South: Empowering the People*, ed. Ponna Wignaraja (London: Zed Books, 1993), 50.

[38] Bishop Luciano Mendes de Almeida, interviewed by Renato Machado, April 17, 1991, Television program, "Noite e Dia."

CHAPTER 4

The external dimension: the growth of popular Pentecostalism

In this chapter I wish to offer some general points about the nature of Pentecostalism in Brazil. The chapter is not intended to provide an authoritative and comprehensive vision of the plethora of Pentecostal practices and forms of organization. Drawing from secondary sources, its aim is far more modest: to explore the causes behind Pentecostalism's rapid growth beginning in the 1940s and to identify certain practices and beliefs that might make it a more viable and attractive alternative to the urban poor than the popular church in the contemporary setting.

Protestantism[1] is not a new phenomenon in Latin America. Its first successful introduction in the area came in the 1800s, via European immigrants with ties to mainline churches, following failed attempts during the colonial period to spread the faith on the mainland using Caribbean islands under British, Dutch and Danish rule as a base.[2] Although in many cases Protestants in this "first wave" played a significant role in the independence process, nourishing anti-clerical and republican sentiments and supporting struggles to institute liberal reforms, Protestantism remained confined to sectors of the emerging national elites and to immigrant pockets in the countryside.

Protestantism's limited impact in the region began to change at

---

[1] Protestantism is a general term that applies to all those Christian traditions that trace their origins to the Reformation. Evangelical Protestantism refers to churches which emphasize the authority of the Bible and evangelization (i.e., missions). Pentecostalism is a type of evangelical Protestantism that, among other characteristics I will explain more fully later, makes the activity of the Holy Spirit in human history the defining element of belief and practice.

[2] On the history of Protestantism in Latin America, see J. P. Bastian, *Breve historia del protestantismo en América Latina* (Mexico: Casa Unida de Publicaciones, 1986).

the beginning of the twentieth century as a result of an evangelical wave originating in the North. This "second wave" had its origins in an earlier faith revival in the United States. In contrast to the first wave, missionaries in the second wave, though instructed within historical Protestant churches, particularly Baptists, Presbyterian and Methodist churches, introduced a strong element of Holiness[3] that separated them from mainline denominations, giving them a strong anti-intellectual and anti-bureaucratic thrust. Rather than attracting followers from the emerging, liberal-leaning bourgeoisie in the area as the mainline churches had done before, the new evangelical missions tended to appeal to the growing urban and rural poor who were beginning to feel the social dislocation caused by rapid and uneven industrialization.[4]

In Brazil, the second Protestant wave brought missionaries such as Daniel Berg, a Swede with ties to W. H. Durham and W. J. Seymour, both of whom were important figures in the formation of modern US Pentecostalism, and Gunnar Vingren. Working in the north-eastern state of Pará, Berg and Vingren founded in 1911 what is still the largest Pentecostal church in Brazil: the Assemblies of God. Almost simultaneously, Italian immigrant Luís Francescon, who had lived in the US for some time, founded the Christian Congregration in Brazil, the second largest Pentecostal church in the country.[5]

The importance of this second, mission-based Protestant wave is that it served as the basis for the formation of local, independent churches. Pastors trained during this phase moved on to build a nationally-based Pentecostal movement between the late 1950s and the mid-1970s, a period of intense Pentecostal expansion. Several highly successful churches and movements were formed during this period, beginning with O Brasil Para Cristo (Brazil for Christ) founded by Manoel de Mello in 1956. Brasil para Cristo –

---

[3] I define Holiness as the sanctification of the believer's life in its totality as a result of the purifying work of the Holy Spirit – a sign of the grace of faith and election.

[4] J. P. Bastian, "The Metamorphosis of Latin American Protestant Groups: A Sociohistorical Perspective," *Latin American Research Review* 28, no. 2 (1993), 33–61, esp. p. 37.

[5] On the history of Protestantism and Pentecostalism in Brazil, see D. Reiley, *História documental do protestantismo no Brasil* (São Paulo: ASTE, 1984); A. G. Mendoça, "Um panorama do protestantismo brasileiro atual," in Landim; and P. Freston, "Protestantes e política no Brasil: da constituinte ao impeachment" (Ph.D. diss. Universidade de Campinas, São Paulo, 1993).

together with the Christian Congregration of Brasil, the Assemblies of God, the Four Square Church, and the more recent Igreja Pentecostal *Deus é Amor* (Pentecostal Church "God is Love," c. 1962), and the Igreja Universal do Reino de Deus (Universal Church of the Kingdom of God, *c.* 1976) – have spearheaded Pentecostalism's spectacular growth.

According to IBGE figures, between 1980 and 1990, the number of Brazilian Protestants has jumped from 7.9 million to 16 million, about 10 percent of the country's population. This accelerated growth is all the more dramatic considering that in 1940 only 2.6 percent of the country's population declared themselves to be Protestant. It is estimated now that 600,000 Brazilians convert to Protestantism every year.[6]

Citing data from a survey conducted by the ISER in the greater metropolitan area of Rio de Janeiro in 1992, Paul Freston concludes that "Protestantism is the preeminent religion of the poor and, even more so, of the less educated."[7] This phenomenon, together with the fact that anywhere from 60–80 percent of the country's Protestants consider themselves Pentecostals, leads Rubem Fernandes, the survey's chief researcher, to conclude that Pentecostalism is one of "the most important movements for changing mentalities in contemporary Brazilian society, above all among the poorest urban sectors."[8] Thus, according to both Fernandes and Freston, Pentecostalism is a truly popular religion in Brazil.

Within Pentecostalism, the fastest growing churches are those that can be categorized as *cura divina* (divine healing or deliverance) movements which offer miracles cures and exorcisms to their faithful. These movements tend to assume decentralized, diffuse organizational forms and to rely heavily on the electronic media to spread their gospel.[9] According to Antônio Gouvêa

---

[6] The statistics come from the IBGE and the CNBB. They are cited in "A fé que move multidões avança no país," *Veja* (Rio de Janeiro), May 16, 1990, 46–52.

[7] P. Freston, "Pentecostalism in Latin America: Characteristics and Controversies," unpublished manuscript, 1994, 12.

[8] Fernandes quoted in Freston, "Pentecostalism in Latin America," 7.

[9] These movements and ministries are part of yet another revival wave that started in the 1960s. To differentiate them from more "classical" Pentecostal movement such as *Brasil Para Cristo*, some experts use the term neo-Pentecostalism to describe them. Typical examples of these "churches" are the Igreja Pentecostal Deus é Amor which now draws

Mendoça, who teaches ecumenics at a Methodist institute in São Paulo,

The charismatic leaders of the divine cure [movement] establish shopping counters where religious goods are offered to a fluctuating and non-committed clientele, setting a relation of quid pro quo between the faithful and the sacred. The praxis of divine cure groups comes close to those in magic . . . Although some of these groups keep their discourse within the parameters of the Christian faith, their praxis sometimes distances them from it. Moreover, other groups show a discourse and practice almost irreconcilable with the Christian worldview.[10]

What are the causes behind the accelerated Protestant growth in Latin America in the last three decades? Why are Pentecostal churches, particularly those that center their pastoral activities around miracle cures, the fastest growing segment of Protestantism? Why are poor people increasingly "opting" for Pentecostalism? The earliest attempts to address these questions are the now classic studies of Christian Lalive D'Epinay and Emilio Willems in the late 1960s.[11]

Although the two authors draw contrasting conclusions about the social function of Protestantism, both assume that the latter's growth is a response to the anomie generated by the transition from an agrarian mode of production to an urban-based, industrialized mode of capitalist accumulation. Whereas the rural model of production relied on hierarchical and rigid bonds of organic solidarity for its reproduction, industrialization and urbanization require and produce secularization and differentiation, forcing the individual to assume a multiplicity of roles. For both Lalive D'Epinay and Willems, the transition produces a break-

---

about 500,000 followers, and the controversial Igreja Universal do Reino de Deus with 2,000 temples across the nation and three million followers. Recently, the latter's founder has become a target of a police investigation over the embezzlement of large sums of money in the purchase of a TV network for $45 million.

[10] Mendoça, "Um panorama do pentecostalismo brasileiro," 80. Freston has challenged Mendoça's view of the divine healing churches, arguing that as they evolve they begin to show a institutional stability and doctrinal sophistication. Freston, "Pentecostalism in Latin America."

[11] C. Lalive D'Epinay, *El refugio de las masas. Estudio sociológico del protestantismo chileno* (Santiago, Chile: Editorial del Pacífico, 1968) and E. Willems, *The Followers of the New Faith. Cultural Change and the Rise of Protestantism in Brazil and Chile* (Nashville, TN: Vanderbilt University, 1967).

down of the old rural order without providing new axiological and cognitive elements to guide thought and action *vis-à-vis* the highly differentiated emerging context. This transitory condition in turn generates a situation of disorientation and meaninglessness for the individual, for whom Protestantism could supply a new set of principles to regulate praxis and cognition.

Lalive D'Epinay and Willems disagree on the role this set of principles plays in integrating the individual to the changing social environment. For Lalive D'Epinay recent forms of Protestantism such as Pentecostalism are essentially conservative: they serve to "reconstitute" the hierarchical relations that structure the old agrarian order in the new context generated by industrialization. In the face of increasing secularization and social differentiation, Pentecostalism responds by harkening back to the past, reconstituting, albeit in a modified manner, the patriarchal forms of organization that ordered rural life. In place of the local rural boss (*patrón*), the pastor assumes the role of powerful parental authority, protecting, disciplining, and providing for his flock. This reconstitution offers a "refuge" to the displaced rural masses as they enter the baffling and precarious urban world.[12]

Willems, on the other hand, sees in Protestantism, and particularly in Pentecostalism, a progressive force opening and diversifying a cultural arena that has been dominated by Catholic conformity. Pentecostalism's appeals to individual conscience in matters of faith and ethos and its emphasis on a democratic and participatory community life stand in stark contradiction to Catholic forms of thinking and organization. Catholicism is characterized by a hierarchical form of organization which makes it possible and necessary for institutional reproduction to form alliances with authoritarian socio-political orders. These alliances allow the ruling classes to legitimize their domination over and exclusion of subordinate groups. Pentecostalism, in contrast, thrives on local, independent forms of lay leadership and relies on networks of self-help that make it possible for poor people to survive the transition to urban life. By challenging the Catholic monopoly over religious goods and offering alternative, more egalitarian

---

[12] Lalive D'Epinay, *El refugio de las masas*, 71.

forms of organization based on the notion of the priesthood of all
believers and the charisma of the Holy Spirit, Pentecostalism not
only plays an important role in social change but is potentially a
form of popular resistance to the status quo.[13]

The classic works of Willems and Lalive D'Epinay have framed
much of the social scientific discussion on the growth of Pentecostalism. There have been several national studies that sought to
apply their insights. An important example for the case of Brazil is
Judith Hoffnagel's study of urban Pentecostalism in Recife.[14] On
the debate whether Pentecostalism is a conservative or a revolutionary force, Hoffnagel falls in the camp of those who see it as
playing a key role in reproducing the hierarchical relations that
support the authoritarian, corporatist social order. In Hoffnagel's
view, the pastor not only fulfills the function of the lost rural boss,
as Lalive D'Epinay had argued; he also interacts with the elites
within the corporatist, patrimonial state to obtain economic and
political favors for his congregation. In this fashion, Pentecostalism, by adhering to clientelist politics, acts to retard the emergence
of civil society, working against more democratic, participatory
forms of political action.[15]

In the most recent study of Pentecostalism framed within
the Willems–Lalive D'Epinay debate, sociologist David Martin
reaches a conclusion that contrasts sharply with that of
Hoffnagel. Martin draws from Weber's notion of elective affinity –
that a particular religious practice (i.e., Puritan inner-worldly
asceticism) accompanied and reinforced the rise of capitalism and
modernity – to claim that Pentecostalism, rather than being a
conservative force, is potentially a major contributor to the process
of secularization, democratization, and modernization that Latin
American societies are experiencing. Echoing Willems' earlier
argument, Martin contends that Pentecostalism, by challenging

---

[13] Willems, *The Followers of the New Faith*, 249.
[14] J. Hoffnagel, *The Believers: Pentecostalism in a Brazilian City* (Ph.D. dissertation, University of Indiana, 1978).
[15] Peter Fry and Gary Howe elaborate this point. According to them, Pentecostalism's legalist ethics and absolute monotheism correspond to technocratic capitalism's cal-culative, means–ends rationality and the bureaucratic–authoritarian state. P. Fry and G. N. Howe, "Duas respostas à aflição: Umbanda e Pentecostalismo," *Debate e Crítica* 6 (1975), 75–94.

Catholicism's monopoly of the religious field, loosens the latter's totalizing and hierarchical grip on Latin American culture. It helps in the process of individuation and differentiation by introducing a "free, voluntaristic evangelical Protestantism." According to Martin,

> As the sacred canopy in Latin America is rent and the all-encompassing system cracks, evangelical Christianity pours in and by its own autonomous native power creates free social space . . .
>
> What then travels across from the United States [Pentecostalism] . . . is precisely the kind of powerful but fragmented and competitive religiosity bound up in the very emergence of "Anglo" civilization. It will enter into the open spaces, simultaneously enlarging them and operating as a potent competitor within them.[16]

Martin argues, correctly, that Catholicism in Latin America has played historically a consistently conservative role, symbolically sanctioning an exclusionary social order. Moreover, the Catholic Church has allied itself with landed elites to bolster the agrarian model of dependent capitalist production prevalent in Latin American until the 1930s. With the advent of industrialization, this agrarian model is in crisis. The cultural order that supports it no longer seem plausible to the dislocated rural masses who have migrated to big cities in search of work or a better life. Here Martin returns to the familiar concept of anomie.

Because of the breakup of the Catholic, agrarian social order, Martin believes, "the largest conduit for evangelical Protestantism is provided by the massive movement from the countryside . . . to the mega-city." As people's old ties are shaken by the migration, Pentecostalism

> provides a cell taking over from scarred and broken tissue. Above all it renews the innermost cell of the family, and protects women from the ravages of male desertion and violence. A new faith is able to implant new disciplines, re-order priorities, counter corruption and destructive machismo, and reverse the indifferent and injurious hierarchies of the outside world. Within the enclosed haven of faith a fraternity can be instituted under firm leadership, which provides for release, for mutuality and warmth, and for the practice of new roles.[17]

[16] D. Martin, *Tongues of Fire: The Explosion of Protestantism in Latin America* (Oxford: Basil Blackwell, 1990), 280.
[17] Ibid., 284.

Pentecostalism is thus attractive to poor people, especially women, because it is a "symbolical repudiation of what previously held [the evangelical believer] in place, vertically and horizontally." In place of hierarchical relations that guarantee the monopoly of legitimate religious goods for a specialized corps (i.e., the clerics) as in the case of Catholicism, Pentecostalism offers a radically participatory and democratic form of religious practice.

Within the "religious enclaves" that Pentecostalism opens, believers can develop their own models of self-governance, establishing forms of relationality, organization and social activity that contrast with the world that has marginalized them. In this sense, according to Martin, Pentecostalism provides a context where believers can experience democracy and re-enfranchisement. Pentecostalism

offers a network of mutual support which may include a variety of services: groups for female interaction and for training in some skill, a source of information and communication, access to helpful contacts, a brotherhood within which to initiate economic cooperation, reliable friends to help out at home while you're away, and other friends to offer you a second home . . . [The poor] see in Protestantism a new milieu in which to take an active and independent part. For such people it provides an escalator for yet further movement, and a belief corresponding to their raised aspirations.[18]

In sum, Martin's main contention is that Protestantism, especially of the evangelical strand, offers a worldview, an ethos and form of organization that, in contrast with Catholicism, are congruent with changes in the region's socio-economic structure. Evangelical Protestantism is "an advanced form of social differentiation," Martin argues, which "accompanies a stage in industrialization and/or urbanization" in today's Latin America. This elective affinity allows believers not only to adapt to the system, but to act effectively upon it to advance their economic cause. This is why the poor find Pentecostalism so attractive.

At times, Martin makes reductive and ahistorical generalizations about Latin American culture, treating it as a static and homogeneous totality devoid of history and of geographical, political, ethnic, and economic differences prior to the advent of

[18] Ibid., 283.

Protestantism and industrial capitalism. Nevertheless, his conclusions represent an important synthesis of years of field research in various countries in the region. The main weakness of Martin's analysis resides in its sociological functionalism: its failure to take Pentecostalism seriously as a religious worldview. To Martin, Pentecostalism is just another cultural institution, not unlike ideologies and the arts, with a given role in the social organism. Thus, for him, there is no need to look at the internal specificity of Pentecostalism *qua* system of symbols, beliefs and rituals dealing with transcendence and the sacred, that, in Geertz's words, formulates "conceptions of a general order of existence" placing them in a cosmic framework.[19] Rather than looking at the content of Pentecostal theology, which would be more in line with Weber's *verstehende* sociology of religion, Martin limits himself to examining the social effects of Pentecostal practice and organization. In other words, he describes what Pentecostalism "does but not what it is."[20]

This partial view of Pentecostalism leads Martin to postulate that it has an elective affinity with social changes in Latin America, spurring the birth of the modern in the region. I contend that if one were to examine the content of Pentecostal theology, one would obtain a more nuanced understanding of the ambiguous role this religious worldview plays for the disenfranchised in Latin America.

The strengths and weaknesses of the functionalist approach to religion are reflected in sociologist Cecília Mariz's comparative work on base communities and Pentecostals in Recife.[21] Mariz offers arguably the most nuanced functionalist approach to Pentecostalism. Although she acknowledges that Pentecostal groups and CEBs hold different values and worldviews, she argues that "Because they are organized in similar ways and their members have

[19] C. Geertz, "Religion as a Cultural System," in *The Interpretation of Cultures* (New York: Basic Books, 1973), 90.

[20] This is anthropologist André Droogers' critique of functionalist readings. See A. Droogers, "Visiones paradójicas sobre una religión paradójica," in *Algo más que opio: Una lectura antropológica del pentecostalismo latinoamericano y caribeño*, ed. B. Boudewijnse, A. Droogers and F. Kamsteeg, (San José, Costa Rica: DEI, 1991), 28.

[21] C. L. Mariz, *Coping with Poverty: Pentecostals and Base Communities in Brazil* (Philadelphia: Temple University Press, 1994).

many experiences in common, both groups in effect encourage behavior that is surprisingly similar."[22] Since there "are limits on the [CEBs' and Pentecostal groups'] ability to put their ideologies into effect," both traditions end up having, as an "unintended consequence," roughly the same functions for the urban poor. Both groups entail: (1) an experience of renewal, where there is radical break with the past, and the adoption of a new ethos; (2) an experience of religious reflection where the new convert gains a voice and a deeper understanding of the Christian faith; (3) a union of religion with everyday life as believers are required to live the fullness of their religious commitment; (4) an experience of community life that provides not only local but national networks of self-help and spiritual support; and (5) revelation and empowerment whereby believers claim a special access to the true core of Christianity that allows them to play a prophetic role.

Mariz dispels some enduring myths and misconceptions that have colored the discussions about the growth of Pentecostalism and the relative stagnation of CEBs. Her comparative research goes beyond often ideological and self-interested readings that have opposed the two traditions to study the concrete ways in which religious practices and discourses provide "microsocial strategies" for coping with poverty. Moreover, Mariz offers a much-needed corrective to Martin's excessively functionalist reading. Although it is true that religion plays a role in the material survival and/or economic advancement of the poor, she recognizes that one cannot reduce religious practices and ideas to utilitarian interests. According to Mariz, "Despite the materiality of religion, people's religions are not economically determined. No one chooses a religion because of its material advantages. Instead, religion is basically a source of meaning . . . Thus a functionalist model does not offer an appropriate explanation for religious phenomena.[23] Mariz's focus on meaning introduces a healthy dose of *verstehende* sociology to functionalist approaches. In this vein she writes that "In order to understand the meaning of poor people's actions, we must stand in their shoes and see, from their

[22] C. L. Mariz, "Religion and Coping with Poverty: A Comparison of Catholic and Pentecostal Communities," *Sociological Analysis* 53 (1992), S64.

[23] Mariz, *Coping with Poverty*, 155.

perspective, what it means to live in poverty, what it means to attempt to change conditions, and what religious meaning people ascribe to the strategies of survival."[24]

Nevertheless, despite Mariz's rejection of economic reductionism, her reading of base communities and Pentecostalism still shows traces of sociological functionalism. One clear example is her unwarranted assumption that there is a considerable gap between base communities and Pentecostal groups' "ideal, verbalized values" and their actual practice – a gap that allows for commonalities in their function. Such an assumption is possible only because she chooses to bracket what she calls the "ideological elements" of the two traditions. Yet, it is important to bear in mind that both CEBs and Pentecostal groups are, as Mariz herself recognizes, religious approaches entailing a conscious choice, a true conversion experience, which demands that beliefs be put into practice. Precisely because both groups claim to have a special access to the true essence of Christianity, because both assume a prophetic role predicated on religious purity, the link between belief and practice, between ideals and reality, must be strong. This is why both CEBs and Pentecostals bring together faith and life. This link is what distinguishes them from other traditions such as folk and romanized Catholicism, where the believer is born to the faith/culture.

The link between values and practices is made tighter by the stakes involved in the process of conversion. It is not simply a question of material betterment, as Martin would have it, or even of giving meaning to the problem of evil and poverty, as Mariz has argued. In Pentecostal groups and CEBs what drives believers is primarily their thirst for justification and salvation/ liberation. Conversion is ultimately about transcendence, or in Paul Tillich's words, about facing the "threat of non-being," at the moral, spiritual, intellectual, and existential levels.[25] Personal and communal empowerment are mere by-products – clearly important ones – of a deeper quest for eternal life. These ontological, soteriological, and eschatological dimensions of religion, are very

---

[24] Ibid., 9.
[25] See P. Tillich, *The Courage to Be* (New Haven: Yale University Press, 1952).

prominent in both base communities and Pentecostalism, forging a close bond between belief and practice in everyday life.

The intensity, originality, and radicality of the type of Christianity experienced in CEBs and Pentecostalism, thus, renders any attempt to separate ideal values from actual practices and organizational forms problematic. If one agrees that for both groups ideals, values, and worldviews are just as important as practices, for the latter are conscious attempts to live the religious experience in its fullness, then one might turn the tables on Mariz. Rather than assuming that there are limits to full implementation of ideal beliefs – a assumption that allows her to claim that there is a gap between values and practices – one might ask about the limits that religious ideology places on practice. In order to address this question one would have to understand the internal logic of that religious ideology which Mariz has chosen to bracket.

This, of course, does not mean that there are no material determinations of the process of conversion. Material conditions of existence generate a context, exerting pressures, creating needs, and setting the limits of the possible, which poor people must address with the economic, political, cultural, and religious resources at hand. The recognition that there are extra-religious elements that shape religious choice and practice, however, should not lead us to ignore the complexity and depth of religious phenomena. It is not enough to focus on the praxical, organizational, and even psycho-cognitive aspects of religion. Religion, particularly in the case of base communities and Pentecostalism, is a reflection upon the origin, nature and *telos* of being itself.

By bracketing the "ideological elements" behind CEBs and Pentecostalism, Mariz enters a sociological *cul de sac*. If both groups have in the end roughly the same functions for the poor, why is it that we observe a differential in the number of conversions to Pentecostalism and participation in CEBs? What makes a person choose one tradition over the other? Is it the believer's personal trajectory? Is it the fact that one tradition is more visible in the religious market? In response to these questions, Mariz develops two lines of argumentation. The first is economic: whereas CEBs "do not offer immediate solutions to problems of poverty," Pentecostalism shows to be "an efficient strategy for overcoming life crises," a fact that makes it more attractive to the "poorest of the poor" who "have a greater need for immediate support."[26] As we shall see later on, this explanation carries some weight, especially in view of the worsening life conditions of the urban poor in Brazil.

Mariz's second line of argumentation, however, is considerably weaker. Drawing from the Weberian notion of rationalization she claims, that CEBs disenchant and secularize the world with their rationalistic analysis of the causes of (collective and structural) sin, while Pentecostals offer a more affective practice. Pentecostalism's rationalization of the world is more limited than that of CEBs, since it retains a mystical-magical view of reality. Pentecostals, for example, continue to perceive the world as the arena where supernatural forces determine the fate of individuals, a place where the forces of good and evil do battle. Thus, Pentecostalism's mystical-magical worldview connects better with the beliefs of the poor masses who are steeped in folk Catholicism. Yet, as I shall argue in the next chapter, this explanation of the differential appeal of CEBs and Pentecostalism among the poor is problematic: it re-instates the dichotomous thinking *vis-à-vis* CEBs and Pentecostals that Mariz wanted to overcome in the first place.

Without denying the fruitfulness of such, approaches as Martin's and Mariz's, focusing solely on the organizational and praxical aspects of Pentecostalism, I want to offer a reading that takes seriously the density of religious worldviews, values, and concerns. Drawing on the comparative work of sociologist Rowan Ireland in a small town in the state of Bahia,[27] I would claim that what the poor find in Pentecostalism is a theology that blends moral asceticism, Holiness, and eschatological hope. This combination allows the believer to be "in this world but not of this world,"[28] that is, to assume a position of continuity and rupture with social reality. The believer can thus navigate and survive psychologically and physically the perils of late capitalism (i.e., the twin dynamics of fragmentation and globalization and the crisis of modern projects),

---

[26] Mariz, *Coping with Poverty*, 156
[27] R. Ireland, *Kingdoms Come: Religion and Politics in Brazil* (Pittsburgh: University of Pittsburgh Press, 1991).
[28] See Jn. 17:14–15. The theme is also echoed in several Pauline letters (see 1 Cor. 5:10 and 7:29–35; Phil. 2:15; Col. 2:20).

while distancing him/herself from human history and preparing
for the coming of a qualitatively different spiritual order. Pentecostalism thus simultaneously responds to concrete material and
psycho-cognitive needs, which is what functionalists have argued,
and to the existential anxiety generated by the threat of non-being.

To support my contention I will first review briefly the main
theological tenets of Pentecostalism and then show how these ideas
both respond to the believer's material needs and structure social
action. Before embarking on this theological reconstruction, it is
necessary to acknowledge that more than a tradition that centers
around doctrine, Pentecostalism is a charismatic religion, built
around performative aspects such as baptism in the Spirit and
glossolalia. It is a religion built more around the body than the
mind. Moreover, Pentecostalism is an extremely heterogeneous
phenomenon at the grassroots. At the local level Pentecostalism
presents multiple forms of organization, a cross-fertilization of
doctrines and liturgical styles among various churches, and some
syncretism with other grassroots forms of religiosity with which it
shares a pluralistic religious field. As Freston observes, this heterogeneity poses severe challenges to typologies or totalizing readings
of the phenomenon.[29] In this context, my theological reconstruction of Pentecostalism can only be an "ideal type" in the Weberian
sense, which does not always fit neatly in every instance with
reality on the ground. However, I want to argue that recent
research on Pentecostalism shows that this worldview is not only
present in particular Pentecostal communities, but that it is in
many cases normative. While we need to be cautious in generaliz-
ing about Pentecostalism, we should not abandon all attempts at
providing a coherent picture of the phenomenon. To disregard
theology as a unifying force in the face of praxical heterogeneity
would be tantamount to saying that in understanding Protestantism Luther's ideas do not matter.

With these caveats in mind, we can begin our reconstruction of
the "Pentecostal worldview." Theologian Donald W. Dayton
identifies four tightly intertwined themes in Pentecostal belief and
doctrine: salvation/justification, baptism in the Holy Spirit, divine

---

[29] Freston, "Pentecostalism in Latin America."

healing, and the imminent second coming of Jesus.[30] A discussion of how these themes come together to articulate a worldview that serves, in Geertz's words, as a "model of" and a "model for" the world may help us understand better the appeal of Pentecostalism for the poor in Brazil.

In contrast to Catholicism's emphasis on works, Pentecostalism adheres closely to the Lutheran doctrine of justification by grace through faith alone. This adherence is the logical result of a strong reading of the doctrine of divine dispensation and of Pauline anthropology. Since "the Fall" has made human beings essentially sinful, or in Paul's words "slaves of sin," Pentecostal theology sees all human attempts at self-redemption as doomed to failure. It is utterly presumptuous to think of human beings as "coparticipants" in the salvific event (*à la* CEB theology), as if they somehow could bring their own salvation through their own fallible actions.

Pentecostalism's conception of humanity as inherently sinful translates into a profound mistrust of human institutions; they are seen as essentially corrupt, part of the evil world that stands against the church of the elect. These institutions can never solve the problem of evil and overturn the conditions of injustice, exploitation, and vice that pervade social life.

This world of suffering and contradiction can only be radically transformed by the irruption of a qualitatively different order, when sacred history supersedes human history, when the second coming of Jesus Christ ushers in the kingdom of God. Only then will the wicked be punished and the righteous redeemed. In this fashion, while there is in Pentecostalism a radical critique of the status quo, active challenge against the sources of injustice is postponed to the ends of time and left ultimately in the hands of God. This is why Ireland finds that "There seems to be no basis in the Pentecostal religious imagination . . . for the pursuit of civil liberty and social justice as a sacred cause." There is nothing in Pentecostalism that gives the faithful a "responsibility to achieve a just order as part of their pursuit of salvation." There are no "myths and symbols that might rally

---

[30] D. W. Dayton, *Theological Roots of Pentecostalism* (Metuchen, NJ: The Scarecrow Press, 1987).

the faithful for social transformation in the name of this-worldly utopia."[31]

Pentecostalism's eschatology shifts the believer's focus away from this world, which becomes a mere testing ground to prepare her/him for the next life. This *vida passageira* (fleeting life) is just a place for the believer to demonstrate his/her faithfulness to Jesus, staving off the temptations posed by the devil. Preparation in this life for the reign of God is fundamentally a personal matter, taking the form of a sanctified life: the adoption of a strict moral asceticism that keeps the believer "on the narrow path" awaiting the second coming. It is true that moral asceticism has social consequences, as it transforms the individual into a disciplined, sober and law-abiding citizen. However, these consequences tend to support the status quo because the new ethos, based as it is on obedience to a sovereign God, demands respect for authorities.

It would seem, then, that Pentecostalism, by offering redemption and consolation in the beyond, is functioning, in Marx's famous words, as the "opiate of the masses." Not only is Pentecostalism the "justification" of the present unjust world, functioning as a theodicy (i.e. injustice issues from humanity's sinfulness, which is part of God's plan), but it becomes "the fantastic realization of the human being inasmuch as the human being possesses no true reality."[32]

This is, in fact, the conclusion that Brazilian sociologist Francisco Rolim reaches in his studies of urban Pentecostalism. According to Rolim, Pentecostalism, by focusing on the spiritual manifestations of evil without looking at the structural causes of injustice and inequality and by attributing these manifestations to the work of supra-social forces (the devil), produces what he calls a "sacralization of the social:"

We are referring here to the emphasis placed on the direct and immediate effects of a condition of lack and not on social roots of the condition. What is sacralized is the appearance of the social. An appeal is made to an extra-social power. But what is check-mated is not the dominant

---

[31] Ireland, *Kingdoms Come*, 107.
[32] K. Marx, "Contribution to the Critique of Hegel's *Philosophy of Right*: Introduction," in *The Marx-Engels Reader*, ed. Robert C. Tucker, (New York: W. W. Norton and Company, 1978), 54.

power but that of a mythical figure, the devil. Since what is challenged is the appearance [the malady as an expression of the latter's work], the social is denied in its specific structure.[33]

Thus, for Rolim, Pentecostalism offers a mere symbolic critique of oppression, which, in displacing the locus of struggle for Christian fullness to the beyond, clothes the status quo with, in Geertz's words, "an aura of factuality."[34] This factuality induces believers to adopt a quietist political attitude. The existence of social evil is the work of the devil, part of God's plan to separate redeemed from sinner.

In his later work, Rolim takes his hypothesis of Pentecostalism's sacralization of the social a step further. He argues that Pentecostalism's magico-religious practices represent an impotent symbolic response to the disenchantment of the world brought by the instrumental rationality that accompanies capitalism. For Rolim, there is "an elective affinity between the Pentecostal vision, which focuses on what is immediately present and individual, and the capitalist vision of economic progress. In both visions, human existence does not have meaning [in itself]."[35]

Although Rolim points to some interesting ideological homologies between the spirit of late capitalism and the Pentecostal worldview, his Marxist-Weberian reading of Pentecostalism is too simplistic. As Willems, Martin, and Mariz have shown, Pentecostalism can empower poor people in ways that make it possible for them to attain some measure of control over their lives in the here and now. In the capitalist world described by Rolim, where the poor's fate is increasingly subject to decisions made by global actors such as international organizations and transnational corporations, Pentecostalism offers tangible strategies, forms of organization and solutions to everyday predicaments. For instance, the charismata, or gifts to the Spirit, are signs of election, which not only set the true believer apart from a world destined to wither away, but transform the believer's everyday life, exorcising the demons that lead to infidelity and alcoholism and healing bodies

---

[33] F. C. Rolim, *Pentecostais no Brasil, uma interpretação sócio-religiosa* (Petrópolis: Vozes, 1985), 230–31.

[34] Geertz, "Religion as a Cultural System," 109–118.

[35] Rolim, "Pentecôtisme et vision du monde," *Social Compass* 39, no. 3 (1992), 419.

broken by long working hours and the precarious living conditions. In a continent where the poor confront the double jeopardy
of endemic diseases and of an inadequate and unresponsive health
care system, divine healing, the fourth major theme of Pentecostal
doctrine, represents one of the few psychologically and sometimes
physically effective ways available to them to cope. This fact may
account for the great success of *cura divina* movements such as *Deus
é Amor* (cf. n.9).

Furthermore, as Brusco's work in Colombia and Gill's study of
evangelical Protestantism in La Paz show, Pentecostalism brings
significant benefits to poor Latin American women, who are the
catalysts for frequent family conversions.[36] According to Gill,
Pentecostal asceticism

> reforms male behavior in accordance with some of the needs and the
> desires of women. Married women and their children, for example,
> benefit from an improvement in the material circumstances of their
> households because male resources previously spent on alcohol, ciga-
> rettes, gambling, and extramarital liaisons are directed back into the
> domestic unit.[37]

Pentecostal moralism preserves and/or restores the integrity of the
family unit, which represents one of the few remaining relatively
safe spaces for women and children, who, as we shall see later on,
have been the main victims of economic restructuring and neo-
liberal policies. Within the family, Pentecostalism "domesticates"
male dominance and abuse over women, because its makes men
accountable and submissive to God. In Pentecostalism, men are
"forced to cultivate some traditionally 'feminine' traits."[38] In contrast, some scholars have argued that CEBs, with their stress on
political organization and structural change, have failed to address
adequately women's needs in the domestic sphere.[39]

The benefits for the here and now are not only connected with
Pentecostalism's organizational forms and praxis. Beyond func-

---

[36] E. Brusco, "The Reformation of Machismo: Asceticism and Masculinity among Colombian Evangelicals," in *Rethinking Protestantism in Latin America*, ed. V. Garrard-Burnett and
D. Stoll (Philadelphia: Temple University Press, 1993); and L. Gill, "'Like a Veil to
Cover Them': Women and the Pentecostal Movement in La Paz," *American Ethnologist* 17,
no. 4 (Nov. 1990), 708–721.

[37] Gill, "'Like a Veil to Cover Them,'" 132.   [38] Ibid.

[39] Burdick, *Looking for God in Brazil*.

tionalist explanations, there are in Pentecostalism theological elements that empower the poor in the face of the encroaching economic logic of late capitalism. Pentecostals are fully certain of their salvation: they have already been redeemed by the blood of Christ. They need only accept Jesus Christ as their Savior, living out this conversion with purity of heart and eschewing the corrupting influences of the outside world. This certainty gives the believer a great sense of security and stability in a world characterized by suffering and confusion. The believer acquires, as it were, a sense of control over – or at least certainty about – her/his destiny that is reflected in the strict ethos s/he practices.

Conversion, redemption by the blood of Jesus, is accompanied by a baptism in the Holy Spirit through which believers both accept and transcend their prior lives of sin and brokenness – lives in which they were weak and marginalized – and reconstitute themselves anew as unified selves with a sense of purpose. By becoming divinely chosen citizens of the Kingdom, believers acquire a strong sense of self-worth, as their lives come to be intertwined with sacred history. As Richard Schaull writes, in a context of social disintegration and exclusion which has "left people so destroyed that they are even incapable of doing anything to change their fate," Pentecostalism provides the hope and energy not only to survive but to build a new life.[40]

The believer's sense of self-worth is enhanced further by the centrality of the Holy Spirit in Pentecostalism, which gives religious life a "powerful immediacy and presentness."[41] According to Quentin Schultze, "Pentecostals experience faith . . . as a living, dynamic work of the Holy Spirit in their everyday lives. God is present in their midst both as a community and, more directly, in each of their lives."[42] Armed with this confidence and spiritual empowerment, the believer can confront the tribulations of this fleeting world, confident that in the end her/his life of righteousness will lead to the only salvation that really matters. Her/his life of righteousness may have concrete social effects; it may lead to

---

[40] R. Schaull, "La Iglesia, crisis y nuevas perspectivas," *Vida y Pensamiento* 15, no. 2 (1995), 8–48.

[41] Q. J. Schultze, "Orality and Power in Latin American Pentecostalism," in *Coming of Age: Protestantism in Contemporary Latin America*, ed. D. R. Miller (Lanham, MD: University Press of America, 1994), 75.   [42] Ibid.

economic improvement or may foster the ideals of self-governance. However, as I argued earlier, economic improvement and
empowerment are by-products, rather than the causes, of religious
choice and practice.

Even though eschatology is central to Pentecostal doctrine,
orienting the believers toward the end of times, conversion turns
them *ipso facto* into soldiers in God's army ready to spread the
Gospel and to do battle against Satan wherever he may be. The
struggle to wrest souls from Satan's grip redirects the believer's
activities to this world. Even when s/he is ultimately seeking
eternal life in heaven, s/he does not withdraw from this world, for
it is here that the apocalyptic battle between good and evil is being
waged. As one of God's warriors in this epic battle the believer
must be in this world. Yet, s/he must be alert, lest earthly lures
ensnare her/him. It is in this sense that the believer is very much
"in this world but not of this world."

John Burdick makes the same point on his comparative study of
popular religions in the Baixada Fluminense. Commenting on the
combativeness and critical consciousness shown by some of his
Pentecostal interviewees, Burdick writes:

> While Catholics are taught to think in conciliatory terms, Pentecostals see
> the world as a divine battleground in which the Devil plays a constant
> role. *Crentes* [literally the believer, but the term refers mainly to Pente-
> costals] are thus able to claim with relative ease that many of the rich are
> in league with the Devil. The [P]entecostal in politics speaks of the
> politician or captain of industry as a "tool of the Devil," while the
> Catholic emphasizes only that "we are both children of God."[43]

This observation leads Burdick to dispute the claim made by
Brazilian sociologists and progressives that Pentecostalism is a
"'religion of the status quo.'"[44] For Burdick, Pentecostalism "includes a number of tensions, contradictions and sources of empowerment that facilitate rather than hinder participation in social
movements. In some cases these may even nurture the development of a highly critical social consciousness."[45]

---

[43] Burdick, *Looking for God in Brazil*, 218.   [44] Ibid., 226.
[45] Ibid., 206. There is evidence that Pentecostalism may inspire contestation of the status
quo. In her study of rural Pentecostalism in northeastern Brazil, Regina Novaes found
crentes actively participating in collective struggles over land tenure. See *Os escolhidos de
Deus* (Rio de Janeiro: Marco Zero, 1985).

Recognizing that Pentecostal ideology may sanction both conservative and progressive political action, Burdick recommends
that rather than trying to determine once and for all the socio-
political nature of Pentecostalism, it is better to study the latter's
effects in particular, historical settings. It would be more fruitful to
"investigate the conditions under which any given [political] tendency prevails."[46]

Burdick makes a sound recommendation. Unfortunately, despite his intentions to "examine closely whether, when, and how
[P]entecostals come to participate in collective action for social
change," he does not identify, even in the case he has studied, the
specific conditions that determine when Pentecostals engage in
conservative or progressive politics. He is satisfied with just demonstrating that Pentecostals can become involved in neighborhood organizations, labor struggles, and radical political parties.

I would venture to say that one of the conditions that shapes the
type and range of political action for Pentecostals is precisely
religious ideology. While it is true that ideology can be appropriated differently – stressing various aspects within it – given the
demands of everyday life, the Pentecostal worldview limits the
scope of legitimate socio-political appropriations because of its
tendency towards fundamentalism. Religious ideology demands
that the believer stay on the narrow path, restricting the ways s/he
can translate theology into social action and political praxis. In
other words, not just any appropriation goes.

This is, in fact, one of the important points that Ireland makes.
He argues, correctly in my view, that Pentecostalism's this-worldly
activism on God's behalf does not lead the believer to become
involved in politics in the macro sense, as it is traditionally construed, for s/he has a profound mistrust of human institutions and
initiatives. As Ireland notes about one of his interviewees: "*crente*
[evangelical] dualistic moralism and eschatological despair feed a
radical distrust of democratic politics and politicians."[47] Inspired
by a Pauline anthropology, the believer avoids investing all his/her
efforts and aspirations on political institutions and social solutions
to evil. Rather, the faithful directs her/his work toward her/his

---

[46] Burdick, "Struggling Against the Devil," 21.   [47] Ireland, *Kingdoms Come*, 53.

immediate others, toward her/his loved ones, her/his neighbors, seeking to make them participants in Jesus' salvific work. The believer thus works mainly at the personal level, transforming his/her surroundings while eschewing work for structural and systemic transformations. In Ireland's words, the believer "trims the notion of justice to its local dimensions." Ireland adds: "under the incessant scrutiny of God [the believer] prepares himself and those for whom he is immediately responsible, family and neighbors, to be considered worthy of Divine justice."[48] This local/personal focus results from Pentecostalism's conception of faith as fundamentally a personal matter, a matter between each individual and God. Moreover, since suffering is in large part the result of personal sin, it is necessary (though not sufficient) to transform the sinner's heart in order to deal with the problem of evil.

Pentecostalism thus empowers the poor mainly at the micro and symbolic levels. At the personal and everyday level, it addresses such problems as alcoholism, illness, domestic violence, and the breakup of the family due to sexual promiscuity, gambling, and unemployment. At a community or neighborhood level Pentecostalism's "fervent moralism" may inspire "a politics of local resistance," by which the *crente* calls to task corrupt local officials.

Nevertheless, because of the sharp limits the Pentecostal worldview imposes on this-worldly transformative activity, challenges to the structural and systemic conditions that generate inequality and injustice tend to remain merely symbolic. In Ireland's words, "there is no place for a city upon a hill, to be constructed and defended by God's faithful."[49] This does not mean that Pentecostals cannot or do not in fact get involved in traditional politics. Freston has shown how some Pentecostals have become involved in party politics in Brazil. Furthermore, as theologian Juan Sepúlveda writes, since Pentecostalism is not a static set of doctrines but a faith experience, it changes constantly to adapt and respond to the challenges posed by everyday life.[50] As life conditions

---

[48] Ibid., 58.

[49] R. Ireland, "The Crentes of Campo Alegre and the Religious Construction of Brazilian Politics," in *Rethinking Protestantism in Latin America*, ed. Garrard-Burnett and Stoll, 62.

[50] J. Sepulveda, "Pentecostal Theology in the Context of the Struggle for Life," in *Faith Born in the Struggle for Life*, ed D. Kirkpatrick (Grand Rapids, MI: William Eerdman, 1988).

deteriorate further for poor people who have joined Pentecostal churches, there is a strong possibility for the emergence of a popular Pentecostalism that could take a more historicized vision of evil in the world (i.e., seeing it more as the result of the action of power groups working against God's plan than of Satan's activities).[51] Such vision could lead to a concern for integral liberation from sin, injustice, and oppression. In his more recent work, Ireland has, in fact, stressed the existence of a current within Pentecostalism which sees conversion not as a finished event that separates the elect from a fallen world, but as an on-going moral struggle in everyday life. Ireland suggests that this type of Pentecostalism might create a predisposition towards radical, critical citizenship.[52]

While acknowledging the potential for the development of a powerful liberationist current at the grassroots within Pentecostalism, I want to argue that Pentecostal theology tends to favor local action. It is not that Pentecostals are automatically apolitical or conservative, or will never engage in capital "P" politics but that, because of the emphasis on a personal relation with God, they will tend to focus on moral issues of personal, family, and community control. The aggregate activity around local moral issues may have an impact on larger social questions, but this impact is mostly indirect and long term.

Pentecostalism thus contains conceptions of agency, social change, and history which differ markedly from the progressive Catholicism's emphasis on the effectiveness of human works, intra-historical transcendence, and social change (through the actions of a collective emancipatory subject struggling to change social structures). Is Pentecostalism's worldview more suited to deal with the conditions the poor face in the context of contemporary capitalism? Is it immune to the crisis of modern emancipatory discourses?

I shall argue later on that Pentecostalism's stress on the local and the personal resonates with the poor's loss of control over their

---

[51] For the first signs of this transformation, see C. Alvarez, ed., *Pentecostalismo y liberación* (San José, Costa Rica: DEI, 1992).

[52] R. Ireland, "Pentecostalism, Conversions, and Politics in Brazil," *Religion* 25 (1995), 135–145.

lives and with the dimming possibilities of transforming a capitalist system that is simultaneously becoming more decentered and more all-encompassing. In the absence of the possibility of effecting structural change because of the decline of collective actors such as trade unions, political parties, and social movements, and because of the crisis of emancipatory meta-narratives, poor people seek empowerment at the micro level. Pentecostalism provides one of the few vehicles available for them to reach this more modest, but more realistic empowerment. Pentecostalism helps the poor negotiate the perils of contemporary capitalism by keeping the present and the beyond in tension. While it tends effectively to the believer's concrete psychological and physical needs in the here and now, giving her/him a certain level of empowerment with personal, household and local dimensions, it offers a radical break with the broken, unjust present, promising fullness of life with Jesus Christ's second coming. On the one hand, the unresolved tension between the present and the future in Pentecostal theology provides the poor an ethos of discipline, a strong sense of self-worth, and a plausible theodicy to explain and make bearable the problem of evil and to negotiate the conditions imposed by late capitalism. On the other hand, it formulates a total rejection of the status quo as part of humanity's fallen history, offering a utopian vision where injustice and sin are vanquished. The apocalyptic nature of Pentecostal eschatology makes it possible to eschew the fate of modern emancipatory discourses which draw their inspiration from progressive historical march to utopia.

Having characterized the external dimension of the crisis of the Catholic popular church (i.e., the dynamics of Pentecostal growth), we can now turn to the central focus of this book: the crisis of participation and mobilization within progressive Catholicism. Keeping in mind that the growth of Pentecostalism is an important background condition to the crisis, we can now concentrate on elucidating the intra and extra-ecclesial obstacles and pastoral contradictions that have hindered the popular church's transition from a *pastoral de grupos pequenos* (CEBs and *círculos bíblicos*) to a *pastoral de massa*. Before offering my own reading of the internal dimension of the crisis, I present in the next chapter two readings proposed by ecclesial actors. After a discussion of the strengths and weaknesses of these two readings, I offer my own interpretation based on a case study in Nova Iguaçu in chapters 6 and 7. Once I have presented my reading of the popular church's crisis, I return to my discussion of Pentecostalism in chapter 8 to reformulate the insights above and to propose some hypotheses for further investigation in the light of my findings.

PART III

Explaining the crisis

CHAPTER 5

Intra-institutional explanations

CONFLICTING FORCES WITHIN THE BRAZILIAN
CATHOLIC CHURCH

In this chapter I discuss attempts by key actors within the Catholic church to make sense of the crisis of the *igreja popular*. This discussion will help identify elements of the crisis that I will later explore in more detail when I offer my own explanation.

Although various intra-institutional readings of the crisis of the popular church have been proposed, two main lines of argumentation can be discerned in the Catholic reaction to the crisis. The first line emerges from the progressive wing of the church, which since Medellín has come to organize its pastoral and ecclesial initiatives in the *igreja popular*.

In contrast to the popular church's perspective, a competing reading of the crisis emerges from the conservative or more traditional sector of the ecclesial body, which has gathered considerable strength during John Paul II's papacy. In chapter 3, I characterized the various institutions, pastoral initiatives, and levels of action that constitute the Brazilian popular church. Just like the *igreja popular*, the conservative sector of the Catholic church is diverse. However, because of its quest to re-centralize power in clerical hands, the conservative sector has a strong episcopal accent. Its core is a group of newly appointed bishops and cardinals, among whom José Cardoso of Olinda and Recife, Boaventura Kloppenburg of Nova Friburgo, Freire Falcão of Brasília, Amaury Castanho of Valença, Lucas Moreira Neves of Salvador and Eugênio Sales of Rio de Janeiro are the most prominent.[1]

---

[1] A 1991 survey conducted by *Veja* showed that of the 270 voting members of the CNBB, 31 percent are progressive, 53 percent are moderates and only 16 percent are conservatives.

Supporting the initiatives of these prelates are fast-growing, internationally-based church movements such as the Charismatic Renewal Movement and Opus Dei, which in Brazil tend to target the urban middle class. At the grassroots level, acting among the rural and migrant poor, there are other pre-Vatican II movements such as the Vicentinos (Society of Saint Vincent De Paul), the Legião de Maria (Legion of Mary) and the Apostolado da Oração (Apostolate of Prayer), based either at national or diocesan levels.

The progressive and conservative explanations of the crisis have been in fierce contention since roughly the early 1980s, with the final outcome still to be determined. The stakes of this struggle are high: the sector that succeeds in making its reading normative will have a greater hand in shaping the future configuration of the Brazilian Catholic church and in determining the role it will play in Brazilian society.

THE PROGRESSIVE READING

For the progressive wing of the church, the crisis of participation in the popular church stems from four interrelated factors: (1) a continued shortage of priests to engage in sustained pastoral work among the poor, (2) institutional constraints to the full implementation of the CEB model, (3) the conservative Vatican offensive against liberation theology and the *igreja popular* as the most powerful instance of these constraints, and (4) a massive evangelization campaign supported principally by North American Evangelical churches.

Traditionally, the Catholic church's clerical hold in Brazilian society has been weak. The chronic shortage of priests, the excessive reliance on foreign pastoral agents, and the vastness of the territory have combined to give Brazilian Catholicism a particular configuration.[2] Catholicism in Brazil has become more the under-

In recent years, however, the conservative sector has gathered considerable strength, culminating with the election in 1995 of Lucas Moreira Neves as president of the CNBB.

[2] According to the Catholic Centro de Estatística Religiosa e Investigação Social (Center for Religious Statistics and Social Research, CERIS), in 1985 Brazil had only 13,155 priests to tend 6,838 parishes spread across 8,511,965 km². The same source indicates that in 1970 the ratio of priests to Catholics was 1:7,151. Almost 21 percent of those priests were foreign-born. By 1985 the ratio had decreased to 1:10,000, while the percentage of

lying, taken-for-granted cultural fabric of national identity than a matter of conscious choice and practice. Within this all-pervading cultural background, there are two dominant forms of practice.

The first one is a traditional folk Catholicism which blends elements of pre-Trent Portuguese Catholicism and native religious beliefs and practices. Since in many cases the natives' conversion to Catholicism occurred in the absence of priests who could correct erroneous readings of orthodoxy, the indigenous people had some space to appropriate the Christian message through their own religious categories. Also, very often, the missionaries, in trying to explain church teachings, drew from autochthonous practices and beliefs to establish parallels with the Christian message.

Central to the traditional, popular strand of Brazilian Catholicism is the cult of the saints. Believers have direct access to the supernatural through personal relationships with their patron saints. These relationships are of exchange or alliance: the saint provides protection, health, and/or success to the believer and the latter reciprocates with devotion. The cult of the saints has not only an individual component, but also involves a collective dimension. Some saints have come to be identified with the particular locality in which they appeared or performed a miracle. At these sites, communities built shrines and temples to venerate the saint, which, depending on the latter's power and the sacredness of the place, draw many pilgrims. Until the nineteenth century, these shrines were in the hands of laypeople, who often organized themselves in autonomous brotherhoods (*irmandades*), charged with overseeing the devotion to the local saints. Priests had only very circumstantial contact with the Catholicism surrounding these sacred places, i.e., when they were invited by the lay organizations to celebrate mass on the patron saint's day.[3]

Despite the post-Vatican I reforms, this type of folk Catholicism has persisted to this day, undoubtedly due to the fact that it requires minimal clerical intervention. Folk Catholicism has

---

foreign-born priests had jumped to 40.6 percent. *Anuário Católico de 1985* (Rio de Janeiro: CERIS, 1985).

[3] M. de Theije, "'Brotherhoods Throw more Weight around than the Pope': Catholic Traditionalism and the Lay Brotherhoods in Brazil," *Sociological Analysis* 51, no. 2 (1990), 189–204.

developed its own pastoral/religious agents, such as *benzedeiras* (healers) and *rezadoras* (local prayer leaders), who have preserved its practices and worldview.[4]

The second dominant form of Brazilian Catholicism is a more privatized type, in which the believer lives his/her faith primarily at a personal level, seeking clerical and institutional services only at crucial moments of the life cycle (i.e., birth, adolescence, marriage, and death), or during moments of stress (i.e., illness). This privatized form of practice results from an incomplete "romanization" of Brazilian Catholicism.[5]

Romanization describes a process in the nineteenth century whereby the Vatican sought to impose its hierarchical and clerical model of ecclesial organization on the various national churches. This process had it roots in the Council of Trent (1545–1563). Reacting to the Protestant Reformation, the Council sought to define sharply the limits of orthodoxy and establish the church as the only legitimate interpreter of Scripture and Christian tradition. By reaffirming the centrality of the sacraments, the Council transformed clerics into a core of specialists empowered to produce and deliver religious goods. The clergy became the only sanctioned mediators between the human and the divine worlds. Efforts to consolidate clerical power in the Americas gained momentum during the independence period, as the separation of church and state allowed Rome to take a firmer grip on the emerging national churches. Among the strategies to romanize Catholicism was combating local forms of syncretic practice and expropriation by the clergy of many of the shrines and pilgrimage places in the hands of *irmandades*.

Although post-Trent, romanized Catholicism directly contradicted folk Catholicism's reliance on lay leaders and personal devotion, it had a limited impact in Brazil. Due largely to the shortage of priests, traditional popular Catholicism was not eradicated. In fact, it appropriated central elements of romanized practice (i.e., the sacraments) under its own logic, giving them a

---

[4] See L. van den Hoogen, "Benzedeiras within the Catholic Tradition of Minas Gerais," in *Social Change in Contemporary Brazil*, ed. G. Banck and K. Koonings (Netherlands: CEDLA, 1988).

[5] On the romanization of Brazilian Catholicism, see P. R. de Oliveira, *Religião e dominação de classe* (Petrópolis: Vozes, 1985).

different flavor. The faithful, instead of strictly adhering to church teachings, continued to have only irregular contact with the priest. Nevertheless, the expropriation of local shrines and pilgrimages from lay Catholic groups tended to curtail the collective element of rural practices, leading to a more privatized type of Catholicism.

The contemporary popular church has sought to overcome the logistical limitations of romanized Catholicism, attempting to evangelize the Brazilian masses without appealing to a hierarchical and centralized ecclesial model. Through CEBs and *círculos bíblicos*, the *igreja popular* has attempted to make faith a matter of conscious choice and collective practice, privileging the laity's role within a new, more democratic and participatory church. In this sense, the contemporary popular church recovers traditional, popular Catholicism's emphasis on lay autonomy and group *praxis*, without getting caught in the latter's excessive mysticism and devotionalism. The *igreja popular* historicizes the practices of traditional, popular Catholicism, adding a socio-political element to religious practice.

Nevertheless, for all its stress on lay pastoral and political activity, the popular church has also suffered the consequences of the chronic shortage of priests. Some observers have argued that the creation of base communities throughout Brazil rested on the initiatives of pastoral agents acting with the support of the CNBB.[6] Political scientist Daniel Levine argues, furthermore, that the role of these pastoral agents in the maintenance of CEBs and *círculos* cannot be underestimated: they mediate between institutional and everyday levels. According to Levine, pastoral agents play a mediating role because "they are part of the institutional church while also operating between it and popular groups. Legitimacy, resources and moral strength are drawn from their connection to each."[7]

---

[6] In a comparative research project undertaken in 1984 on a sample of twenty-two CEBs in the Archdiocese of São Paulo, W. E. Hewitt found that local priests and nuns played an instrumental role in the formation of well over three-quarters of the CEBs studied. W. E. Hewitt, *Base Christian Communities and Social Change in Brazil* (Lincoln: University of Nebraska Press, 1991). In addition, a national survey of CEBs conducted by the CNBB found that only 21.8 percent of the communities sampled were founded by lay people. *Comunidades: Igreja na base* (São Paulo: Paulinas, 1981).

[7] D. H. Levine, *Popular Voices in Latin American Catholicism* (Princeton: Princeton University Press, 1992), 270.

Sociologist Madeleine Adriance makes an even stronger case for the centrality of priests, sisters, and lay agents in the promotion of Catholic grassroots organizations. According to Adriance, even in dioceses where the bishop has not been supportive of innovative pastoral approaches, CEBs have flourished through the determined efforts of pastoral agents. The pastoral agents' relative autonomy *vis-à-vis* their bishops, particularly in the countryside, and their direct, day-to-day contact with the laity give them a level of influence among the poor that sometimes transcends episcopal authority.[8]

As we shall see later, Adriance underestimates the important role of progressive bishops when she states that "the key actors in the CEBs are not the bishops, but rather the pastoral agents."[9] However, she is correct in stressing the importance of priests, nuns, and lay people in the advancement of grassroots pastoral initiatives. At the very least we can say that pastoral agents both translate national and global church pastoral proposals into concrete praxis and influence the decisions of ecclesial elites by confronting them with needs and expectations felt at the base. At the micro, everyday level, the pastoral agents' constant efforts to introduce ecclesial and liturgical innovations and to train lay leaders among the poor are central to the CEB experiment.

Reliance on pastoral agents to implement initiatives on the ground and to train lay "organic intellectuals" contrasts with Pentecostalism's proselytizing practices. The latter does not require members to receive special training for critical consciousness *vis-à-vis* the church and the social world. In Pentecostalism, each new convert becomes an *ipso facto* evangelist baptized in Holy Spirit and charged with saving souls and fighting evil wherever it may exist. In this light, according to the progressive wing of the church, the crisis of participation results from Catholicism's failure to compete effectively with Pentecostalism at the base. The Catholic church's inability to increase its presence among those at the margins of society stems from the fact that not enough lay leaders have been trained to make up for the shortage of clerics. In addition, those who have been trained have faced obstacles within the institutional church to advance their alternative pastoral and ecclesial projects.

---

[8] Adriance, "Agents of Change," 302–303.   [9] Ibid., 293.

From the perspective of progressive Catholicism, the growth of Pentecostalism in no way points to the failure of the CEB and the popular pastoral model. Rather, it evinces the need to implement this model in a fuller fashion, as a truly concerted pastoral strategy to work with and among the poor. Only by strengthening the laity's position within the church, that is, by unequivocally using lay movements and groups at the base as a powerful evangelical catalyst, can Catholicism restore its presence among the poor.

However, strengthening the laity's position would demand a radical restructuring of the church's hierarchical configuration. It would call for a drastic decentralization of institutional resources, so as to shatter the "monopoly of legitimate symbolic goods"[10] held by priests and bishops. The focus on intra-ecclesial power dynamics brings us to what progressives consider to be the second contributing factor in the crisis. The popular church has not succeeded fully in its evangelizing efforts precisely because it has operated within the constraints of a heavily bureaucratized institution, whose top–down logic makes it ineffectual on the ground.

One of the most visible signs of the persistence of top-down arrangements within the popular church is its reliance on the power and charisma of progressive bishops to carry out work at the diocesan level. Political scientist Jean Daudelin notes that "in progressive dioceses, the bishop is still the absolute ruler of his church. The same applies to the priest or the pastoral agent in the parish of the local community."[11] The heavy reliance on personal charisma and goodwill of the local bishop is aggravated by a "practically total" "financial dependence of the popular church on foreign Catholic institutions" that channel resources mostly through the episcopal office.[12]

Drawing from the work of Brazilian sociologists of religion who serve as CEB advisors, Daudelin concludes that

---

[10] P. Bourdieu, "Genèse et structure du champ religieux," *Revue Française de Sociologie* 12 (1971), 295–334.

[11] J. Daudelin, 'L'Église progressiste brésilienne,' 678. The same argument is made by Novaes, "Nada será como antes."

[12] In the case of Nova Iguaçu, many diocesan projects have been financed through the German Catholic funding agency Adveniat, which has a close relationship with Bishop Adriano Hipólito. On the Brazilian Catholic church's reliance on European funding agencies, see R. Della Cava, "Financing the Faith: The Case of Roman Catholicism," *Journal of Church and State* 35, no.1 (1993), 49–52.

there has not been a transfer of power, even in the most deeply involved sectors of the Church . . . no bishop seems to be in the process of realizing such a change and many of the bishops who promote political and social involvement have no intentions to encourage a revolution which would threaten their dominant position.[13]

According to Daudelin, "the bishops' preponderance" in the popular church has deleterious consequences: it "narrows its demographic base" and curtails "its autonomy in relation to Church authorities," making it unable "to resist Vatican pressures."[14] An example of this inability is the precipitous collapse of progressive initiatives in Olinda and Recife – the diocese that many claim gave rise to the CEBs – with the naming of José Cardoso Sobrinho to replace Hêlder Camara, arguably one of the most visionary innovators within the popular church. Shortly after his installation, Dom José took forceful action against the local popular church, closing the Theological Institute of Recife (ITER) and the Seminary of the North-eastern Region II (SERENE II), both crucial for training the region's progressive pastoral agents.[15]

For sociologist Regina Novaes, the centrality of the progressive bishop in the advancement of the popular church points to a serious internal contradiction between the institutional imperative to reproduce a hierarchical structure and the desire to decentralize the church by encouraging lay participation at the base. Novaes writes:

Precisely because the Catholic Church is hierarchical and authoritarian, the bishops have necessarily assumed a vital role in the dissemination of liberation theology. Generally, CEBs only become a visible presence in the local church under the auspices of the progressive bishop . . . How [then] can [the popular church] propose that power be decentralized when at the same time it is clear that it is the power concentrated in the bishop . . . that legitimates and ensures, *vis-à-vis* the hierarchy and the Catholic masses, the viability and reproduction of the network that sustains the progressive sector of the church?[16]

In other words, by working to decentralize power within the universal church, the *igreja popular* ends up delegitimizing and

[13] Daudelin, "L'Église progressiste brésilienne," 678.   [14] Ibid., 68off.
[15] See SEDOC (Documentation Service), "Dossiê: Crise na Arquidiocese de Olinda e Recife," *SEDOC* 22, no. 220 (1990), 693–747.
[16] Novaes, "Nada será como antes," 53–54.

undermining the position of those who have been vital to its establishment, a process which, in turn, weakens the progressive pastoral initiatives. This contradiction has made both the progressive bishops and CEBs vulnerable to attacks from conservative sectors within the church. To shore up their position against conservative episcopal offensive, progressive bishops have had to reclaim their legitimacy, recentralizing power to the detriment of CEBs and other lay organizations. We shall see in the next chapter the consequences at the local level of this attempt by progressive bishops to recentralize power and shore up their position *vis-à-vis* a growing conservative faction in the episcopal body.

To avoid linking the fate of the popular church to charismatic progressive bishops, theologian and pastoral agent José Comblin has suggested that CEBs become a truly national *lay movement* with its own juridical identity, institutional weight, and its own mechanisms for harnessing resources and electing its leadership.[17] Hitherto, CEBs have been a patchwork of diocesan initiatives without a coordinating body to oversee a balanced, nation-wide implementation. While bishops such as Pedro Casaldáliga and Luís Gonzaga Fernandes have made CEBs the pastoral priority in their diocese, others, like Dom Eugênio Sales, boast that there are no CEBs in their dioceses. So far, the only national forum for CEBs has been bi-annual inter-ecclesial meetings, starting in 1975, in which they exchange experiences and reflect on the social and religious situation. In any case, Comblin and other progressive Catholics suggest not a rejection of the popular church's model, but rather its deepening. Such a deepening, they believe, can provide the solution to the crisis of participation.

Daudelin's and Novaes's discussion of the popular church's vulnerability within a hierarchical institution points to the most radical constraint the *igreja popular* faces: a conservative offensive within Catholicism to rein in the historicizing consequences of the church's openness to modernity with Vatican II. Although this offensive predates John Paul II, it has gained considerable momentum during his papacy. Historian Ralph Della Cava has

---

[17] See J. Comblin, "Algumas questões a partir da prática das comunidades ecclesiais de base no nordeste," *Revista Eclesiástica Brasileira* 50, no. 198 (1990), 335–381; and Van der Ploeg, "A Igreja dos pobres no nordeste," 61–71.

identified four key issues in this "Catholic restoration":[18] (1) the careful regulation of the formation of pastoral agents, (2) control of the level of collegiality within the church, (3) the relative diversity of liturgical, pastoral and organizational practices within Catholicism, and (4) the range of application and validity of papal *magisterium*.[19]

In broad terms, the conservative offensive seeks to reaffirm the universality of the church by restoring the symbolic power of the priest's office – a power that arises from the priest's unique access to sanctioned religious goods – and by reaffirming the unchangeability of Catholic values.[20] Thus, grassroots pastoral initiatives, such as the CEBs, which challenge the clergy's monopoly of symbolic power by opening sacraments and teachings to lay experimentation and by fostering autonomy at the base, must be reined in.

In Brazil, the conservative restoration has taken many forms.[21] Besides the highly publicized drive to discipline Leonardo Boff, which recently ended with his voluntary withdrawal from priesthood,[22] the Vatican has applied strong pressure on liberal bishops to bring their pastoral activities into the papal line. The Vatican has issued strong warnings to liberal bishops and decrees to divide their diocesan base, and, most importantly, it has appointed a considerable number of conservative bishops.[23]

---

[18] The term restoration has been endorsed by Cardinal Joseph Ratzinger, the prefect of the Sacred Congregation for the Doctrine of the Faith and one of the chief architects of the offensive. According to Ratzinger, restoration means "the search for a new equilibrium after all the exaggerations of an indiscriminate opening to the world." J. Ratzinger, *The Ratzinger Report* (San Francisco: Ignatius Press, 1985), 37–38.

[19] Della Cava, "Vatican Policy 1978–90," 178–183. See also C. L. Mariz and L. D. G. Sobrinho, "Algumas reflexões sobre a reação conservadora na Igreja Católica," *Comunicações do ISER* 9, no. 30 (1990), 73–78.

[20] The drive to assert the universality of church teachings is evident in the latest Vatican documents: in the "Instruction on Christian Freedom and Liberation" (1986) on the question of teaching Catholic doctrine, in the new *Catechism for the Universal Church* (1990), and in *Veritatis Splendor* (1993) on matters of morality.

[21] For an overview of the extent of the conservative Vatican offensive in Latin America, and particularly in Brazil, see P. Lernoux, *The People of God: The Struggle for World Catholicism* (New York: Viking, 1989).

[22] See H. Cox, *The Silencing of Leonardo Boff. The Vatican and the Future of World Christianity* (Oak Park, IL: Meyer Stone, 1988).

[23] Letters of warning were forwarded from the Prefect of the Holy See's Episcopal Congregation to at least ten progressive bishops, including Nova Iguaçu's Hipólito. See "Outro pito de Roma," *Veja* (Rio de Janeiro), October 26, 1988, 108–109. In 1988, the

The Vatican restoration has had dire consequences for the Brazilian popular church. It has brought to the surface and intensified latent divisions within the CNBB, putting stress on the delicate alliance between progressives and moderates within the episcopal body which have made possible the implementation of pastoral innovations at the base.[24] In the midst of a polarized episcopal conference, and with the number of conservative bishops on the rise, progressive forces have found themselves increasingly isolated. Thus, progressives have tended to retreat from more radical proposals to be able to connect with moderates. The progressive bishops' isolation and retrenchment has in turn affected CEB work, which, as we saw, is heavily dependent on episcopal support. The case of Pedra Bonita in the next chapter exemplifies the impact of this dynamic at the grassroots.

The final outcome of the Roman restoration is still uncertain. At present, the conservative bishops' inability to articulate a coherent alternative vision, together with the crisis of the progressive sectors paradigm, has led to fragmentation, confusion, and even gridlock in Catholic pastoral work. This, in turn, has aided, indirectly, the spread of other religions.

Progressive Catholic circles trace the roots of the popular church's crisis not only to intra-ecclesial constraints. The final cause, they claim, comes from an external source: an orchestrated and well-financed campaign by conservative evangelical churches in North America to evangelize the Third World, especially Latin America. Progressive Catholic intellectuals believe that this campaign has been shaped by US geopolitical interests in the region, which in the 1980s meant the containment of communism through counter-insurgency operations and the spread of democracy,

---

archdiocese of São Paulo, a bastion of progressive Catholicism, was dismembered into five smaller areas. W. E. Hewitt, "Popular Movements, Resource Demobilization, and the Legacy of Vatican Restructuring in the Archdiocese of São Paulo," *Canadian Journal of Latin American and Caribbean Studies* 18, no. 36 (1993), 1–24. In the meantime, since 1979, the pope has appointed more than 130 bishops. K. Serbin, "Brazil Bishops' Vote May Mask Future Power Shift," *National Catholic Reporter*, May 3, 1991, 12.

[24] Edward Cleary observes that "progressives in the Latin American church have always been in a minority, but were able to ally themselves with a large group of moderates in the leading progressive churches." "Conclusion: Politics and Religion – Crisis, Constraints, and Restructuring," in Cleary and Stewart-Gambino, *Conflict and Competition*, 201.

understood very narrowly as the implementation of electoral processes and of free market-oriented economic reforms.[25]

Although the most visible example of the link between evangelical missions and US counter-insurgent foreign policy is Central
America,[26] the Brazilian case shows some parallels. Progressive
Catholics point to the Banzer Plan, adopted by the Brazilian
military after a meeting in Asuncion, Paraguay in 1977. This plan
called for a systematic campaign of harassment and intimidation
against church members critical of the status quo. Governments
were instructed to smear progressive bishops, detain pastoral
agents and deny entry visas to foreign priests and nuns coming to
work in troublesome dioceses. At the same time, they were to
facilitate the work of evangelical missionaries from the US.[27]

Aided by local authoritarian governments, supported by an
influx of resources, and using the proven methods of the US
electronic church, the more aggressive and exclusionary forms of
evangelical Protestantism (i.e., Pentecostalism) have apparently
commodified salvation, turning the whole religious field into a vast
market where the poor purchase temporary relief for their afflic-
tions. In the eyes of progressive Catholics, the popularity of forms
of Pentecostalism which offer cures and miracles rests mostly on
the unscrupulous commercial manipulation of the people's most
cherished spiritual needs.

It should be noted that this reading of the rapid growth of
Pentecostalism is not restricted to the progressive sector of the
church. In their 1992 meeting in Santo Domingo, the Latin
American bishops concluded that the "problem of sects has
reached dramatic proportions and has become truly worrisome,"
due mostly to the proselytizing activities of "fundamentalist
sects." These sects

---

[25] Progressive Catholics point to the document produced by the Committee of Santa Fe in
1980 where foreign policy experts linked to the Reagan administration pledged support
for the spread of conservative Pentecostalism as a counterweight to "Marxist-oriented"
teachings of liberation theology. The Committee of Santa Fe, *A New Inter-American Policy
for the Eighties* (Santa Fe, NM: np 1980).

[26] See E. Domínguez and D. Huntington, "The Salvation Brokers: Conservative Evangelicals in Central America," *NACLA: Report on the Americas* 18, no. 1 (1984), 2–36.

[27] See P. Lernoux, *Cry of the People: The Struggle for Human Rights in Latin America – The Catholic
Church in Conflict with U.S. Policy* (New York: Penguin Books, 1980), 142–145.

[a]re characterized by their very enthusiastic proselytizing through persistent house visiting and large-scale distribution of Bibles, magazines and books; their presence and the opportunistic help they provide at times of personal or family crisis; and their great technical skill in using the media. They have at their disposal immense funding from other countries and the tithes they obliged all their members to pay.

Other features are . . . their aggressive stance toward the Church; they often resort to defamation and material inducements. Although they are only weakly committed to the temporal realm, they tend to become involved in politics with a view to taking power.[28]

In sum, progressives within the Brazilian Catholic church link the crisis of the *igreja popular* to a combination of intra-ecclesial contradictions and extra-ecclesial obstacles that have hindered the full implementation of grassroots initiatives. The pastoral void left by this partial implementation has been filled by alternative traditions such as Pentecostalism and African-based religions which show greater organizational flexibility.

How are we to assess the relative merit of this explanation of the crisis? The explanation certainly goes a long way toward uncovering the institutional limitations and obstacles that have constrained the production and circulation of the popular church's liberationist message among the poor, just as it highlights some of the external advantages that Pentecostal churches have enjoyed to carry out their missionary work. We shall see in the next chapter that in order to understand truly what is happening at the grassroots, it becomes necessary to take into account the institutional constraints faced by popular church initiatives such as CEBs.

The progressive reading, nevertheless, only accounts for the differential availability in the "religious market" of progressive Catholicism's and Pentecostalism's messages. It fails to explain adequately why the poor find Pentecostalism attractive – and Catholicism less so – in the first place. To say that the attraction to Pentecostalism is solely predicated on "the opportunistic help" it provides in times of personal and family distress is to ignore the centrality of the experience of conversion in Pentecostal practice.

---

[28] A. T. Hennelly, ed., *Santo Domingo and Beyond: Documents from the Historic Meeting of the Latin American Bishops Conference* (Maryknoll, NY: Orbis Books, 1993), 112. The pope has even used sharper rhetoric, calling the sects "rapacious wolves." See his opening address to the Santo Domingo conference in *Origins* 22, no. 19 (October 22, 1992), 326.

Conversion is a complex liminal process, which in the case of Pentecostalism is a powerful experience of baptism in the Spirit, by which the believer repents of his/her sinful life and becomes a new person with a new ethos that separates him/her from the rest of the world. Contrary to what economistic approaches to religious choice presuppose, conversion is not just a matter of utilitarian considerations; it is not the simple purchase of a commodity that has attained high visibility in the religious market. Thus, any attempt to understand Pentecostalism's rapid expansion will have to examine carefully its inner logic and how this logic moves the believer.

The attribution of Pentecostal growth to the willful deception and exploitation of thousands of believers acts more to block a critical self-examination of the popular church's pastoral practices than to explain the intricate combinations of micro- and macro-processes, of socio-economic and religious variables that structure patterns of mass conversion. At its worst this explanation may fall into a kind of "conspiracy theory" that imputes the causes of religious dynamics to only exogenous factors. David Martin makes the same point, though in a more polemical fashion, when he attacks conspiracy theories that suggest "that the conversion of forty million Latin Americans can be explained by subventions from the CIA, and more broadly by American imperialism. The favoured explanation of Roman Catholic apologists and cultural nationalists is adopted to avoid the work of sociological revision."[29]

Furthermore, as I argued in chapter 4, Pentecostalism is a truly popular religion, at least in Brazil. Despite the central role of foreigners such as Berg and Francescon in the formation of the early congregations, at present most of the emerging Pentecostal temples are local and autonomous initiatives. They have very little to do with concerted international plans to challenge the Catholic church hegemony. According to Freston, "in Brazil as a whole, no newly-arrived foreign church has established a significant presence in over forty years. Protestant (and especially Pentecostal) religion is a *national, popular,* and *rapidly expanding* phenomenon."[30]

[29] D. Martin, "Evangelicals and Economic Culture in Latin America: An Interim Comment on Research in Progress," *Social Compass* 39, no. 1 (1992), 10.
[30] Freston, "Pentecostalism in Latin America," 7.

The progressive reading also fails to address a second, more important aspect of the crisis for our purposes. At issue is the cultural distance generated between the *fermento de massa*, the "popular elite" acting in the CEBs, and the masses. Why are CEBs and *círculos bíblicos* "very far from representing the majority of the Brazilian Catholic population," if they are indeed a "popular form of Catholicism?"[31] As I argued in chapter 3, the inability to transform the *pastoral de grupos pequenos* into a *pastoral de massa* is the defining element of the crisis. It is not sufficient to propose, as some progressive Catholics do, that fuller implementation of the *igreja popular* will solve the problem. It may, in fact, be that the problem lies precisely in the model of the *pastoral de grupos pequenos* itself. There may be contradictions within the CEB model that inhibit its effectiveness given the present conditions in which the Brazilian urban poor find themselves.

The next chapter, in fact, represents an attempt to explore this possibility by focusing on the evolution of a particular base community. Chapter 7 then places my findings at the local level in the larger context of contemporary Brazilian society. I hope it will become clear that, without discounting the determining weight of the institutional obstacles identified by progressive Catholics, there are indeed impasses and limitations within the CEB model which need to be corrected in order to maintain its viability.

THE CONSERVATIVE READING

The conservative wing of the church blames the popular church's ecclesiology and methodology for the crisis.[32] Conservatives believe that the popular church's single-minded emphasis on orthopraxis and its unrestrained use of rational-critical social scientific tools to understand the world has resulted in a radical relativization of the Catholic universal message and in a stark disenchantment of reality. Add to this the excessive politicization of faith and the political instrumentalization of such notions as "the people of

---

[31] Oliveira, "Religiões Populares," 125.
[32] On the conservative Catholic critique of the popular church's model, see F. C. Rolim, "Neoconservatismo eclesiástico e uma estratégia política," *Revista Eclesiástica Brasileira* 49, no. 194 (1989), 259–281.

God," "the poor," and "works," and what results is a lifeless religion, lacking a sense of mystery, awe and dependence, which cannot connect with popular religiosity. An instance of this argument can be found in John Paul II's complaint during the meeting of the Latin American bishops at Santo Domingo that one of the reasons the faithful turn to Protestant "sects" is that they "do not find in pastoral agents that strong sense of God that such agents should be transmitting in their lives."[33]

According to traditionalists, religions like Pentecostalism and the African-based *umbanda* flourish because they show a remarkable continuity with the deeply ingrained popular Catholicism of saints and pilgrimages. Pentecostalism and *umbanda* share with folk Catholicism a strong emphasis on the affective component of ritual practice and the psycho-cognitive force of symbols. All these religions favor a direct, intense and personal experience of the sacred, which unlike the highly mediated and rationalized vision of reality offered by liberation theology, and sometimes by CEBs, is accessible to the believer regardless of his/her level of education and *conscientização*. Only a short step separates the traditional Catholic world populated by apparitions and subject to the miraculous interventions of God through saints from a world pregnant with the "gifts" of the Holy Spirit or with the activities of the *orixás* (African spirits). Traditionalists conclude, then, that Pentecostalism and African-based religions grow by leaps and bounds because they speak to the poor in their own language, taking advantage of their fervent spirituality.

This argument would certainly explain why the poor convert to Pentecostalism rather than join the CEBs. It would also explain why Pentecostalism shows such a strong animosity toward African-based religions: since they fulfill similar religious functions for the poor, they are open competitors. But why then are people converting *en masse* to Pentecostalism, for instance, rather than continuing their practices within traditional popular Catholicism? Here once again the church's conservative wing points to liberation theology and the popular church. By portraying the church as a human institution susceptible to ideological manipu-

---

[33] 'Opening Address to Fourth General Conference," 326.

lations, deeply immersed in a stratified society, liberation theology and the popular church have in effect delegitimized Catholicism, robbing it of its main claim to truth: its universality.[34] Such a delegitimization disarticulates the Catholic sacred canopy, weakening the effective power behind the priestly *magisterium*. The emptying and disenchantment of Catholicism has left the poor hungry for the sacred, for a sense of transcendence that the overly politicized discourse and practice of the CEBs cannot satisfy.

Evidence from the field seems to confirm the conservatives' argument. Comparing CEB attitudes toward popular religion with the approach taken by Pentecostalism, sociologist Cecília Mariz notes that the "secularized vision of the CEBs may have weakened faith or the religious concern of their members. The secularizing elements of that vision give the sacred and religion a lesser role in human life than that which they play in popular culture."[35]

Chief among these secularizing elements, Mariz claims, is the "assumption that truth is reached not only through revelation, but also through theoretical knowledge and rational analyses." Since the progressives' vision "proposes in many aspects the disenchantment of religion . . . the proposal of liberation theology, even when translated to a popular language, is not totally understood and accepted by the population in general and by poor Brazilians in particular."[36]

For conservatives, the church's loss of universality, the disenchantment of the world, and the fracturing of the sacred canopy result directly from a political instrumentalization of the preferential option for the poor. This instrumentalization proceeds through what Bishop Boaventura Kloppenburg calls the "ideologization of

[34] This seems to be the point conservative Bishop Boaventura Kloppenburg wants to make when he criticizes Leonardo Boff for writing that "Jesus Christ did not found the church and that, as such, there is no divine law [*direito divino*] in the church. [Boff] said that the dogmas formulated in the past have only a relative value for a time, but not for all times and all places." Boff "denied the unity of the Church of God." "O Marxismo na Igreja. Entrevista com Dom Boaventura Kloppenburg," interview by J. A. Dias Lopes (Rio de Janeiro), *Veja*, January 9, 1985, 3.

[35] C. L. Mariz, "CEBs e pentecostalismo: Novas reformas da religião popular," *Revista Eclesiástica Brasileira* 51, no. 203 (1991), 609.

[36] Mariz and Guerra Sobrinho, "Algumas reflexões sobre a reação conservadora," 77.

the concept of the people of God."[37] In a series of unwarranted interpretive steps, liberation theology and the *igreja popular* first reduce the people of God to the poor, identifying the latter only as the economically oppressed. Then the liberationist camp equates the economically oppressed to the poor in the Gospel. This allows it to turn the poor as economically oppressed into the privileged subject of God's salvific work and the only valid locus of prophetic action and theological reflection.[38] Thus, the ideologization of the concept of the people of God, its transformation to a "class option" functions to exclude rather than to open the church to the world. Under these terms the preferential option results in the "the exclusion of those not poor . . . [in] a classist attitude contrary to the universality of the evangelizing activities of the church."[39]

For Kloppenburg, the term "people of God" applies to the entire church, and the notion of "the poor" goes beyond mere material considerations to include the "spiritually poor," i.e., sinners, whom the church must save also. He argues that "The social condition of poverty is not sufficient to enter the Kingdom of God: it is still necessary to be poor in spirit. And to be poor in spirit it is not necessary to be indigent and oppressed: it is sufficient to be open to God and to man [*sic*]."[40] Thus, for the conservative Catholic wing, liberation theology and the *igreja popular* have divided the holy church, forcing it to abandon its true and universal spiritual mission and thrusting it into the fractious world of politics and power relations. In the words of Amaury Castanho, bishop of Valença in the state of Rio de Janeiro,

The preferential option for the poor, adopted by the Latin American pastors gathered in . . . Puebla . . . in consonance with the messianism characteristic of Christianity, regrettably ended for many Christian and Catholics as more ideological than pastoral, more politically oriented than evangelizing. It became an option that discriminated the rich, that is

[37] For a full presentation of his position see B. Kloppenburg, "Influjos ideológicos en el concepto teológico de 'pueblo,'" in *Otra iglesia en la base?* (Rio de Janeiro: CELAM, 1984), 97–142.

[38] José Freire Falcão, a conservative archbishop, states that "[w]hen poor is taken to be synonymous with 'working class' [*classe operária*] according to Marxist categories, one ends up taking class struggle as the only key or privileged explanation of society and history and as the only path of liberatory practice and social transformation." *Jornal do Brasil* (Rio de Janeiro), July 27, 1984.

[39] Boaventura Kloppenburg, quoted in *Jornal do Brasil* (Rio de Janeiro), July 7, 1983.

[40] Kloppenburg, "Influjos ideológicos," 130–131.

aggressive, "excluding and exclusive," as Pope John Paul II has insisted repeatedly and incisively . . .[41]

Conservative Catholics argue that a divided church only interested in this-worldly activities is no longer open to everyone, for it can no longer appeal to humanity's universal quest for salvation. It appeals only to the particular material interests of a social class (the poor). This is why religions like Pentecostalism, which respond to the deep yearning for individual salvation, have overtaken the popular Catholic church. It follows, then, that the solution to the twin problems of the growth of Pentecostalism and the crisis of participation in the popular church demands a return to the sacred, to the mystical, symbolic and affective elements of Catholicism so dear to the impoverished masses, and a recovery of the Catholic church's universality through a reaffirmation of its privileged access to the Christian tradition. In the words of Archbishop Falcão of Brasília, "Politics is the task of political parties. Priests and bishops must concern themselves with saving souls and preaching the Gospel."[42]

The church's extrication from politics may take different forms, ranging from the virtual elimination of liberationist initiatives, as in the Archdiocese of Rio de Janeiro, to their cooptation into more traditional structures. The latter option is advocated by Bishop Amaury Castanho, who thinks that the problem lies not with the CEBs themselves, but in the *assessores* who have accompanied them. These advisors are "known for their ideological, political and partisan convictions and for their leftist activism." Castanho sees two possible ways to deal with the advisors:

[T]o try through dialogue to bring them back from their radicalism, bring them into the ecclesiology and christology of the Vatican II Council, and to a pastoral practice corresponding to the Church's sentiment; or to separate them from the CEBs, substituting them with theologians and sociologist really identified with the Gospel, who may guide CEBs to diverse and safer paths.[43]

Clearly, this effort to recast progressive initiatives into a more traditional, hierarchical mold and to recover the liturgical and

[41] A. Castanho, *Caminhos das CEBs no Brasil: Reflexão crítica* (Rio de Janeiro: Marques Saraiva, 1988), 136–137.
[42] J. F. Falcão, "A distância da política. Entrevista com Dom Freire Falcão," interview by L. Gomes (Rio de Janeiro), *Veja*, June 8, 1988, 5.
[43] Castanho, *Caminhos das CEBs no Brasil*, 146.

sacramental elements of Catholicism dovetails nicely with the pope's restoration. It resonates with his support for movements such as Opus Dei and the Charismatic Renewal, which emphasize personal and spiritual salvation, and subscribe strongly to a pyramidal ecclesial model. Support for these groups coincides with declining favor for progressive orders such as the Society of Jesus (Jesuits) who were instrumental in the implementation of the pastoral directives coming from Medellín and Puebla.[44] The concern expressed by progressives about the obstacles and danger that the conservative restoration poses, therefore, appears justified.

If the conservative sector's reading of the crisis of Catholicism in Brazil is correct, then Catholicism's loss of hegemony rests ultimately on the popular church's world view and methods. Thus, only the abrogation of these methods will restore the Brazilian Catholic Church to its original primacy in the religious field.

Although the conservative reading points to some troubling pastoral and methodological impasses in the popular church's approach, highlighting the troubles the latter is having in connecting with the religiosity of the poor, it suffers from serious flaws. To begin with, the charge of religious disenchantment and political instrumentalization levelled against CEBs is overstated. As we shall see in the next chapter, CEB members construct a popular theology that sustains them in their long struggles. Despite their critical social consciousness, their central point of reference continues to be Gospel histories in which they find metaphors, characters and events that help them make sense of their everyday world. The life of Christ continues to serve as the wellspring of inspiration for Christian engagement in the world.[45]

To be sure, CEBs produce a disenchantment of the world of folk Catholicism that is common to all forms of Catholic modernism. According to anthropologist Carlos Rodrigues Brandão, this post-Vatican II Catholicism has tended:

1) To not associate the person's fate after his/her death with individual religious and ethical sins (the great sins are political and salvation is collective);

[44] See Della Cava, "Vatican Policy, 1978–1990."
[45] C. C. Macedo, "CEBs: Um caminho ao saber popular," *Comunicações do ISER* 9, no. 35 (1990), 26.

2) To ignore intermediary places where the dead purify themselves, of which Purgatory is the best example;

3) To overlook the existence or power of supernatural evil forces, beginning with the devil.

"Vanguard Christians" [of the CEBs] forget without any regret the devil and its subordinates, just as they disregard traditional saints. These Christians prefer to deal with the Hebrew prophets. They prefer to attribute the evils of the world to political and economic causes, that having a social origin, should be resolved among humans.[46]

CEBs' disenchantment of popular Catholicism is not, however, as total as the conservative forces and some sociologists suggest. What CEBs actually do is "re-enchant" folk Catholicism. They preserve traditional popular Catholicism's central idea that the divine is near, that it manifests itself in the everyday life of the Catholic activist. God is with the people accompanying and legitimizing their long struggles for justice and equality (the *caminhada*); *ergo* the term "people of God." For CEBs, the sacred continues to intersect with the human realm, but not primarily through the miraculous actions of saints or the mischievous activities of Satan. Rather, this intersection comes through the insertion of human liberation within the history of divine salvation. The world, the present, and human works become in CEB theology part of the fulfillment of the reign of God.[47] I argued in chapter 1 that these notions of the unity of salvific history, intra-historical transcendence, and the effectiveness of human works lie at the core of both liberation theology and the *igreja popular*.

In the previous chapter I noted that Mariz attributes the failure of base communities to compete effectively with Pentecostalism partly to the type and level of disenchantment and rationalization of folk Catholicism. According to Mariz, whereas Pentecostalism produces just a "normative" and individual break with folk Catholicism, CEBs foster a cognitive and collective rupture with tradition that leads to a "higher degree of secularization."

[46] C. R. Brandão, "O festim dos bruxos," *Religião e Sociedade* 13, no. 3 (1986), 131.

[47] Nicaragua offers an extreme example of this intersection. Anthropologist Roger Lancaster notes that during the insurrection against Somoza, Marxist revolutionary ideology fused with the millenarian element of popular Catholicism. This interpenetration made it possible for the working classes to identify the construction of a new socialist order with the coming of the Reign of God. *Thanks to God and the Revolution: Popular Religion and Class Consciousness in the New Nicaragua* (New York: Columbia University Press, 1988).

Pentecostalism preserves the notion, central to folk Catholicism, that supranatural forces play a determining role in human history. CEBs, in contrast, propose a humanist, voluntarist view of the world in which individuals pursue salvation through the power of their intellect and the consequences of their strategic activities. In Mariz's opinion, the vision espoused by CEBs does not "recognize miracles and supernatural occurrences in everyday life." In addition, it does not "assume any relationship between miracles and God's plan. God does not use miracles to help human beings carry out his plan; instead, he uses human beings and relies on their abilities."[48] In contrast,

The Pentecostal idea that God's plans or Providence must rely on supernatural means is quite plausible in popular culture, which is grounded in the assumption that the supernatural can be experienced in everyday life. For both Pentecostals and Afro-Brazilian spiritists, miracles and supernatural experiences are common place, and members of both groups have visions, hear prophesies, and perform supernatural cures.[49]

Mariz is correct in highlighting the voluntaristic stress in popular church's worldview. Nevertheless, as the case of Pedra Bonita's base community will show in the next chapter, she incorrectly assumes that reliance on human works translates into a rejection of miracles and supranatural experiences. We shall see how, in Pedra Bonita, community members stress conscious praxis while preserving their faith in divine and saintly intervention. In one case, it was a miracle cure that led a community activist to become involved with the CEB.

The fact that CEB members can hold both a rational-instrumental and a magico-mystical approach to reality should come as no surprise. The tension between works and miracles/sacraments is inherent to Catholicism. Even conservative, traditional forms of Catholicism which place a heavy emphasis on miracles and saints, retain the idea that human works are effective, that they can somehow improve our lot. Belief in supernatural forces does not preclude strategic action to improve one's and one's neighbor's situation. That is the whole point of charity. In the next chapter we will meet the *Vicentinos*, a group that centers its activities around the

[48] Mariz, *Coping with Poverty*, 67.   [49] Ibid.

cult of saints. We shall see how the *Vicentinos*, despite their emphasis on miracles and prayers, see their charity work within the CEB as a key element in God's salvific work.

Furthermore, it can be argued against Mariz that one of Catholicism's strengths is its flexibility, its capacity to incorporate and blend with local beliefs and practices. This syncretic flexibility allows it to interact with the "polyphonic composition"[50] of the Brazilian religious and cultural fields. One of the most visible example of Catholicism's ability to embrace the country's religious and cultural *melánge* is the fact that practioners of Afro-Brazilian religions and spiritists can claim simultaneous membership in the Catholic church. Catholicism's will to encompass autochthonous practice is carried on to base communities. They are constantly looking for ways to incorporate the central elements of popular culture, trying to give them a liberationist interpretation. Although it is fair to say that these efforts are not always successful, Mariz's assertion that "there is no continuity between the CEB message and the values of popular culture"[51] is extreme.

In contrast to CEBs, Pentecostalism, with its strong sectarian orientation, tends to show a negative attitude toward folk religions, seeing the latter as part and parcel of the sinful world. This negative attitude translates into an outright rejection of saints, religious symbols, and rituals, all of which play a central role in folk Catholicism and Afro-Brazilian religions. In place of folk Catholicism's traditional elements, Pentecostalism introduces a stern ethic, sparse liturgical spaces, and a drastic reduction of the objects of veneration. Pentecostalism thus creates not only a normative and individual break with folk Catholicism, as Mariz argues; it also produces a symbolic rupture. This rupture is as profound as the CEBs' cognitive break with folk Catholicism. I would even say that Pentecostalism's rupture is more radical because it aims at the heart of popular religiosity: the symbolic. Popular culture is after all not primarily a matter of cognition, but an affective, expressive matter where the body is the central actor, where the senses are fundamental. Of course, Pentecostalism re-introduces the affective and expressive components of religion in a modified form via holiness.

---

[50] Fernandes, "Santos e agentes," 11.   [51] Mariz, *Coping with Poverty*, 78.

The point that I want to make here is that the use of the concept of rationalization to explain the differential appeal of CEBs and Pentecostalism is problematic. It sets up a false dichotomy between an allegedly rationalistic religion (CEBs) and a more affective one (Pentecostalism). In my view, both traditions have complex relations of continuity and rupture with folk Catholicism. The hypothesis of disenchantment, thus, cannot explain by itself the CEBs' troubles (in comparison to Pentecostalism) in connecting with the poor masses. There must be other factors that account for this situation.

Given these reflections, it is fair to conclude that the charge of disenchantment leveled by conservative bishops against CEBs is not altogether sound. At best it may apply to some pastoral agents who by virtue of their formal education acquire a more secularized, instrumental view of the world. Helena, whom we will meet in chapter 9, certainly underwent this kind of transformation. Pastoral agents, theologians, and *assessores* have more often struck instrumental and reductive stances, "ontologizing the poor" and constructing an inflated and radical image of CEBs which contradicts their more modest, but nevertheless real, achievements and potentials. The idealized image of CEBs created and projected nationally and internationally by some liberation theologians, pastoral agents, and *assessores* has opened base communities to attacks from the conservatives within the church and has contributed to disappointments and the current crisis of motivation for Christian activists at the base. Faustino Teixeira recognizes this problem when he criticizes pastoral agents for adopting a "pastoral rationality" based on a means-ends, instrumental logic. This "Cartesian logic" and means-ends rationality have produced an arrogant attitude toward popular religiosity among some pastoral agents.[52]

Certainly, the consequences of such rationality have filtered down to the base, as the various levels in the popular church are in close interaction. Nonetheless, to say that CEB members at the base simply mimic the reductive stances of pastoral agents is to deny the power of the laity to appropriate institutional messages

[52] Teixeira, "CEBs: Recriação evangelizadora," 31.

according to their own experience. In Pedra Bonita, we shall see that despite the central role of pastoral agents in initiating and determining the course of CEB life, the community's lay leaders have achieved a level of autonomy and critical clarity that allows them to contest the priest's designs.

In a sense, Bishop Amaury Castanho is correct about the perils involved in the work of CEB advisors and pastoral agents. His solution, nonetheless, is tantamount to throwing the baby out with the bath water. I will argue in chapter 9 that CEBs need not cast out their socially critical advisors. Rather, CEBs should reformulate their range of political action and revise their understanding of the poor. Placing the blame for the disenchantment of the world on some pastoral agents does not mean that there are not tensions and misunderstandings at the base that hinder effective evangelization of the poor. Again, the case of Pedra Bonita's CEB in the next chapter will illustrate some of these contradictions.

I contend that the crisis of the popular church results not so much from disenchantment as from the loss of plausibility for the poor of the CEBs' particular form of re-enchantment of the world. The trouble is that the CEBs' re-enchantment of the world (through the notion of this-worldly transcendence) does not seem to resonate with poor Brazilians material and spiritual needs at this juncture. The poor's experience of increasing loss of control over their lives stands in stark contradiction to CEBs' teleological view of history in which human actions point to the realization of the reign of God on earth.

There is another, arguably more disabling, flaw in the conservative reading of the crisis. The implementation of a strict traditional pastoral approach does not in any way insure that Pentecostalism will be kept at bay. The case of the archdiocese of Rio de Janeiro is very instructive in this regard. Archbishop Eugênio Sales, a well-known conservative, has favored from the very beginning of his tenure an orthodox pastoral line centered around the concept of charity (which his progressive critics have labeled "assistentialist" and "paternalistic") and around the veneration of saints (especially Mary and St. Sebastian, the city's patron saint). He has repeatedly boasted that in his archdiocese there are no CEBs.

If the conservative wing of the church is correct in their assessment of the crisis, one would expect to see a weak Pentecostal presence in this archdiocese. Nevertheless, studies of Pentecostalism in Brazil indicate that Rio de Janeiro has in fact been one of its strongholds.[53] Thus, there must then be other factors contributing to the growth of Pentecostalism. Furthermore, these factors must be extra-pastoral, since this growth affects both progressive and traditional dioceses. We will see that in the case of Pedra Bonita, groups which uphold more traditional forms of Catholic practice are not immune to the pull of Pentecostalism. Several of their members acknowledged that people whom they evangelized converted to Pentecostalism. In one case, the husband of one of the groups' leaders converted to Pentecostalism.

Thus the conservative wing's reading of the crisis fails to take into account the fact that the crisis of participation affects not only the progressive sector but the whole Catholic church, including traditional pastoral approaches. This failure to understand the growth of Pentecostalism and other forms of popular religiosity as a global Catholic problem is no doubt connected to the conservative wing's mistaken assumption that the popular church's project achieved full hegemony, at both the elite and grassroots levels, in the seventies and eighties.

I have shown how the implementation of grassroots pastoral initiatives and the creation of CEBs has been more a collage of diocesan initiatives, heavily reliant on the figure of the charismatic progressive bishop, than part of a homogeneous, well-orchestrated national movement with its own institutional autonomy. In Bruneau's and Hewitt's words,

> The degree of success the CNBB has had in converting the entire church to the preferential-option approach has, of course, been questioned. It is well-known that the actual implementation of most programs, including the CEBs, has varied from diocese to diocese. Some dioceses are known as progressive . . . other are conservative . . . These designations normally refer to the orientation of the local bishop. When the bishop is changed for one with a different orientation, it is not long before the overall orientation of the diocese changes . . .[54]

Even in those dioceses that have adopted the progressive project as their central pastoral orientation, the CEB model has encountered

---

[53] See Rolim, *Pentecostais no Brasil*.
[54] Bruneau and Hewitt, "Catholicism and Political Action in Brazil," 50.

institutional impediments that have limited its full deployment. As a result, it has had to co-exist with more traditional pastoral forms. One could not expect things to be otherwise: twenty years of *aggiornamento* cannot undo patterns of organization and power distribution that have been solidifying in Christendom for nearly two millennia.

The conservative reading loses plausibility as soon as one takes into account the fact that the popular church's project achieved dominance only at the two elites levels: (1) in theological production (for indeed, liberation theology achieved a considerable degree of international recognition); and (2) at the episcopal level as a general pastoral framework to operationalize the conclusions of Medellín and Puebla supported by an alliance between a small group of progressives and larger contingent of moderates within the CNBB. At the base, reality has been far more ambiguous, often marked by the co-existence of contradictory pastoral methods in the same parish.

The case of Pedra Bonita illustrates the juxtaposition of pastoral approaches even in a progressive diocese: a politically-militant segment represented by activists of Catholic Action exists side by side with the more traditional *Vicentinos* and is subject to pressures emerging from changes in the parish composition. We come, thus, full circle, to the progressive wing's claim that the problem lies not in the nature of the model but in its incomplete implementation. I have already shown that this position also has its shortcomings.

In sum, the conservative Catholic fraction, though raising the thorny question of the gap between CEB spirituality and popular religiosity, offers a simplistic reading of the crisis. It absolutizes the popular church's hegemony, a rhetorical strategy which allows it to lay the blame squarely on the latter for the current crisis. Such a reading may, in fact, serve conservatives' own restoration efforts.

Both intra-institutional explanations leave many important questions unanswered. How are we then to understand the crisis? In the next chapters I offer my own reading, drawing from a fieldwork in Nova Iguaçu and placing the crisis in a socio-economic cultural and context. My reading does not necessarily disqualify intra-ecclesial interpretations. It is meant, rather, to supplement and correct them, adding a new angle that may help select the most persuasive elements in them.

CHAPTER 6

The crisis in local perspective: a Brazilian base community

To explore how the crisis is experienced by the actors who embody the popular church's project among the poor, I will focus on the evolution and structure of a basic ecclesial community in a small working-class neighborhood I shall call Pedra Bonita.[1] This focus will allow us to identify some of the conditions that hinder the reception of the popular church's message among the poor and open spaces for the emergence of alternative religious worldviews.

Pedra Bonita is a settlement of about 300 families located in the southeastern tip of the district of Nova Iguaçu, itself part of a vast low-lying area at the outskirts of Rio de Janeiro known as the Baixada Fluminense. Although Pedra Bonita is part of an area that is becoming rapidly urbanized, the neighborhood retains a rural feeling, still surrounded by a couple of decaying *fazendas*. Several methodological reasons justify the selection of a neighborhood in Nova Iguaçu as my object of study. First, the district has witnessed the formation of influential grassroots movements, the most important of which has been the powerful and highly successful Movimento de Amigos do Bairro (Friends of the Neighborhood Movement, or MAB), which between 1974–1985 mobilized up to 120 neighborhood associations around bread-and-butter issues.[2] Second, the Catholic church has played a major role in the articulation of these popular movements. From his appointment in

[1] I conducted research in Pedra Bonita between January and June 1991. Field work included numerous informal conversations with residents, participant observation of CEB meetings and activities, 16 in-depth interviews with base community members and two with priests who served the parish.

[2] For an account of the genesis and evolution of MAB in Nova Iguaçu, see S. Mainwaring, "Grassroots Popular Movements and the Struggle for Democracy: Nova Iguaçu," in Stepan ed., *Democratizing Brazil*.

1966 until his retirement in 1995, Bishop Adriano Hipólito was in the forefront of the struggle to democratize the country and to carry out the CNBB's progressive pastoral guidelines. These two conditions guarantee the selection of an instance where the project of the *igreja popular* has been vigorously pursued. Thus understanding the obstacles faced by pastoral agents and Catholic activists in Nova Iguaçu will help us make sense of the larger crisis of the popular church.

Moreover, because of its location on the outskirts of one of the country's largest cities, Nova Iguaçu suffers many of the socio-economic contradictions generated by unequal, dependent development. Problems such as overpopulation, inadequate housing, lack of basic services, high crime, and poverty are endemic in the district, affecting the majority of its inhabitants. It is precisely these problems that the popular church has sought to address, especially through the CEBs, in its efforts to identify and critique "structural sin." In other words, there is in Nova Iguaçu a convergence of appalling living conditions and a tradition of grassroots resistance that should, in theory, facilitate the reception of the popular church's work and message among the poor. Finally, because of their urban location and legacy of political activism, both Nova Iguaçu and the Baixada Fluminense have been the subject of many studies on phenomena such as migration, religious/cultural change, and marginality – studies that provide the context for my local study.[3]

I chose to focus on Pedra Bonita's CEB specifically because, as we shall see below, it offers a clear example of a mature ecclesial community actively engaged in both political and religious practices, serving as a model for other pastoral initiatives in the diocese. Pedra Bonita's CEB is one of the poorest and most remote of the seven base communities in the parish of Ocampo. Since Ocampo encompasses relatively economically-stable households close to the center of Nova Iguaçu and poor areas in the periphery of the

---

[3] For a study of socio-economic conditions in the Baixada Fluminense, see J. E. Perlman, *The Myth of Marginality: Urban Poverty and Politics in Rio de Janeiro* (Berkeley: University of California Press, 1976). On Nova Iguaçu's popular church and its relation with the popular movement and the state, see Mainwaring, *The Catholic Church and Politics in Brazil*. On the religious arena, see Burdick, *Looking for God in Brazil*.

district, the case study should also serve to document the effects of socio-economic differentiation on local religious practices. Located at the edge of the district, diocese, and even the parish, Pedra Bonita also mirrors the precarious situation of Nova Iguaçu: a human settlement at the periphery of a great urban center in a semi-peripheral country within the capitalist world-system.

PEDRA BONITA'S BASIC ECCLESIAL COMMUNITY

The beginnings

Pedra Bonita's basic ecclesial community, like many others throughout Brazil, finds its origins in the organizing activities of a pastoral agent. In the early 1970s, Father Claúdio, a diocesan priest familiar with the experiences of Catholic Action in his native France, came to Pedra Bonita seeking to purchase a plot of land to build a church in the neighborhood (*bairro*). His initiative was part of a diocesan plan designed by the new bishop of Nova Iguaçu, Adriano Hipólito. In 1968, in the wake of the Medellín Conference, he had declared the creation of base communities a priority in the diocese.[4]

Pedra Bonita was, at the time, just a haphazard collection of dwellings connected by precarious dirt roads. The nascent neighborhood did not have even the most basic infrastructure: there was no potable water and sewage system, no street lighting, and no direct bus service to the district seat. The nearest school and church were several miles away.

Cléa, one of the first to arrive in the area, recalls coming to Pedra Bonita in 1973 and finding "a swamp with a dense undergrowth, few houses, few inhabitants."[5] In many ways, Cléa and her husband Gerson fit the profile of the first wave of Pedra Bonita settlers who eventually became the main participants in the ecclesial community. Typically, the settlers came from rural areas in the states of Minas Gerais and Espírito Santo and from the

---

[4] For a history of Hipólito's tenure in Nova Iguaçu, see N. V. Chaverra, "As CEBs nos caminhos do pírito," Ph.D. dissertation, Pontifícia Universidade Católica, Rio de Janeiro, 1985; and Diocese of Nova Iguaçu, *O povo de Deus assume a caminhada* (Petrópolis: Vozes, 1983).

[5] All interviews were conducted and tape recorded by the author.

Northeast, especially from Ceará and Paraíba. Very often the men moved in first, living temporarily with relatives or friends already established in the neighborhood and working as carpenters, masons, and machinists in Nova Iguaçu's incipient industrial park or in the factories that line the main thoroughfares connecting the district to Rio. Once they had saved enough money to buy a plot of land and enough materials to build a couple of rooms in their spare time, they brought the rest of the family. In Cléa's case, her sister Amélia served as the "gate" to facilitate her family's entry to Pedra Bonita.

The majority of the early settlers had attended school in their home states, yet very few had gone beyond the fourth grade. The settlers' worldview was informed heavily by the devotional folk Catholicism practiced in Brazil's countryside. It was a Catholicism of saints, pilgrimages, cures, *promessas* (vows to saints), and routine church attendance. Otília, a seamstress and one of the founders of the ecclesial community, characterizes this type of Catholicism thus:

I know that all my life I was Catholic. My mother was Catholic . . . we lived very close to the church, and went to mass every Sunday. When I grew up I stopped going to the nine o'clock mass, because I would go there and didn't pay attention because I was just going to see how the others were dressed, their shoes, if they were pretty. Well, at that time the priest would say the mass with his back to the people. I knew that I was in mass and that the priest was doing something up there, but I couldn't participate. The priest didn't let the people participate in preparing the mass.

Against this background, Father Cláudio's new, radical pastoral approach can be properly understood. He had been ministering to the neighbors for some time, even before his plans to build a church materialized. To compensate for the lack of a central place of worship, he visited the most established families in the area and celebrated mass in their houses. This strategy allowed him to build a small network of five women who held weekly meetings to study the gospels. This *grupo de reflexão do Evangelho*, as it was called, became the community's first building block and its core, as each of its members became a leader in evangelization teams that operated in the main sections of the *bairro*.

Claúdio established a pastoral methodology that would remain unchanged for more than a decade. After he left in 1973 a succession of three French priests, all with strong ties to Catholic Action, ministered to the community, building on his groundwork. Basically, Claúdio used the *grupo de reflexão* and the evangelization teams to train lay leaders according to the pedagogical model of reflection-action-reflection. Every Friday, the pastoral agent met with the women coordinating the evangelization teams to prepare the activities for the following week. In Amélia's words:

We used to take everything that happened in our evangelization groups to these meetings. There would be someone from the outside [a pastoral agent] who would talk to us. He would raise our consciousness [*conscientizar*] more. And we would take in more ideas to pass on to our groups. We prepared readings of the Gospel there, so that when we got to our group with that text we would be prepared. It was a sort of a walking stick [*bengala*] in our hands to prepare the people.

The next Tuesday the women went out visiting their neighbors to invite them to participate in the evangelization groups. If the neighbor accepted the invitation the next group meeting was held at his/her home. Ana, who came to Pedra Bonita in 1977, when the various groups had consolidated, remembers that

there were only women in the group because on Tuesdays men were working. Every Tuesday at three o'clock in the afternoon we left to do our visits. And it was interesting because in each house people were so concerned with participating, not only offering their homes, but participating within the group, fixing a snack. It always ended up with everyone coming together and sharing [*confraternização*]. We used to take last Sunday's gospel reading.

Claúdio followed all meetings very closely, participating in some of them. In addition to the weekly preparatory meetings, he organized a general meeting of all evangelization groups every three months. Those meetings served to evaluate pastoral work and to link the various groups in the neighborhood with those in the vicinity and with diocesan activities.

Father Claúdio's strategy proved to be highly successful. Each evangelization group attracted between 18 and 30 women. Before too long, the sons and daughters of these women had formed catechism groups which, during the community's peak years in the late 1970s, prepared up to forty youngsters to receive their first communion. The level of lay involvement was so high that Pedra Bonita became a model for surrounding neighborhoods and earned the bishop's recognition.

This remarkable level of mobilization, however, did not occur overnight. It required repeated house calls by the pastoral agents inviting and even coaxing the women, the backbone of the community,[6] to put aside their daily chores and household responsibilities, break the traditional roles that limited their world to the home, and attend the Bible meetings. Otília's reluctance to participate is typical.

Father Márcio [the second French priest] called me to go to the evangelization meetings, that is, to coordinate them. I would tell him that I wouldn't go, that I didn't have the skills, that I found it all very difficult. Before that Father Cláudio had called me many times, but I didn't go. I would tell him that I would go, but on the day of the meeting I wouldn't go, I stayed at home sewing. Then he would come back and ask me: "Did you like the group meeting?" "Ah, I didn't go" "You didn't go? Why? Go, you're gonna like it". Finally, I put away my sewing machine and my children, and went. I liked the meeting.

Even after attending the meetings, Otília was hesitant to assume the position of group's coordinator. Only after her five-year-old son recovered from a severe state of lassitude, probably due to intestinal parasites, did she become fully involved in the community. For two years she kept trying various methods to cure the child, from expensive medicines to visits to *umbanda* centers,[7] all to no avail. Finally, during a "strong" moment of prayer in her evangelization group, she "felt the presence of God," and from

---

[6] In her research in the periphery of São Paulo, Carol Ann Drogus found that "as many as 90 percent of the most active [CEB] members are women." Drogus, "Popular Movements and Limits of Political Mobilization," 67.

[7] Brazilian African-based religions, such as *umbanda*, include many practices, i.e., *consultas* (consultation with spirit mediums), animal sacrifices, herbal baths and other rituals, oriented towards healing and the resolution of personal and domestic problems. The rituals and other religious events take place at centers or *terreiros* presided by a hierarchy of mediums. See D. Brown, *Umbanda: Religion and Politics in Urban Brazil* (Ann Arbor, MI: UMI Research Press, 1986).

that day the child began to improve with the medicines he was receiving. She credits his cure to a "miracle" in response to her prayers and her participation in the evangelization group.

Otília's history of involvement with the community is not uncommon. Many members of the ecclesial community trace their full-fledged involvement in it to a critical personal or family event like a disease or a death, and describe the experience as a true conversion. Through this conversion, divine intervention comes together with human action, as very often community members see God acting in their lives, sending them signs such as illness and cures, for instance, to become active in the CEB. The experience of Otília, thus, contradicts the charge that CEB members do not "recognize miracles or supernatural occurrences in everyday life."[8]

As the French priests' pastoral work began to take hold, a relatively stable ecclesial community emerged. Father Miguel, the last of the French priests, characterizes this early community as a flexible "polycentered web," with some of the threads serving as the structural support for a whole array of activities, groups, and levels of involvement. The central threads converged in a "nucleus" or informal "directorate" consisting of the families of the five women who founded the base community.

The central strands radiated in several directions forming subsectors or patches of activity coordinated by each of these families. This is what Miguel calls the "periphery" (*coroa*) of the community. While there was a certain level of instability at the periphery, where branching allegiances were weaker, with people entering and exiting according to their needs, sometimes attending community services only occasionally, the nucleus remained intact, pulling the entire web together.

To center the CEB web geographically, Cláudio purchased a plot of land to build a church, but his plans were altered by community needs. During a meeting of the *grupo de reflexão*, the women complained that the neighborhood did not have a school. Cláudio encouraged the women to go to the mayor of Nova Iguaçu to request at least a classroom, "orienting them how [they]

---

[8] Mariz, *Coping with Poverty*, 67.

should talk to him." Thus begins the "political component" of their community life. When the mayor indicated that he did not have the resources to build a classroom for the neighborhood, but that he would try to provide a teacher if the community furnished the locale, Claúdio and the women in the *grupo de reflexão* decided to build a room that could serve primarily as a school, but that on weekends could also be used as a place of worship. The construction of this room was a *mutirão*. (This term orignates in northeastern Brazil. It designates mutual assistance activities undertaken by rural workers in response to the harsh environment and economic conditions in the area. The term has been appropriated by the popular church to highlight poor people's self-empowerment.) Claúdio brought money from the diocese, his contacts with Catholic Action in France, and from his own labor, since on weekdays he worked in a nearby factory. The community also pitched in, organizing small raffles. The construction project would eventually produce a five-room school which became, as we shall see later, a focus of community struggle.

Once the "church" was built, Claúdio proceeded to introduce some important liturgical innovations, stressing spontaneous participation in various pedagogic and liturgical exercises. Laura, one of the five women who founded the CEB, recalls how the priest left all preparations for the mass to an *ad hoc* group of community people. They decided what would be done, setting up an informal rotation of duties.

We would do everything for the mass . . . we were a liturgy team, only that we did not call ourselves that. When time came we would have things ready. "Dona Otília, you're going to do the first reading of the Bible. Dona Cléa, you'll do the second. Vitória will read the Gospel." The priest would just help people to speak and discover.

Instead of delivering a traditional sermon, Claúdio sought ways to encourage participation from a barely literate population, borrowing techniques from Paulo Freire's method. According to Gabriela, Laura's youngest daughter,

Father Claúdio was sensitive to the difficulty people had in reading, people of the Northeast who came here. He would take the gospel reading and would write it in a big brown poster and would place it in the front of the room during the mass. And then people would read each word slowly, discussing it, linking it with our reality. People would even decorate the gospel text. He even had to bring paper so that people could draw what they understood from the readings. And it was a long process to make people understand that the end was not just to decorate the gospels, but to read it, to enjoy it and to link it with our lives.

Thus, for Pedra Bonita's CEB, the initial period of growth marked the gradual formation of a core of lay activists whose *ad hoc* attribution of responsibilities and roles allowed the base community to achieve continuity without reification. The pastoral-political training of this emerging leadership took another step towards the mid-1970s with the formation of a group of the *Ação Católica Operária* (Workers' Catholic Action, or ACO) in the neighborhood.

The formation of the ACO: the CEB enters politics

Cláudio's standing in the community was greatly enhanced by his activism alongside the people he served. This activism came to be symbolized by his employment in a nearby factory. For Vitória, "Father Cláudio had a working-class life [*uma vida operária*]. He suffered what the worker felt when taking the train [to Rio] crawling with people. He even said that there nobody knew he was a priest, that he was equal to his colleagues at work." This direct involvement with the everyday life of the working class in the community helped him to organize an ACO group in the neighborhood.

The ACO group started as a *grupo de trabalhadores* (a workers' group) where the heads of four of the community's main families would get together to swap impressions and opinions about their daily experiences at the workplace. Since the various Catholic Action movements were still subject to persecution by the military government around that time,[9] the group could not declare its identity openly. According to Gerson, group meetings were "very close during those years. We had to close our doors. If a strange person arrived we would stop talking. Our meetings were like small family reunions, only for those already in the group." This family atmosphere was well-suited to the ACO methodology of

[9] Mainwaring, *The Catholic Church and Politics in Brazil*, 129.

consciousness-raising in the context of small groups sharing common experiences and working-class links.

Although this secrecy enabled the *grupo de trabalhadores* to survive and eventually become a full-fledged ACO group in 1976 during the *abertura*, it set the families apart from the rest of both the community and the neighborhood. They were perceived as a highly politicized, and thus potentially dangerous group, within what was fundamentally a religious community. This perception was bolstered by their untiring activism, as they were the driving force in all the community's bread-and-butter struggles, and by their keen knowledge of local and state power dynamics. They began as a group of neighbors who "would come together to talk about the difficulties of life in the *bairro*," and became through the use of the see-judge-act method in the *revisão de vida operária* (i.e., reflection on the workers' daily life) "politically literate [*alfabetizado politicamente*]." In Ana's words, the group began to "awaken [*acordar*] to the discrimination and repression that [poor] people confront when [they] demand [their] rights." According to Cléa, the ACO group became a vanguard within the community that would "show the people that it is us, the neighbors, who have to struggle to gain our rights."

A clear example of the deleterious effects of the ACO's semi-clandestine nature early on is the case of Ana and Ernesto, the last couple to join the original group. Ana was invited by Laura to attend one of the their meetings. She went and found the gathering "boring" and "horrible: it didn't do anything for me; it didn't have any aim, it was bland [*sem sal*]." Her reaction was due to the fact that the participants would not explain to her what the movement was about. Fear of government repression led group members to make the ACO a "mystery" for her.

Always at the behest of the pastoral agent, Ana continued to attend ACO meetings, bringing her reluctant husband along. Her engagement in earnest with the ACO, however, was marked by the accidental death of one of her daughters. "That event left a deep and painful scar, but the support of the community helped. They supported me 24 hours a day, every single day. I began to value life in community even more." Ernesto, Ana's husband, was "desperate." He remembers that on the night of the vigil,

[a]ll members of the ACO came to our house, which by midnight was packed. Father Miguel brought other priests with him. The next day ACO took charge of the burial, paying for everything. They told me: "Don't worry about a thing, we'll take care of everything. Now you just want to think, grieve and pray to God." Then I knew those people better. I asked myself: "Who are those people who have such a great solidarity with us?"

As in Otília's case, a trying moment of bafflement and pain accompanied by caring pastoral and group assistance shaped Ana's conversion to community life. Out of that experience Ana and Ernesto emerged as full-time activists for the ACO, rising through its ranks to become the movement's representatives in the Workers' Party.

Despite the constraints experienced by the ACO, the growth of the movement was a turning point for Pedra Bonita's CEB, for it encouraged the five families that formed the community nucleus to link religious practices with everyday concerns in the neighborhood. Ecclesial and liturgical matters resonated with the situation in the *bairro*, transcending the traditional view of religion as just the realm of prayer and the contemplative life. Through the ACO, the community nucleus added a definite political component to the reflection and evangelization tasks of the first groups organized by Claúdio. Because of its more sophisticated pastoral-pedagogical methodology, the ACO eventually replaced the *grupo de reflexão* as the community's anchor.

This political component reached its full maturity with the formation in March 7, 1982 of a neighborhood association which linked Pedra Bonita's community activists with other grassroots organization in Nova Iguaçu.[10] The association became the privileged vehicle to "oversee [*zelar*] the rights and well-being of the *bairro's* population" and to create "organizations to promote educational, recreational, cultural, and health-related programs" in the neighborhood.[11]

It is important to note that the community's interventions in the political sphere did not signal the abandonment of religious

[10] On August 29, 1982 the association hosted a regional lecture on the relevance of the popular movement sponsored by the MAB. Article no. 13 of Pedra Bonita Neighborhood Association's *Libro de atas* (Book of Proceedings), 1982–1991.

[11] Ibid., article no. 6.

practices.[12] Community members continued to prepare mass, study the Bible, and teach catechism, while lobbying for better social services. Even though during this phase in the CEB's development the ACO substituted the *grupo de reflexão* as the community's new center of gravity, activities were not limited to secular, political matters. For example, the evangelization teams continued to function as a key pastoral outreach strategy. Thus, CEB members used the ACO and the neighborhood association as the main vehicles to tackle bread and butter issues, while operating in the religious field through the evangelization teams. The balance between religious and political activities came from a reading of the Bible that linked Christian symbols, events, and teachings with the life of the poor in the community. Ernesto, for instance, thinks that there is

a close link between Christ and today's worker. Today's worker is crucified by the system. Christ is a friend [*companheiro*] who is fighting on the worker's side, because he came to get rid of the oppression of people of his time, because he wanted to make an alliance with the world. So just as the worker now fights for justice so did Jesus Christ. He said: "those who are hungry for justice will be satisfied." And we too are hungry for justice, for a just wage. He also said: "I came so that all have life and life in abundance." So we fight for life. No one came to the world to suffer, to not have a house, to not have education for his children, to not have a place where his children could play, and injustice takes all that away from the worker.

Out of a reading the Bible that brings together faith and the community's everyday life, a "popular theology" emerged that placed people at the heart of sacred history, intertwining their fate with God's salvific work in history.[13] The struggles of everyday life became embedded in a divine plan leading to a qualitatively different form of life with the coming of the kingdom. In Ana's view, this popular theology taught people to "recognize their self-worth, that they have strength. They say to themselves: 'Hey I too can do things, I am a person, I am here, I too have a voice, I

[12] Levine makes the same point in his work on Venezuelan and Colombian CEBs when he states that, for all their political impact, they maintain "their original and enduring religious nature." Levine, *Popular Voices*, 46.
[13] See A. L. Peterson, "Religious Narratives and Political Protest," *Journal of the American Academy of Religion* 64, no. 1 (1996), 27–44.

too can start to say what I think.'" They came to see that "human beings are valuable [*tem muito valor*] . . . that life is valuable." Laura provides a striking example of this popular theology:

The Gospel is in the life of the worker. The worker's life is all in the Gospel. I remember the words of Our Father, the only prayers Jesus taught us, he didn't say anything to discriminate against anyone. He didn't say: "He is my father, not yours." He is father to everyone, the high, middle or low class. He is our father and he wants everyone to have bread. "Give us our daily bread." So, I think that God's wish is that all of us would eat as equals. He wants equality.

In the popular theology of Pedra Bonita's CEB there is no contradiction between supernatural occurrences and rational human activity. When asked about the possibility that the belief in saints may contradict the struggle for liberation because rather than stressing the need for involvement it emphasizes dependence on the saint, Gerson laughed and added:

Yes, maybe there is a contradiction, but I don't believe so. I believe in the saints, you know . . . in the fact that they perform miracles. They perform miracles according to the person, to the faith of the person. Sure, it is not that there is a miraculous saint you just ask and he'll give. I don't believe in that. But if you have a deep faith and you call the name of the saint, I believe you'll receive a grace . . . [you] can even be cured and everything.

Thus, in the case of Pedra Bonita the hypothesis that CEBs disenchant and rationalize the world is not confirmed. Furthermore, the relation between CEB theology and traditional popular Catholicism is more complicated than observers such as Mariz argue. True to its Catholic roots, CEB theology is able to hold in tension the notion that human works are effective and important and the idea, central to popular culture, that there are sacred forces that may alter the course of human life. What CEB members reject is not the power of the supernatural and its irruption in history, but the notion that one can take a purely magical, instrumental approach to it. One cannot obtain miracles just by praying or making an occasional *promessa*, without leading a fully committed Christian life that includes concern and care for fellow human beings. In the words of an ACO activist in Rio de Janeiro, miracles do not "drop from the sky as consummated deeds [*pratos feitos*]."

Ana, for instance, believes that "miracles only come from Christ Himself, not from an image." When she goes to church, she does not like "all that stuff of kissing and kneeling in front of [the image] of the saint." She does not "bring flowers to the saint or place a coin to ask him for something because it is not fair to say: 'O.K. if you give me such and such St. Francis, I'll give you, I'll pay you and I'll do this for you.' But that faith can bring you something, that's true."

As I argued in chapters 4 and 5 in my discussion of Mariz's rationalization hypothesis, it would be more accurate to claim that CEBs re-enchant the world, re-interpreting folk Catholicism's notion of the sacred and of the latter's relation with secular history, than to affirm that they disenchant reality. The CEB world is still "enchanted," imbued with the sacred, but now the sacred is linked to human action in a new cooperative fashion. Disenchantment is more a problem for pastoral agents and national lay leaders, to the degree that they have been influenced by social scientific knowledge. Certainly for Pedra Bonita's base community, where most of its members come from the north-east and have not gone beyond the fourth grade, it is baseless to suggest that there has been a radical cognitive break with folk Catholicism's worldview. People do not abandon all at once the culture that has oriented them for most of their lives. Rather, they re-interpret it in the light of new challenges. To an outside observer this re-interpretation may be contradictory, but to the believer it is part of the mysterious nature of religion. Laura, for example, while involved in political and consciousness-raising activities, keeps an ornate altar at home where she prays daily. She also lights candles and gathers her family in the backyard to hold yearly prayers in commemoration of the death of her mother and father. Laura wants her children "to know, preserve, and respect history, tradition."

The centrality of CEB theology in guiding the activities of community members cannot be underestimated. The quest for equality, sanctioned by God, that Laura evokes in her theology inspired Pedra Bonita's base community to become active in the political sphere. Of the many struggles Pedra Bonita's CEB fought, I will focus here on the efforts to bring a school to the neighborhood, to obtain direct bus service to Nova Iguaçu and

Rio, and to curtail delinquency and violence in the area. These struggles evince the potential as well as the limits and obstacles of grassroots activism in Brazil.

"Our Long, Difficult Struggles"

After completion of the community room that was to serve as a place of worship and a school, CEB members returned to city hall to demand the teacher they had been promised. The mayor's office responded that it did not have money to hire teachers. With this new refusal the community learned their first lesson about one of the preferred strategies of city, municipal and state officials in order to deal with the growing popular movement. Officials always found an excuse to delay or minimize government involvement, forcing local communities to draw from meager internal resources to provide for their own services.[14] According to Gerson,

What happened after the room was ready was that we didn't have a teacher. The municipality did not want to give us one because, first we did not have a room. Then when we had a room, we had, as a matter of fact, five rooms with a bathroom, they claimed that we didn't have potable water. Just like everybody in the neighborhood, the school had well water! But the municipality didn't want to pay the teacher's salary.

The fight to establish the school lasted about a year, finally taking them to the state seat in Rio, where Father Miguel used his personal contacts to bring a teacher. Even then, the state government agreed to pay only the teacher's salary. The community had to pay for water, electricity, and general maintenance of the school. The school functioned under these terms for nearly ten years, until a school principal with ties to district politicians started to build a room on school property. As Gerson recounts the story, the principal

[14] In her study of a neighborhood in northeastern Brazil, Nancy Scheper-Hughes notes that, "[f]ootdragging, lies, and false compliance are not only the tactics of the oppressed, the weapons of the weak, as James Scott's analysis would seem to imply; they are also of strategic importance to politicians and bureaucrats . . . hostile to the demands of the poor and the popular classes." See N. Scheper-Hughes, *Death Without Weeping: The Violence of Everyday Life in Brazil* (Berkeley: University of California Press, 1992), 514; and J. Scott, *Weapons of the Weak: Everyday Forms of Peasant Resistance* (New Haven: Yale University Press, 1985).

began to build without telling anyone in the community. She claimed it was a lunch room, but we already had one. Her interest was not to improve the lot of the children. It was to sell building material, because her husband had a building material factory. So she would bring material, without any outside control, and charged [the municipality] whatever she wanted.

Since the land on which she was building was the diocese's, Father Miguel forced her to suspend all construction. Working through her political connections in Nova Iguaçu, she convinced the government in Rio to buy land for a state school. The school was built under a cloud of secrecy to avoid opposition from the neighbors.

She didn't tell us that they were building a school there. When it was almost time to inaugurate it, she came to tell us that it was a state school, that all the material we were using in our own little community school had to go there, that we had to vacate here and take everything there. She said that the community had to give up its [class] materials because there was nothing at the new school.

Laura recalls that on the day the moving was to take place, she confronted the principal and told her: "'You will have to leave some things here for our people because you were here for 10 years and didn't pay a penny on water and electricity. You didn't do anything, not even building maintenance.'" The principal agreed to leave some "old, rickety chairs," but asked Laura to sign receipts, to which Laura responded: "We will sign nothing!"

The school moved but almost immediately began to have problems. In the rush to close down the little community school the new building was left unfinished. Located in a dangerous part of the neighborhood, the new school had no perimeter wall to protect the building and students from burglars and prowlers. To build a wall, the principal started charging parents a monthly fee. Once again her husband became the main supplier of construction materials. To address these irregularities members of the newly formed neighborhood association requested a meeting with the principal. When they confronted her about the fee, she claimed it was to build the wall and protect the school. The neighbors did not accept this explanation. Gerson remembers how as a member of the association he challenged the principal:

"You moved the school before the building was finished, it was your decision. Why didn't you let them finish it?" She said it was necessary. I said: "It wasn't necessary, there was nothing wrong with our community school? It was because of shameless [*sem vergonha*] politics in Nova Iguaçu. You had to inaugurate the school to win votes for the politician. He didn't win and he disappeared, lost interest. The politician who won has nothing to do with the school, that's why they haven't finished it even now."

The principal promised to discontinue the fee in exchange for the association's help in lobbying state authorities to finish the school. After several trips to Rio they convinced the state to hire a private firm to do the job. However, changes in Rio politics stopped work once more, so that the association finally had to propose to the state that they would have a *mutirão* to finish the school themselves if the state just provided the material. After much prodding the state agreed and the association completed construction of the school.

The school continued to function, receiving maintenance only when the principal had connections with politicians in city hall. The association all but withdrew from their monitoring activities because around that time Leonel Brizola, the populist governor of Rio de Janeiro, built a CIEP, Centro Integral de Educação Pública (Integral Center for Public Education), in Pedra Bonita.[15] Most community children moved to the CIEP, which functioned relatively well, with neighbors having considerable access to activities inside the school. But then, in the 1988 governatorial elections, Brizola was defeated by conservative Moreira Franco.

Moreira Franco saw CIEPs as wasteful ploys devised by Brizola to build an electoral base among the poor. So he proceeded to close many CIEPs and installed his allies in school boards across the state. These boards were less open to outside intervention and generally less responsive to community concerns. In addition, despite serious irregularities with the distribution of food in Pedra Bonita's CIEP, the association was reluctant to act because of fear of police brutality. According to Laura, the neighbors "discovered

[15] The CIEPs, popularly known as "Brizolões," were designed to provide not only primary and secondary education, but to offer vocational programs for up to 1,000 youths per center. The idea was to have several school shifts to engage youngsters in pedagogic exercises the whole day. They would also receive meals and basic medical attention.

that the principal's husband owned a restaurant. He lives by a police station and he would come in a patrol car to get the leftover food. We were concerned, but what could we do?"

The long struggle to bring a school to the neighborhood demonstrates, on the one hand, the CEB's tenacity and its capacity to defend the neighbors' interests against the truculent maneuvers of political elites. It is clear that the "political literacy" developed by consciousness-raising activities in the ACO was instrumental in enhancing this capacity. It is a case where the existence of a popular, politically acute vanguard in the neighborhood makes it possible to hold politicians accountable for their broken promises and devious actions. This is precisely what lies at the heart of the model of representative democracy, so foreign to Brazil.

On the other hand, the struggle also shows how grassroots efforts can be coopted, diverted and/or blocked at every turn by populist and clientelistic strategies. The exhausting, uphill battle against selective and arbitrary solutions imposed from above is also poignantly illustrated by the community's effort to establish a bus service to Nova Iguaçu.

In 1981, the association began to lobby the private bus company that serviced the route between the center of the district and Cabuçu. This route touched Pedra Bonita only tangentially. The company responded that it would be willing to establish a service to the heart of the neighborhood if they could have an uninterrupted circuit. Such a circuit required the construction of a bridge linking Pedra Bonita with other neighborhoods to the south. The association then took its fight to build the bridge to the municipality, and later to the state level with no tangible results. Only after Brizola became state governor was the bridge built, ostensibly to facilitate access to the CIEP.

Since the bus company was still refusing to serve Pedra Bonita, even after the bridge was finished, the association decided to contact another private transportation company working in the general area. The latter indicated that they would be ready to provide a unit immediately. Faced with this competition, the original company mobilized its connections in Nova Iguaçu to reassert its monopoly over the area. The association's next move was to network with other neighborhood organizations affected by the monopoly. Together they exerted pressure on the state trans-portation secretary, inviting him to tour the area on foot.

After his visit, the transportation secretary decided to allow the competing bus company to service the Pedra Bonita route. The original company still resisted, taking its case to the state court and finally to Brasília, but losing both legal battles. Finally, on April 9, 1986, after five years of struggle, the first buses began circulating in Pedra Bonita's dusty roads under the watchful eye of the federal police. But as Laura recalls, the community's victory was bitter-sweet, as it turned out, for when the first bus made its way to Pedra Bonita, it

> was packed with politicians [*politiqueiros*] who were claiming that they had fathered the project [*que eles eram o pai da criança*], and it was the neighbor-hood association, the ACO group, that had fought long and hard for it. One of them said: "Listen, this here is my struggle, I was the one who fought for this route to open." And at home we had all the documents showing our struggle! But we couldn't speak, they wouldn't let us. They scream so loudly. They behave like the Pentecostals [*crentes*], reaffirming things so strongly, and then it is difficult for us.

Thus, in addition to having to sustain long, at times hopeless, struggles, the association has had to fight against what Laura calls "the dirty tricks of politicians [*a sujeira dos políticos*]." Local bosses and outside politicians have been consistently trying to coopt or delegitimize the association's initiatives. There have even been cases where food, cement and other goods have been offered as a politician's personal gift, bypassing the association's lobbying ef-forts. At other times, the gifts have been made to association leaders to secure political allegiances. Each time the ACO group has had to "clean the brains of those with a 'rusted head [*cabeça enferrugiada*]' among us who still believe in politicians and who don't believe in the people."

As in the case of the school, the conflict over bus service shows the fragility of grassroots activism. Stacked against such activism is not only a well-established network of patron–client relations, but a whole political culture in which elite control of resources rather than popular pressure largely determines public policy.

In addition to these two struggles, the association sought to curtail the high level of violence in the neighborhood. This was an important effort, given the insecurity that permeates everyday life in the community. According to Father Patrício, the current pastoral agent, the neighborhood has witnessed "a lot of violence ... a lot of people killed. Even some of our community people [have been] badly affected and held hostage in their homes." In 1981 Gabriela, one of Laura's daughters, witnessed their house being robbed by youngsters. When the local drug bosses learned about the robbery they picked up the youngsters and beat them severely, making them return all the items they had stolen. Local drug bosses do not approve of this type of action on their turf. They have to show they have control over the area; they "want to have the sympathy of the neighbors. They want to appear as the defenders of the causes of the locals" so they would be shielded against outside police intervention.

For Gabriela and Vitória, this experience became another point of transition from ecclesial, community-centered activities to political, neighborhood-based *praxis*. From then on Vitória

opened [her] eyes to the reality faced by children and adolescents. They are used, they become hooked on drugs. Children live in a difficult situation, earning a salary that doesn't allow them to get their food, to buy clothes. So they feel that they must steal to sell some stuff in other neighborhoods. We [also] discovered that our catechism classes were too disconnected from the situation of children in the periphery [of Nova Iguaçu].

To address the situation of the youth in Pedra Bonita, Gabriela and Vitória began to organize the Movimento de Adolescentes e Crianças (Children's and Adolescents' Movement), more commonly known by its acronym: MAC. MAC is a kind of a junior partner to the ACO; its leadership and ranks are made up of the sons and daughters of the first generation of community activists. It represents, in Cléas's words, "the new blood that is coming slowly to the movement." Its methodology combines play with consciousness-raising. Vitória offers the following characterization of MAC's aims and methodology:

I began to invite children I saw wandering in the streets, whom their mothers would leave with an aunt or a neighbor while they went to work as maids. These children lived on the streets. Their mothers only came to get them on weekends. So we got together and began to see the situation they were experiencing, why that was happening. We wanted to discover together why children so young got involved with delinquents and what we could do about it. The children proposed some activities: "Let's organize a dance. Let's put together a group to go to city hall and demand a school for the neighborhood."

Despite the success of the MAC experience in Pedra Bonita, violence in the neighborhood intensified. The root causes of this violence clearly lay outside the purview of MAC action. They were connected to vicious turf battles waged among drug bosses operating in the Baixada who had chosen Pedra Bonita as their hideout. These bosses formed armed groups (*quadrilhas*) for personal protection and to enforce their control of different neighborhood sectors by recruiting from the impoverished local youth. The latter were merely foot soldiers in gang wars, seeking to escape indigence and attracted by the lure of money and drugs.

In July 1985, the neighborhood association called for a meeting to discuss the issue. Seeing that it was impossible to end the cycle of violence, the association decided to launch a campaign to warn both inhabitants and visitors of the danger, recommending in posted signs throughout the neighborhood measures to insure personal safety.

The situation deteriorated further at the end of the 1980s; Ernesto recalls that the situation "was very dangerous. There was hardly a weekend when you wouldn't find two, three, four people killed by the side of the road. We even thought of moving out of the neighborhood." Even if community members were not involved they could be "at the wrong place and at the wrong time" and be in harm's way. Faced with this critical situation the association took its case to the diocesan chapter of Justice and Peace Commission, which during the 1970s had taken a very active role denouncing the work of death squads linked to the military regime. This time the Commission proved unhelpful, for it advised the community to confront the drug traffickers and racketeers directly, denouncing them to the police. Given the high level of corruption and incompetence in the police department, however, this "principled stand" would only imperil community members more.

The community decided, instead, to hold an ecumenical celebration, inviting various movements and organizations in the neighborhood. There was a proposal to do a walk for peace throughout the neighborhood after the service, but it was not taken up for safety reasons. According to Ernesto, this service "at least calmed us spiritually, soothing our fears because we saw that we were together in this."

Selective violence has continued into the 1990s, tempered only by an uneasy truce between *quadrilhas*. When the precarious balance of power established between local drug bosses changes, it is very likely that Pedra Bonita will suffer another cycle of death and delinquency. Just as in the case of the school and the bus, the effort to make the neighborhood a safer place shows that community struggles require constant follow-up work, lest the gains made be canceled or coopted by a political establishment/culture characterized by authoritarianism and corruption. This inconclusiveness, added to the emergence of new problems in the neighborhood, has brought considerable fatigue and frustration to Pedra Bonita's activists. According to Tina,

[People in the neighborhood say:] "I won't go to that neighborhood association any longer because it doesn't do anything." But it is not like that, I was there in the association and saw the work. It is very tough, you have so many meetings, you get tired. You have to run after things. They [the authorities] bounce you here and there. All that to benefit the community and we don't get anything. I think, in the end, we don't get anything. It is just a never-ending fight, a walk [*caminhada*] all in vain.

A mature, diverse ecclesial community

During the late 1970s and early 1980s, Pedra Bonita's community continued to expand, adding new groups and movements. Developing parallel to the more politically engaged current of the base community – constituted by the ACO-CEB nucleus and the MAC – was a more traditionally religious group: the Society of Saint Vincent de Paul. In Pedra Bonita, the *Vicentinos*, as they are known in the *bairro*, number approximately 10–12 persons. The leaders of this lay movement – Tina, Antônia and João – are among the poorest members in the base community. They are also older than the majority of the ACO activists.

Vicentino practice is intensely spiritual. It is supported by two pillars: the devotional cult of saints, expressed in prayer and ritual activities, and the Holy Spirit, as the force that unifies the group. The *Vicentinos* understand the *caminhada* not as the on-going religio-political struggle to build the reign of God, but as a personal journey of conversion and renewal. In the *caminhada*, according to Antônia, "one is born, dies and is resurrected, and you know, São Vicente was the one who helped me to be born again."

Social outreach among the *Vicentinos* is more assistential, modeled along the lines of traditional Catholic charities. Every week they prepare food packages, purchased with money contributed by group members, and distribute them to the poorest families in the community. They also visit the sick and destitute in the neighborhood, praying and reading the Bible with them, and more generally, giving them encouragement in hard times.

For ACO members, this kind of work raises some troubling questions. In Ernesto's opinion, the *Vicentinos* "are still too attached to the cult of saints. They don't want to go out and confront present reality, or to link faith and life. You have to take your faith inside your union, association, workplace . . ." His wife, Ana concurs, adding that the *Vicentinos*

concentrate in giving the fish already caught. They don't concern themselves with discussing with the poorest families the causes of the problems they are facing, making them reflect on the causes and consequences of the unemployment they are suffering. I am not against giving food to the hungry and clothing the naked, but you have to discuss the underlying causes of unemployment and hunger, and derive an action. Finding someone a job through a friend solves the problem only for the moment. But it wasn't clear to him why he was unemployed.

Tina, the president of the *Vicentinos*, acknowledges that some of the members in her group "sometimes don't participate in other movements and that obstructs [*atrapalha*] community work. But I, as a *Vicentina*, participate in all neighborhood activities. I'm in the liturgy group." She also rejects the charge of assistentialism:

[Some say:] "Ah! That's all foolishness [*bobagem*]! To buy provisions doesn't help anything because you give today a food parcel and it won't be enough to eat for a month, not even for a week." But what is important is the love that goes with that package. When we give that package, we lift up the person because we read the Gospels with them.

The person unburdens [*desabafa*] himself, talking about the problems he's having. He might need reassurance or if he's sick he might need to go to the doctor and we take him.

Some members of the CEB nucleus in the ACO recognize the merits of the *Vicentinos'* social and pastoral work. According to Vitória, "The *Vicentinos* are very important in the neighborhood because they really work hard at visiting people, something that we [the ACO] haven't paid enough attention to." Thus, despite mutual suspicions, the two currents have managed to work together for the benefit of the base community: while the ACO concentrated more on political activism, the *Vicentinos* focused on spiritual matters. Moreover, although the ACO's vision dominated CEB life, the informal rotation of liturgical activities set up by Cláudio allowed the *Vicentinos* to contribute actively to the base community.

Even though the ACO and the *Vicentinos* differed in the *modus operandi* they shared an understanding of what, according to Tina, "Christ demands of us: to learn to forgive and love our neighbors. Because He said: 'where you see a brother suffering, I am suffering myself.'" Both groups see this-worldly actions, particularly those that bring the betterment of the most downtrodden, as fundamental to God's salvific work. Both groups express involvement in these activities as "commitment [*compromisso*] ... a responsibility to give to others as if [they were] standing before God."

As one can see, human and sacred history intersect once more in CEB theology, this time with Christ as the central metaphor of the communion between God and humanity. Where the two currents differ is in the ways they conceive Christ. The ACO sees Christ along more specific class lines, in Gerson's words, "a working-class Christ, a carpenter working in his adoptive father's shop ... a Christ who helped, who didn't just stand there, and because of that He was crucified by jealous and egotistical kings." The *Vicentinos*, on the other hand, see Christ embodied in the suffering neighbor on whom the true Christian, like the good Samaritan, must bestow care and love. The christologies, in turn, lead to different forms of intervention in the social arena: for the ACO a politically militant approach that seeks to change the structural sources of sin, and for the Vicentinos a more assistentialist strategy aimed at soothing the most severe effects of poverty.

The diversification of Pedra Bonita's CEB was not restricted to the base community's core, with the development of the *Vicentinos* as a counter-balance to the ACO. There were also alternative voices at the CEB's periphery, which share some of the beliefs and practices of the ACO and *Vicentinos* but have their own character. An example is Dulce, a widow who supports her two children by patching together cleaning, sewing, and laundry jobs for better-off families in Nova Iguaçu. Up until the death of her husband in 1984, Dulce's participation in the community was limited to regular attendance at community masses and celebrations. Her husband, in contrast, participated actively in the ACO's struggles for the neighborhood's school and bus along side Gerson and Laura. The death of her husband brought Dulce closer to the community, especially to the ACO, as the group sought to help her secure her husband's pension. Despite this new closeness, Dulce does not belong officially to the ACO, nor does she fully understand the nature and significance of its pastoral-pedagogical method. When asked to explain what the see-judge-act method and the *revisão de vida operária* mean, she finds herself somewhat at a loss.

INTERVIEWER: What is the see-judge-act method of the ACO?
DULCE: See, judge . . . I don't know . . . it is to see things as a group, to build together something better. All of a sudden one sees a thing and tries to get it. We go slow, carefully, until we all come together as a community. And it is only God himself who helps us and shows us the way.

Instead of articulating a coherent popular theology that links explicitly political action with religious images as Gerson and Laura do, Dulce speaks of the personal faith that has sustained her and her family through the difficult times. Here Dulce's religious worldview approximates that of the *Vicentinos*. Nevertheless, Dulce does not think that distributing food to the poorest families in the neighborhood and praying are sufficient to lead a truly Christian life. For Dulce there must be a community of the faithful working together. She envisions this community not primarily in political or ideological terms or as a group constituted around a saint, but as an extended family, a support network, where the "little ones [*os pequenos*]" help each other to lead a "human life [*vida digna*]." Thus, while Dulce endorses the aims of the more politically militant sector of the community (i.e., the ACO) in terms of grassroots empowerment, she has a more modest vision of community life: the goal is not to produce a "politically literate" vanguard but to provide a nurturing context. For Dulce, "the community gives one [*a gente*] support, a word of encouragement, fellowship [*companhia*] for one to continue in the struggle, for one not to go on alone."

Such alternative visions of community life at the periphery, along with the consolidation of the *Vicentinos* and the ACO at the CEB nucleus, indicate that by the early 1980s Pedra Bonita had become a complex, highly differentiated community. It was capable of holding in productive tension seemingly conflicting forms of religiosity and approaches to social-pastoral action. The balance between the various currents was maintained until 1985, when pastoral changes in the diocese and the parish collided with the ACO's *modus operandi*. These changes dovetailed with socio-economic transformations in the Brazilian society at large to bring in a period of decline to Pedra Bonita's ecclesial community.

The decline of Pedra Bonita's community: pastoral changes and economic straits

In 1981, the French pastoral agents who had been working the area for more than ten years returned to France and were replaced by Irish priests of the Order of the Holy Spirit. The latter, intent on giving "each community its independent type of life" took a more distant pastoral approach. In the Irish priests' view, the CEBs in the parish had achieved a level of maturity after the initial push provided by the French. Father Patrício, the last Irish priest to come to Pedra Bonita and the community's current pastoral agent, likens the communities to a car: "you [the pastoral agent] are driving the car, the car is doing everything, the engine is going, the wheels are going around and all you do is to get your finger in the steering wheel. So, here . . . we strongly insist that the community do everything. We have as little presence as possible."

This approach generated discontent among some community

members, especially among ACO activists in the CEB nucleus. In Teresa's opinion, "the French priests had us spoiled, they were so good with the people." They were good because, in Gabriela's words,

They had a [pastoral] method which took them to our homes. They would bike around the neighborhood visiting, inviting people to come. They would participate in our moments of happiness and sorrow. And you know, Brazilian people are very hospitable. They like to be visited in their homes, to strike conversations. And the Irish seem to be colder [*mais frios*]. They only come to say mass twice a month and leave quickly.

Father Patrício believes that Father Jaime, the first Irish priest to arrive in Pedra Bonita, sought to address problems of dependence, favoritism, and monopoly of activities:

The French priests were very keen on being warm, protecting priests. They were successful in the sense that they got a tremendous life from some few people there. But there was also one or two people there who got a bit dependent on them. They had money from France. So they depended on the priests. So they never got the people to get the *dízimo* [tithe] going, to get the collection going to try to become an independent community.

It appears that the French priests favored certain families, giving them a monthly installment to augment their meager incomes. In addition, the priests' reliance on a community nucleus to undertake pastoral work in the neighborhood had resulted in a concentration of initiatives and activities in the hands of a few activists. This concentration of responsibilities on the CEB nucleus was a necessary organizational phase before the CEB could turn its attention to the world at large. As we saw in chapter 3, the popular church, and CEBs in particular, worked with a small group pastoral approach, which selected individuals among the poor to train them through a consciousness-raising pedagogy to become lay leaders. These leaders would later on act as "organic intellectuals," or as Catholic activists say, *fermento de massa*, educating and inspiring those around them to become involved in the building of the reign of God. The ultimate objective of forming small groups like CEBs was, thus, to evangelize and mobilize the masses.

The Irish priests had misgivings about the transition from a *pastoral de grupos pequenos* to a *pastoral de massa*. Like the French priests, they also hoped to evangelize the larger community, but they favored different methods. The Irish priests wanted to open up the community, to avoid, Father Patrício's words, the danger of it becoming "a small sect. . . taken over by one or two families who [were] stronger." As a first step, the Irish priests shifted to the base community the burden of responsibility for evangelization and raising money for the parish fund.

Unfortunately the strategy had unintended consequences, as the collapse of the Brazilian economy and the structural adjustment and neo-liberal policies adopted to resolve the crisis beginning in the mid-1980s placed a tremendous pressure on the working poor, limiting their leisure time and their capacity to contribute financially to their communities. Although CEB members often do not fully grasp the causes and effects of this collapse, they sense how economic variables have intersected with pastoral changes to create obstacles to community work. As we shall see, the economic theme resurfaces periodically in discussions about pastoral method.

Otília's case provides an example of the powerful influence of the economic crisis. As one of the CEB's founders, she played a key role in the formation of one of the most successful and durable evangelization groups in Pedra Bonita. She was known for her dynamic style of leadership and her willingness to set aside her seamstress work at home and attend community meetings. This willingness, however, has been severely undermined by the fact that her husband, an electrician, was laid off from his job at a neighboring construction company. For more than two years he has been practically unemployed, with only occasional odd jobs in the district. So, whereas before Otília's sewing work served to supplement her husband's steady income, now she and her twenty-year-old daughter have become the main breadwinners in the household. Faced with this pressure, feeling "tired" of the wear and tear of pastoral visits and "despairing" over the "great suffering of families around [her]," she decided to pass the leadership of her group to another woman, who could not keep up with the visiting routine. In the absence of consistent lay work and without the direct involvement of the priest, the evangelization group, the essential instrument of community growth, all but collapsed.

Teresa, another CEB leader, highlights the economic situation's implications for community action. For her, the inability of people to participate has to do with

[t]he social side of things: the need people have to work at the sewing machine, washing clothes, that doesn't give time to go to there [the community]. The need to work takes time away from the community. There are several [women] who can't take time off. If they don't work that day, they will not have anything to eat at home. The woman has to stay home washing clothes to be able to provide some change [*trocado*] for household expenses since her husband doesn't make enough money to buy bread.

In addition to re-allocating financial and logistical responsibilities, the Irish priests, following directives from the diocese of Nova Iguaçu, implemented pastoral and organizational changes in the community. In response to pressures generated by the Vatican restoration offensive, the diocese sought to regularize the practices of base communities and their links with the hierarchy. This effort provided viable institutional spaces for CEBs to continue their work in the face of increasing reluctance from the National Conference of Brazilian Bishops to support progressive grassroots initiatives. These spaces, however, came only at the cost of re-centralizing authority in clerical hands.[16]

Before the diocesan changes, CEBs in Nova Iguaçu, while receiving assistance from the hierarchy, had operated with a great deal of autonomy. This had created significant pastoral heterogeneity at local levels. Activities within each base community depended more on the personal approach of the pastoral agent, which was itself determined by the specific character and needs of the neighborhood. Thus, while diocesan changes in response to Vatican pressure legitimized the existence of base communities by making

---

[16] Recent Vatican documents affirm the value of CEBs but only under the hierarchy's close supervision. For instance, *The Instruction on Christian Freedom and Liberation* (1986) states that "The new basic communities . . . are a source of great hope for the Church. Their fidelity to their mission will depend on how careful they are to educate their members in the fullness of the Christian faith through listening to the Word of God, fidelity to the teaching of the Magisterium, to the hierarchical order of the Church and to the sacramental life" (no. 69).

them part of the church's institutional structure, they also increased hierarchical supervision and control over progressive grassroots pastoral work.[17] This, in turn, allowed the clergy to force heterodox local beliefs and practices to conform to official orthodoxy. Drawing from our discussion of the history of Brazilian Catholicism in the previous chapter, we can say that the transformation of base communities in Nova Iguaçu represented a "romanization" of CEB discourses and practices. Just as in the mid-nineteenth century, the attempt is made to control local religiosity by clericalizing and sacramentalizing it.

The case of Pedra Bonita illustrates how the recent Vatican drive reflects a trend towards a new romanization. Among the changes the Irish priests introduced was a renewed emphasis on the importance of liturgy in CEB life.[18] The rationale for this shift was *prima facie* coherent and convincing. Father Patrício remarks:

I think we lost sight of popular religiosity, we took away a lot of the piety, the statues and all that sort of stuff. We're [always] talking about the struggle [*luta*] for better transport, better schooling, getting together to fight for this, having a parade about that. . . And then we forget that it is important to have a good liturgical celebration. That's important to [the people]! It is important to them because there is where they talk to their God.

The strategy chosen to bring this renewed emphasis on liturgy was twofold. First, the priests sent community members to the diocesan training center in Nova Iguaçu, where they took short courses on the proper ways to assist and conduct liturgical celebrations (in the

---

[17] There is increasing evidence throughout Latin America of the constraining effects of the restoration movement at the grassroots, particularly in parishes where progressive Catholic pastoral strategies had held sway. See, for example, M. Peña "The Sodalitium Vitae Movement in Peru: A Rewriting of Liberation Theology," in W. H. Swatos, ed., *Religion and Democracy in Latin America* (New Brunswick, NJ: Transaction Publishers, 1995).

[18] In an address during his trip to Brazil, John Paul II reminded the nation's bishops of "the utter importance of teaching clearly on the sacredness of the eucharistic mystery and of liturgical worship." "A Pressing Hunger for Bread and Justice," *Origins* 21, no. 21 (October 31, 1991), 332. A year later in Santo Domingo, the pope stated that CEBs "must be stamped with a clear ecclesial identity and find in the eucharist, presided over by a priest, the center of their life and communion among their members, in close union with their pastors and full harmony with the church's magisterium." "Opening Address to Fourth General Conference of Latin American Episcopate," *Origins* 22, no. 19 (October 22, 1992), 331.

priest's absence). In this manner, the diocese would strengthen its lay leadership, while at the same time creating lay agents capable of reproducing orthodox liturgical practices on their own. The second aspect of the strategy was the adoption of *A Folha*, a periodical publication put out by the diocese since 1972 containing the weekly service, as the heart of the liturgical celebration. Under the French, *A Folha* was more a pedagogical aid than a strict guide. With the Irish, in contrast, it becomes the defining nexus between priest and community. Vitória noticed this change: "Before, with the [French] priests, we reflected on the gospels, they would have us say what we understood when reading it. Now he [the Irish priest] only reads the gospel text and gives a sermon. People don't speak up their minds [*se colocam*]."

In Pedra Bonita the new strategy had, once again, unintended negative consequences. For one thing, it challenged the *ad hoc* rotation of liturgical functions already existent among the community nucleus. Laura expresses her disappointment with the new strategy:

Our work all that time with the [French] priests . . . we were the ones who prepared mass. The gospel text was read, but it was reflected by the people. Each one would speak a little about what that reading meant, what Jesus Christ wanted to say with it. And people linked it with the life of the worker. And then when Father Jaime [the first Irish priest to come] arrived he ended all that. He said that we had to organize a liturgy group, take a course to know how to read [*A Folha*] right. So he undid [*desmanchou*] our work, a work that was done for years. We had been working in that fashion for years. We also know that Jesus never took a course at the university to do his work.

The stress on correct liturgical etiquette had also a chilling effect on the more traditional group members who felt that they could not live up to the new "orthopraxis." Laura recalls an episode where Father Jaime scolded Otília, who had prepared mass as she had always done under the French, for not reading the gospel text properly.

"Look! You have a comma there, you have to read using the comma. Periods and commas must be used when reading." We found this absurd because Otília has not gone beyond second or third grade, just like me. Despite that, I'm capable of reading slowly, in my own fashion, but I'm capable of reading during mass. Even more when those who hear me are just like me. But then people were ashamed of reading incorrectly, stuttering, letter by letter. And [so] they went to take the [liturgy] course.

The most important consequence of the pastoral shift, however, was the rupture of the dialectic of action and reflection that Father Cláudio had established. As described above, in the community's early stages reading the gospel had been an exercise in group discussion, where CEB members fashioned their own popular theology to make sense of their everyday lives. When the Irish priests reinstituted the sermon format, in which laypeople were passive for the most part, the loss of lay biblical reflection undermined one of the central ways that Pedra Bonita people inserted themselves into sacred history and understood their experiences – including their political struggles – as meaningful.

Most members of the original community nucleus resisted the pastoral changes introduced by the first Irish priests and politely refused to attend liturgy courses. To many, the courses symbolized a diversion of CEB energy and resources from social action to mere formalities. Father Jaime took this refusal to participate as a willful tactic of a militant political vanguard within the CEB-ACO nucleus to undermine his pastoral work.

The *Vicentinos*, on the other hand, reacted favorably to Father Jaime's proposals, as they resonated with the group's emphasis on the ritual aspects of Christian life. Their participation in the liturgy courses made them the only key players in the preparation of services. Since liturgical preparations until that point had been the responsibility of the community nucleus, this realignment of duties only succeeded in aggravating the tension between the ACO, with its stress on drawing the link between faith and life, and the Vicentinos who placed a heavy emphasis on the formal aspects of worship. The standarization and "professionalization" of liturgy preparation broke the balance between the two main religious currents in the base community.

Thus, a strategy that was initially designed to strengthen and legitimize Nova Iguaçu's CEBs ended up, at least in the case of Pedra Bonita, fostering division on the ground and undermining the autonomy and efficacy of grassroots pastoral initiatives. This paradox illustrates sharply the limits of grassroots innovation in the context of a hierarchical church, whose institutional interest is to reproduce itself by reinforcing the structures already in place. Even when the bishop is sympathetic to grassroots renewal, as it was the case with Nova Iguaçu's Hipólito, the weight of these structures, which are construed as part of a universal, all-encompassing edifice, ends up suffocating the vitality of local pastoral initiatives. In this sense, the progressive Catholic reading of the crisis, which stresses the intra-institutional constraints faced by the popular church's project, finds validation in Pedra Bonita's case.

The roots of the crisis of Pedra Bonita's base community go beyond religious division brought by pastoral changes within the church at large. Other divisions based on socio-economic transformations in the parish have disabled the CEB. Gabriela thinks that the culprit for the situation in Pedra Bonita is Nova Iguaçu's "middle class," which, "trying to escape high rents, has flown to the neighborhood of Ocampo, where they still are close to center of the district, where they have basic services, everything." As I stated above, Ocampo is the parish seat for seven communities, among which Pedra Bonita is one of the most distant. This middle class brought to the parish "different ideas." According to Gabriela, this middle class "wanted to refurbish their church, to add nice, colorful window panes. Suddenly that began to take hold of our people. They started to think that the church was for that." Setting up a beautiful place of worship became important, downgrading social outreach and evangelization, especially in the parish's periphery.

Such an explanation is not farfetched, for in July 1985 the newly formed community council in Pedra Bonita decided, without popular consultation, to build a new church to replace the simple room that had served until then as the place of worship. Father Patrício saw the decision as an opportunity to build up the community's self-esteem and to energize it in the midst of so much violence and poverty.

At one stage I said: "There's a need for a sign of hope there, which is not just in that *sala* [room] we have mass." That's why we're trying to build this church besides it. So we did. Talked about it and they were all so keen on it. I got some money from the collection [and started]. But I want to get them to finish it out. Once you've got the foundations, the walls, the roof, I know they can finish it. There's no more money coming in. They have to get out and get proud about it, finish their church. And I think that will help them become more united as a community.

The problem is that in the worsening economic situation the community saw its financial resources shrink radically. Instead of using these resources strategically to address pressing needs in the neighborhood or to fortify its various entities, the community diverted most of its funds to the new church.

Setting the parish seat as an example of what the church should be brought a shift in pastoral priorities away from peripheral communities to the center, Ocampo. Whereas "before the parish helped a lot, during the time of Father Claúdio, Father Márcio . . . now we have to collect money for the parish fund." So now Vitória, Pedra Bonita's new community coordinator, rather than working to push and pull together various community activities, spends her time "worrying about other things. We need money to buy cement, or to pay electricity and I have to ask during mass. I don't like it. I have to ask for money for the parish fund in Ocampo."

Religious and economic tensions came to a head in Pedra Bonita during a meeting where Father Jaime tried to form a community council in Pedra Bonita, as part of the diocesan plan to establish a more orderly division of labor within the CEB and to bring them under closer clerical supervision. Each movement or group within the community would democratically choose a representative. These representatives would form the community council charged with planning, coordinating and overseeing CEB work. In turn, representatives of each of the seven communities in the parish would form a *conselho paroquial*, thereby connecting each CEB to the diocesan hierarchical structure. Within each base community different specialized groups would assume specific pastoral tasks: baptism, catechism, and liturgy. People in the various groups would receive special training to carry out their functions properly.

What on the surface appeared to be the next natural step for a mature community had disastrous consequences. During the meeting, Father Jaime asked the participants to identify the group they were representing to then draw a list for the community council. When Laura indicated that she came from ACO, Jaime told her that he did not recognize the ACO as a church movement, that it was independent. Presumably, Jaime wanted to marginalize the ACO because its members were the ones that had been opposing the pastoral changes. This refusal led the main families in the CEB–ACO nucleus to retrench, withdrawing their support from the new community council. Without the active participation of the nucleus the community's web began to unravel. The council, rather than serving to coordinate better community activities, became an instance of overbureaucratization, where functions and tasks were well-defined but where there were no committed individuals to carry them out.

Father Jaime's identification of the CEB–ACO nucleus with an intransigent, radical fringe not interested in liturgical matters encouraged more mistrust from the neighborhood at large. We have seen how the ACO group's secrecy during the military regime had already generated suspicion and unease among the neighbors. This added mistrust rendered the work of the CEB-ACO nucleus more difficult. Isolated from the people and at loggerheads with the priest, Pedra Bonita's lay core of activists lost its effectiveness, leaving its progressive initiatives without anyone to execute them. Laura summarizes the effects of the pastoral changes introduced by the Irish thus:

Father Jaime obstructed our work. He created a catechism group, separated a liturgy group, he separated all groups. Before everybody got together without distinction [*discriminação*]. There we had people from the *Vicentinos*, catechism, ACO . . . everybody joined. Then he divided things, each small bunch went its own way. And that finished the [*grupo de reflexão*] which came to be known now as a Bible circle, for which you also had to take a course.

Pedra Bonita's case bears a strong resemblance to the conditions that led to the decline of progressive initiatives in the parish of Pilar, in Duque de Caxias. In his study of Pilar, sociologist José Cláudio Souza Alves describes the tensions created with the introduction to the parish of the preferential option for the poor.[19]

---

[19] J. C. Souza Alves, "Igreja católica: Opção pelos pobres, política e poder – o caso da paróquia do Pilar" M. A. thesis, Pontifícia Universidade Católica, Rio de Janeiro, 1991.

Among the conflicts he identifies is a struggle for power (i.e., control of resources and the capacity to design and execute pastoral plans) between a "hierarchical current" represented by a priest allied with the parish's more traditionally religious fraction, and "a politicized lay vanguard." Because of its experience in intra and extra-ecclesial struggles this politicized lay vanguard was able to challenge the power and authority of the priest. Although this challenge was a positive step in the democratization of ecclesial power relations, it generated division within the parish. Simultaneously, the lay vanguard's politicization and advanced critical consciousness led it to strike "a rhythm [of activity] that did not correspond with the rest of the parish. [The vanguard] wanted to pull the rest [of the parish] so that the latter would match its rhythm; but this did not happen. So the vanguard kept advancing, not noticing that people were falling behind."[20]

In both Pilar's and Pedra Bonita's cases, the downfall of progressive initiatives resulted from the alienation and demobilization of the crucial nucleus of lay activists, who without the support of a hands-on, pastorally-engaged priest, increasingly came to play the central role in anchoring the community's polycentric web of relations. However, the decline of Pedra Bonita's CEB did not stem only from pastoral conflicts: it came from the interplay of ecclesial/pastoral variables (i.e., the Vatican offensive and the diocesan responses to it) and socio-economic changes. Some of the pastoral changes could have had a positive effect on the community, granting it more independence and consolidating its internal organization. Nevertheless, they ended up producing adverse unintended consequences due to a worsening economic situation in the district. Although tensions are understood, expressed, and fought largely in religious terms (i.e., around issues of pastoral method), the roots of the decline reach beyond purely religious dynamics to economic/structural processes. These processes, which I shall characterize in detail in the next chapter, combined with religious variables to make the CEB's work more difficult.

Today Pedra Bonita's CEB is "holding on." With the arrival of Patrício, relations with the pastoral agent have improved. The

---

[20] Ibid., 141.

ACO was eventually accepted as a legitimate group in the community and it now has a representative in the council. Laura and Cléa have begun to participate more actively, though they still refuse to join the council. Otília attends council meetings representing the group in charge of baptism, but very rarely "speaks up her mind." Thus, the council continues to be largely ineffectual.

In Father Patrício's assessment the two currents are once again beginning to "work as a community," but "there are still a lot of weaknesses there":

There's a lack of leadership. I think that's partially because there are hardly any middle class people, they all are very poor. And normally leadership doesn't come from the poor. You need a certain level of education and a certain level of possibility, because if you're very poor your main preoccupation is how are you going to survive. If you're better off, you're middle class, then you have a kind of a guaranteed salary, then you're not too preoccupied. You can give time and space to these other "militant" interests.

Despite these weaknesses, new initiatives have emerged recently. With the new church nearing completion, there are plans to establish an adult literacy school and a community and childcare center in the neighborhood. Residents have also formed a second ACO team in the *bairro's* northern corner. Some CEB members have also spoken of the possibility of creating a local chapter of the Workers' Party.

That the community has been able to survive through such tough times is a testament to the perseverance and power of its members who, in the face of ecclesial and economic obstacles, have made the CEB their own project. The commitment and energy of laypeople has been crucial to the Pedra Bonita CEB's durability. While the various pastoral agents have played a determining role in shaping and supporting – or undermining – community practice, initiatives on the ground have taken a life of their own that seems to belie attempts at control.

Why are Seitas *growing in Pedra Bonita? CEB members reflect*

Beset by internal tensions and outside pressures, Pedra Bonita's CEB entered, toward the mid-1980s, a period of stagnation. All the while, Pentecostal churches in the *bairro* continued growing briskly.

Base community members' explanations for the growth of Pentecostalism in Pedra Bonita range from defensive denunciations of "manipulative pastors" to more thoughtful evaluations that take into account weaknesses in the CEB. For Laura, for instance,

> those sects are nothing more than a right-wing group that is spreading throughout Brazil. I feel that right-wing groups use preachers. I would even say that pastors earn good money to use a certain biblical text. If one takes the Bible, one finds several interpretations. So they select [those texts] that are linked with miracles like Lazarus and others. He [the preacher] gets that stuff into people's heads and begins to bring people, and they are giving him money. You have to give 10% of your own pocket to the church. And I believe that money is used on election days. So to bring this money the preacher uses the people and the Bible.

Without denying the economic motive cited by Laura, Ernesto offers a different perspective. For him the problem lies in "church strategy" that is "limiting community growth."

> Things come already made by the church elites. They come prepared by an elite group within the dioceses, up above. As long as you have that practice of having everything already written, a group that does and controls everything, it will be difficult for the church to grow. Because if everything comes ready for our celebrations, *A Folha* is ready, the people cannot come together as a community and say: "nope, we are going to prepare that mass, that celebration!" Now you prepare based on what's already there, and you have to do it because the priest is used to doing things that way. He just wants to come read the stuff and leave.

Ernesto considers that the current church strategy fits better the people living in the center of Nova Iguaçu. That "middle class" group is interested in looks: in mass they are used to having "an organ, a musical group performing." But people in the periphery want "deeper, more transparent things" from the church. They want a church "closer to the people," "in the midst of the people and made by the people."

Vitória concurs with Ernesto. She feels that, contrary to the established church, Pentecostals "value people" by the way they receive and follow closely the lives of the new converts:

When I go by those temples, I see the youth playing their instruments, they talk to people, they sing their hymns, they have all those welcoming things [*acolhimento*]. And people appreciate that. They [also] go out in the streets, from house to house, knocking doors preaching and reading the Gospels. I'm under the impression that for them it is not important to go up in front and read [the Gospels] beautifully.

According to Vitória, the community "did a good job forming people . . . but what I'm discovering now is that we didn't really value [people]." She gives the example of a neighborhood youngster who died:

We had a mass for him. We prepared everything for his funeral. The mother of the kid liked our work very much, she even wanted a copy [of the service]. Even the father praised the service, he said it was very good. Then it was necessary to accompany this family, to continue preparing masses. But we just talked about it. We didn't prepare anything because when we try in the council to speak about things like that, we have to talk about other things, about the construction [of the church], about a community party. Thus we don't have time to talk about our own community.

This example contrasts sharply with the community's work when Ana lost her child. On that occasion, the CEB's constant presence and solidarity insured Ana's conversion to community life. In other words, for Vitória the problem is a combination of misplaced priorities and time constraints. Rather than "going to the encounter of the people, what Jesus did when he went by the sea to meet the fishermen," the community "is worrying about silly problems like the council, the construction, money." The CEB lost ground to the "sects" in Pedra Bonita because "we didn't make an effort to talk with [the people who converted to Pentecostalism], to continue with our evangelization groups that visited the neighborhood."

According to Ana, part of the blame for this failure falls on the Irish priests for not getting truly involved in the life of the community and the neighborhood – a necessary condition for effective evangelization.

The main problem is that he [Father Patrício] does not even know the people in the community because he only comes on Saturdays to say mass or when there's a meeting. And even then, he does not participate in our community council's meetings, he just goes to meetings at the parish level. But even if he were to participate at our community meetings, I don't think he would get to know who we are. It is not in a meeting that one knows another person. For me to really know a person you have to chat [*bater papo*] with him individually and [ask him]: "how's it going [*como está a tua luta*]? How's your life?" You need to do everything to help your comrade [*companheiro*] express his day-to-day life, his work and life.

In the absence of a hands-on pastoral agent, the level of involvement required to keep the various community activities running proved too much for most community members, particularly at a time of economic hardship and when conflicts over pastoral method had alienated the community nucleus. As we have seen, worsening economic conditions forced women, the base community's pillars, to assume a more central role in supporting their families, limiting their capacity to seize full responsibility for community work.

Gabriela thinks that the only way to solve the community's predicament is to redouble the members' resolve and activism.

We have to fight for that church that Jesus Christ wants, that outward-looking church, that church of the true communities. We are still a community that sticks to our room too much [*a comunidade salão*]. There's still too much passivity [*acomodação*] among us. Even with the growth of sects, we have to go out and meet the people, touch their reality. The church that Jesus Christ wants is really a church of transformation, of change, of the reign of God. But to build that reign is difficult: you have to leave the room and enter in the problems of the people. It is difficult because one has to dedicate oneself to the task, get involved to do the work. And the sects don't have to do it, people arrive there and they get everything ready, they get a miracle.

To build the reign of God requires patience, effort and much dedication. Whether Pedra Bonita's CEB can muster that level of dedication and whether it can inspire the neighborhood at large are serious questions, considering the precarious life conditions of the majority of the population. Gabriela herself appears to be hinting at the difficulty when she observes that in the sects people "get everything ready." When asked why people are making a "preferential option for the sects," ignoring the church's preferential option for the poor as embodied in the ecclesial communities, CEB members respond unanimously that it is because of self-interest. Tina says she has "begun to believe that people are after a quick miracle." Cléa, in fact, has heard many people say: "Ah, I'll go there and pray and I'm going to be healthy again and I don't even have to go to the doctor."

Most people in the community agree that people are joining Pentecostalism in search of solutions to personal problems. Ana connects the search for solutions in the religious field to the unfulfilled needs and dreams of the working class. The pressures of everyday life have become so intense for the poor that there is no chance for them to search for long-term solutions to address the structural roots of their condition. Rather, they are forced to deal with the immediate manifestations of this condition:

I see that the situation of the working class is wrenching [*desgarradora*]. There's so much anxiety in the working class. They would do anything to achieve their longings, to obtain what they are looking for. So, people today are after immediate things. That's the reason why sects are created everywhere. Sometimes people in the community have health problems. Normally it is people who have just arrived to the community and don't have any religious training. And what do they do? They contact other churches. There the preachers tells them that if they are sick, they should come and they will be healthy again. So the search is for solutions . . . not long term ones. I think today immediatism [*imediatismo*] is very strong among people.

Father Patrício agrees with Ana's assessment. The difficult situation of the people in the district has generated a whole host of urgent needs and expectations, especially connected to issues of life and death, that no human initiative or institution appears capable of addressing. Faced with a baffling, threatening world that seems beyond human control they turn to the divine for answers.

People [are looking] for some spiritual, mystical solution to their problems. They are pretty lost psychologically because there are no solutions to their problems and life is really very, very tough. The government isn't solving problems for them, the state isn't solving problems, the church isn't solving problems. And the insecurity is very important. But then they get this thing that says: "It's OK if you just give yourself to Jesus. Raise your hand for Jesus and you will be saved. And that's guaranteed. Damn this bloody life, this existence! Jesus will help me put up with this existence and I'm guaranteed that I'll be saved."

Thus, CEB members believe the crisis in CEB participation stems from an inauspicious economic situation which is placing obstacles to the work of progressive Catholics and encouraging people to turn elsewhere for immediate solutions to their urgent problems. This crisis affects the whole community's pastoral work, and not just that of the most politically militant and religiously innovative groups (i.e., ACO and MAC). Tina, president of the *Vicentinos*, who has seen her husband convert to Pentecostalism and divide the family, complains that "there are people whom the *Vicentinos* helped, raised up [*levantou*], who now have a piece of land and cows, who are doing fine, and are in the Igreja Universal [Universal Church of the Reign of God]."

The crisis, therefore, does not spare community sectors engaged in more traditional religious practices, even those sectors which have a charismatic orientation similar to that of Pentecostalism. Thus, Pedra Bonita's case does not lend support to the conservative intra-ecclesial reading of the crisis. The questions raised by the growth of Pentecostalism do not just pertain to progressive Catholic pastoral methodology. The roots of the crisis run deeper. Otília offers a very poignant theological interpretation of crisis:

Things are tightening [*apertando*] now. We know that [with all that] unemployment here in Brazil it is not easy for a person to have a peaceful life. People are not paid a just wage here in Brazil. It is a miserable wage that does not allow for life that's worthy of human beings [*vida digna*]. People sometimes fall into despair. We sometimes just have to stop, without strength, almost without hope. But when people know the Gospels they get a different perspective. You see how in the Exodus God tests His people making them cross the desert. On the other hand, He gives them food when it is necessary in their march toward the promised land. So it is with our lives. God gives us food. . . He gives us strength to live, for people to struggle to survive.

Otília sees the "people of God," the church, passing through the desert on its way to the promised land. Whether the people of God will be able to keep their faith and emerge intact from this test is an open question. But what are the social causes that have led the people of God into having to cross the desert? What is this economic crisis that hinders Catholic pastoral work and opens the space for the emergence of alternative religions? I turn to these questions in the next chapter.

CHAPTER 7

Brazilian capitalism since the 1980s: redefining the limits of the possible

To understand the socio-economic conditions that have contributed to the decline of Pedra Bonita's CEB, it is necessary to analyze changes in the political economy of the greater metropolitan area of Rio de Janeiro and of Brazil as a whole, especially during the 1980s, the period when the base community began to experience difficulties. As we shall see, the precarious life conditions in Nova Iguaçu stem from Brazil's contradictory position in the world economy. These conditions worsened considerably toward the mid-1980s as people began to feel the effects of the debt crisis and of adjustment measures responding to it. Deteriorating life conditions, in turn, have created additional constraints and pressures at the community and household level that people need to address using the economic, political, and ideological resources at hand. In Brazil, religion is one of the central ideological resources that help make sense of and guide action upon these constraints and pressures. Because of this centrality, any attempt to assess the viability of a particular religious tradition or a pastoral strategy should take into account its effectiveness in dealing with local needs and expectations. I contend that although the popular church's utopian vision and pastoral methodology were designed to fulfill a preferential option for the poor, they were not prepared to deal effectively with the radical changes in the life conditions of the urban poor brought about by the recent shifts in the configuration of the capitalist world-system.

To describe these changes some scholars have referred to a new "post-industrial," "post-Fordist," "disorganized," "late," or

"advanced" capitalism.[1] This new capitalism is characterized by
the emergence of flexible forms of production and capital accumulation that combine highly sophisticated systems (such as a
global financial market connected by advanced telecommunica-
tions) and operations (an information-intensive service sector)
with archaic, "artisanal," and informal activities (such as the
practice of sub-contracting and the putting-out system in Third
World countries to produce the goods for big retail stores in the
US).[2] Because of this flexibility, heterogeneity, and eclecticism, it
seems to me that none of the terms above is able to characterize
adequately the complexity of this new form of capitalism. For
instance, adjectives such as "late" and "advanced" suggest that
capitalism is a monolithic system with a single teleology. Furthermore, although the capitalist configuration is characterized by an
accelerated rate of turnover time in production, heightened global competition, and great capital mobility accompanied by heterogeneous labor and consumer markets, it would be a mistake
to call this capitalism disorganized. As Harvey argues, capitalism
is at present "becoming ever more tightly organized *through* dis-
persal, geographical mobility, and flexible responses in labour
markets, labour processes, and consumer markets, all accompanied by hefty doses of institutional, product, and technological
innovation."[3] For all of these reasons, I will not use any of the
aforementioned terms, limiting myself to talking about the present configuration of the capitalist world-system, with the understanding that its central characteristic is its ability to integrate
heterogeneous productive units, sectors, and regions. In this configuration Latin America continues to occupy a peripheral place,
sustaining overall negative exchanges in the world economy, as
shown by mounting debts, increased dependence on a flighty

---

[1] See among others, D. Bell, *The Coming of the Post-Industrial Society* (New York: Basic Books,
1973); A. Touraine, *The Post-Industrial Society* (New York: Randon, 1971); E. Mandel, *Late
Capitalism* (London: Verso, 1975); C. Offe, *Disorganized Capitalism* (Oxford: Oxford University Press, 1985); S. Lash and J. Urry, *The End of Organized Capitalism* (Oxford: Oxford
University Press, 1987).

[2] D. Harvey, *The Condition of Postmodernity* (Cambridge, MA: Basil Blackwell, 1989), 191.

[3] Ibid., 159. The evolving capitalist configuration also combines Fordist and flexible
arrangements, a fact that contradicts the assertion that we have entered into a post-
Fordist socio-economic order.

international capital, and the fragility of economic restructuring programs.

In the case of Brazil, the emergence of this capitalist configuration has severely affected the urban poor. Although urban poverty is nothing new to Brazil, there is evidence that economic changes in the 1980s, as the country sought to position itself in this new capitalist order through a series of structural and neoliberal economic reforms, qualitatively transformed the lives of poor people. These changes, combined with an acute national political crisis, led to a redefinition of the limits of the possible for the poor. Long-term utopian projects predicated on the notion of human progress, such as those offered by liberation theology and the popular church, have lost their plausibility. This may account in part for the relative decline of the *igreja popular* among the poor and for the search for alternative religious utopias (such as Pentecostalism) to fill the gap.

Although socio-economic variables have played a key role in the popular church's decline, they should not be taken as the sole explanatory principle. To do so would be to fall into a reductive materialism. I argued in chapters 5 and 6 that several other factors beyond the popular church's control, especially at intra-ecclesial level (i.e., the conservative Vatican restoration, divisions within the CNBB), have also conditioned the decline. More than likely, a combination of all these elements – national as well as international, intra- as well as extra-ecclesial – triggered the popular church's crisis of participation. Indeed, Pedra Bonita's case shows that the decline of the neighborhood's CEB resulted from a coincidence of economic pressures and pastoral changes at the global, diocesan, and local levels. In the previous chapters I have discussed the institutional and theological aspects of the crisis. Now I will concentrate on its socio-economic and political facets.

LIFE CONDITIONS IN AN URBAN PERIPHERY IN BRAZIL

Unequal development and rapid urbanization

Located about fifteen miles northwest of Rio de Janeiro, Nova Iguaçu, a sprawling urban area of an estimated 1.6 million people,[4] has experienced a rapid population growth over the last forty years. In 1950, the beginning of Brazil's economic boom, the district had only 145,649 inhabitants. By the 1980s the population exceeded 1 million.

This accelerated urban growth is typical of dependent capitalist development powered by industrial poles.[5] According to the modernization paradigm dominant during the 1950s and 1960s, economic growth and development result only from a gradual and ordered transition from traditional, agrarian economic structures to a modern, highly industrialized society. To ensure such a transition, "underdeveloped" countries such as Brazil had to follow the steps of developed nations, implementing the same strategies that had made the latter economically successful. Chief among these strategies was the creation of large industrial centers to energize the national economy and generate wealth through production, either for domestic or foreign consumption. In the case of Brazil, the creation of these industrial centers fell in the hands of an interventionist corporative state in alliance with national and multinational capital.[6]

In theory, the wealth and economic dynamism generated by these industrial poles would spill into other regions of the country and spur further industrialization. However, Brazil's top-down modernization produced what Aníbal Pinto has termed "structural heterogeneity."[7] The Brazilian economy became a segmented hybrid encompassing some productive sectors/activities and geographic regions showing high rates of capital accumulation through the use of technology and the production of high-priced commodities, and others, such as the north-east, still relying on extractive, labor-intensive production. This unstable juxtaposition of capital and labor-intensive forms of production

[4] Foundation for Support and Research in the State of Rio de Janeiro, *Anuário estatístico do Estado do Rio de Janeiro* (Rio de Janeiro: FAPERJ, 1981). For a fuller description of life conditions in Nova Iguaçu, see Mainwaring, *The Catholic Church and Politics in Brazil*, especially chapter 8.

[5] See F. H. Cardoso, "Associated-Dependent Development: Theoretical and Practical Implications," in Stepan, ed., *Authoritarian Brazil*.

[6] See P. Evans, *Dependent Development. The Alliance of Multinational, State and National Capital* (Princeton: Princeton University Press, 1979).

[7] A. Pinto, "Naturaleza e implicaciones de la heterogeneidad estructural de la América Latina." *Trimestre Económico*, no. 145 (1970), 83–100.

is what, according to Wallerstein, typifies semi-peripheral economies.[8]

Uneven development created severe contradictions in Brazilian
society, perhaps the most visible of which was over-urbanization.
Driven by precarious conditions in the countryside and attracted
by the possibility of securing a job and a better life in the new
industrial poles, unskilled rural workers migrated to urban centers.
Despite impressive rates of growth, the industrial sector could not
absorb the swelling labor force, thus producing chronic unemployment and underemployment and fueling the growth of the service
and informal sectors. The state, for its part, could not guarantee
basic services for the new arrivals.

The location of industrial poles responded to preexisting patterns of economic regionalization. The poles tended to be located
in areas which had been the centers of Brazil's mercantilist economy. They provided an installed infrastructure and the population
density necessary to launch the new phase of industrialization.
One of these centers was Rio de Janeiro. Beginning in the late
1940s, Rio de Janeiro's rapid industrialization brought an increased demand for cheap labor, attracting many migrants from
the countryside. In 1940, Rio's population stood at 1.8 million
inhabitants. By 1960 that figure had mushroomed to 3.4 million.[9]

Despite a considerable expansion of the city's economic base, its
infrastructure could barely cope with such a massive influx of
people. Besides, Rio's geography imposed limits to its territorial
expansion. Faced with a severe land shortage and ballooning real
estate prices, poor migrants had two choices: to build precarious
housing clusters (*favelas*) on the rocky cliffs encircling the city, or to
migrate to the Baixada Fluminense's neighboring lowlands.

The increasing demand for space to build affordable housing
for Rio's emerging working class radically changed the Baixada's
land tenure structure. During the eighteenth and nineteenth cen-
turies the Baixada was an inhospitable, malaria-infested expanse

[8] I. Wallerstein, "Semi-peripheral Countries and the Contemporary World Crisis," *Theory and Society* 3 (1976), 461–483. For an application to Brazil, see B. Becker and C. Egler, *Brazil: A New Regional Power in the World-Economy* (Cambridge: Cambridge University Press, 1992).

[9] State Secretariat for Fiscal and Human Settlement Matters, *Atlas fundiário do Rio de Janeiro* (Rio de Janeiro: SEAF, 1991).

of land controlled by big landholders dedicated to the cultivation of sugar cane and fruits. The rising migratory tide toward Rio combined with a collapse of the world market for oranges in the 1940s destroyed this arrangement and led to a chaotic development of available territories and to land speculation.

Two serious consequences ensued from the Baixada Fluminense's disorderly urbanization. First, fierce land competition and sky-rocketing property prices led to conflicts over land tenure, contributing to the region's chronic violence. Secondly, the sale of land parcels was so rapid that neither federal nor municipal authorities had the resources to provide the basic infrastructure that normally accompanies urbanization. As a result, a large percentage of the population does not have access to running water and a functioning sewage system.[10] Sewage runs in open ditches that overflow with the region's constant heavy rains. Given the terrain's tendency to flood, favorable conditions are present for the incubation of endemic infectious diseases such as typhoid fever and dysentery. The health problem is all the more urgent because of the lack of adequate medical installations. The district has one public general hospital with just 246 beds for its 1.6 million people.[11] Otherwise, the population must rely on very expensive private health care. As we have seen in the case of Pedra Bonita, the precariousness of health conditions, and of life in general, in the district is one of the central concerns people bring into the religious field.

Capitalism in the 1980s: stagflation, structural adjustment and socio-economic insecurity

Nova Iguaçu's precarious social conditions worsened significantly during the 1980s due to changes in the capitalist world-system that affected Brazil negatively. In the 1980s Brazil entered a period of

[10] According to the 1980 national demographic census conducted by the Brazilian Institute of Geography and Statistics (IBGE), only 42.8 percent of all households in the district have potable water delivered through the municipal waterworks. The same census reports that only 30.3 percent of households are connected to the municipal sewage system.

[11] Dados estatísticos Baixada Fluminense (Duque de Caxias, Rio de Janeiro: CEPEBA, 1988).

economic crisis. The roots of this crisis go back to the late 1960s and early 1970s, when overcapitalized foreign banks began lending massive amounts of money to governments and state corporations to provide infrastructural support for industrialization and to mitigate the contradictions generated by uneven development. *Prima facie*, these loans were the perfect formula to foster economic growth, for they came at a time of low interest rates, high commodity prices, and relative success in the import-substitution developmental strategy. Between 1968 and 1973, in what has been described as Brazil's "economic miracle," the country registered yearly rates of growth averaging 10 percent.

Nevertheless, since the loans tended to benefit only a small fraction of the productive sector, going toward the construction of large scale, energy-intensive projects, this developmentalist strategy was inherently unstable. The first major disturbance came with the 1973 world recession, brought on by an Arab oil embargo. The five-fold increase in oil prices between 1973 and 1974 was followed by a second shock in 1979. At that point, talk about economic restructuring began to surface, as countries scrambled to move away from energy-intensive, smokestack industries to energy-efficient and high-technology production. By the early 1980s, when a combination of slumping commodity markets and extremely high interests rates began to empty the coffers of developing nations, it was clear that Brazil did not have the economic resources or the productive flexibility to undergo industrial conversion and retooling without considerable social pain and dislocation. The Brazilian government reacted by printing more currency and borrowing more money to cover state deficits and service its more pressing debts. This strategy, in turn, ignited an inflationary spiral and sunk the nation further into debt.[12]

As Brazil's situation replicated itself throughout the Third World, the possibility of massive default threatened the stability of the international banking system. In an effort to control this

[12] As of 1990 Brazil's total external debt stood at $117,760 million, up from $80,875 million in 1981. See *Economic and Social Progress in Latin America: 1991 Report* (Washington, DC: Inter-American Development Bank, 1991), 311. For a good account of the Brazilian case, see W. Braer, *The Brazilian Economy: Growth and Development* (New York: Praeger Publishers, 1989).

dangerous dynamic, multilateral lending organizations such as the International Monetary Fund and the World Bank centralized all credit activities, forcing borrowing nations to adopt a series of "belt-tightening" measures designed to stabilize and restructure their economies before they could receive any more loans. The idea was to reorganize the debtor nations' economies to produce an export-led growth that would bring quick capitalization. With the cash earned, debtor nations could then service their debts.

Typically, these economic reform packages included devaluation of the country's currency, wage freezes, reduced public spending, privatization of state assets, and tax breaks for the productive sectors. The ideology behind these packages was essentially neoliberal, based on the notion that the invisible hand of the market would in the long run bring wealth to developing countries and improve life conditions for their citizens. According to this ideology, the state's social and regulatory role was not only an obstacle to the opening of free markets, but was itself part of the problem insofar as it led to deficit spending. Thus, in the economic adjustments of the 1980s, the social sector, which serves mainly the poor segments of the population, came under assault, while corporations received tax incentives to invest.

In the case of Brazil, these adjustment measures not only failed to alleviate the problem of inflation, but added another deleterious element to it: they shrank the country's economic output, increasing unemployment and fiscal insolvency. In 1985, when Sarney became president, annual inflation stood at 233.6 percent. By 1990, after four major IMF sanctioned packages,[13] consumer price inflation reached a record level of 2,937.8 percent annually.

By the same token, the combination of a tight fiscal and monetary policy, a lack of foreign investment due to the Brazilian economy's volatility, and the massive shift of financial resources to service the debt starved the domestic industrial sector, producing a steady decline in the country's GDP from 8.3 percent in 1985 to 0.3 percent in 1988. After gaining some ground in 1989, the GDP suffered again a sharp 4.4 percent fall in 1990.[14] Parallel to this decline the contribution of the industrial sector to the GDP shrunk

[13] The packages were the "Plano Cruzado" implemented in 1986, the "Plano Bresser" in 1987, the "Plano Verão" in 1989, and the "Plano Collor I" in 1990.
[14] *Jornal do Brasil*, 01/11/91.

from 40.3 percent in 1984 to 25 percent in 1991,[15] indicating the deterioration of the manufacturing sector, the stronghold of the proletariat.

In contrast to the 1970s, when the secondary sector was the main source of new jobs, in the 1980s the distinction fell on the tertiary sector. In 1981, the industrial sector accounted for 23.7 percent of the employed population. By 1990 its share was down to 21.9 percent. In the meantime, the tertiary sector went from 47.1 percent to 55.2 percent during the same period.[16] According to the IBGE, this "tertiarization" of the Brazilian economy is the result, on the one hand, of "the amplification and diversification of commerce and service networks which serve the urban middle and upper classes," and on the other, from the "expansion of precarious activities traditionally included in the so-called informal economy. The notable increase of people engaged in street commerce during the period (91.3 percent increase) provides the best example of this [last component]." Thus, the tertiarization that has occurred in Brazil in the last decade "is associated with the creation or amplification of modern and organized activities as well as the permanence or recreation of unorganized activities, many of which would be linked to survival strategies of some [social] agents."[17] As I discussed above, this mixture of activities characterizes the new configuration of capitalism.

How has this new capitalist configuration affected the life conditions of Brazil's working class? The first serious consequence has been a widening gap between declining wages and an escalating cost of living. In 1958 the minimum wage reached its highest point of $185.90 per month. From 1960 to 1980 it dipped to $147.50. In the next eight years, it fell to its lowest point in recent history: $68.87.[18] In the meantime, prices of basic subsistence goods rose dramatically as part of intense inflationary pressures.

The second consequence is a sharply reduced access to public

---

[15] The Economist Intelligence Unit, *Brazil: A Country Profile 1991–92* (London: EIU, 1991).

[16] According to a study published by the IBGE, between 1981 and 1990, the secondary sector only accounted for 20 percent of the newly employed population. In contrast, the tertiary sector absorbed 78 percent of the newly employed population (a total of 13 million people). J. S. de Oliveira, *O traço da desigualdade social no Brasil* (Rio de Janeiro: IBGE, 1993).

[17] Ibid., 23.

[18] "Tempestade de areia," *Veja* (Rio de Janeiro), April 29, 1990, 19. These figures are adjusted for inflation. Overall, between 1980 and 1988 real wages have fallen 30.9 percent. See *Economic and Social Progress in Latin America: 1991 Report*, 54.

services due to deep cuts in state subsidies for health, education, housing and transportation. For inhabitants of dormitory cities and the poorest neighborhoods like Pedra Bonita, this has translated into an almost total abandonment by the state, shifting the burden of the reproduction of the working class to communities and households. It is in this context that there has been an intensification of domestic work and an increased participation of women in the work force. From 1981 to 1990 women's percentage of participation in the labor force jumped from 31.2 percent to 35.6 percent, with a concomitant decline in male participation. More than 50 percent of the women who have entered the labor force during the last decade are engaged in manual labor that requires low levels of qualification. This situation leads some analysts to conclude that the increased participation of women in the labor market, rather than being a sign of advancement, indicates a general "pauperization, a result of the erosion of the wage level," as women "represent a cheaper work force [that may] contribute to lowering the mean wage of the entire labor force."[19] This reading finds validation in the fact that in the 1980s the richest 10% of the population increased its share of the national income from 44.9 percent to 48.1 percent. The share of the poorest 1 percent, in contrast, fell from 0.9 percent to 0.8 percent.[20]

The country's industrial paralysis has also led to massive layoffs, a trend reinforced by the program to downsize the state and to privatize its assets undertaken by Collor's neoliberal administration. It is estimated that in 1990 alone 312,613 jobs were lost.[21] It is interesting to observe here that, although the rate of unemployment for the secondary sector went from 4.5 percent to 7 percent between 1988 and 1990, the overall unemployment rate has held steady at around 10 percent.[22] This discrepancy can only be explained by rapid growth of the service and informal sectors: job

---

[19] Oliveira, *O traço da desigualdade*, 25.   [20] Ibid., 32.   [21] *Jornal do Brasil*, 12/31/90.

[22] These data come from the *pesquisa mensal de empregos* of the IBGE. A survey conducted by the independent Brazilian Institute of Social and Economic Analyses (IBASE) found that in 1988 Nova Iguaçu's unemployment rate was 27.9 percent, indicating the precariousness of the job market in the district. See IBASE, *O mercado de trabalho em Nova Iguaçu* (Rio de Janeiro: IBASE, 1988). It should be added here that the IBGE counts the self-employed as employed, even if they have not held a job during in the period covered by the survey.

losses in the industrial sector and in the state apparatus have been offset by the creation of low paying, unstable jobs in the tertiary and informal sector. The growth of the informal sector, which encompasses activities not legally or officially recognized by the state, is particularly significant.[23] According to the IBGE, in 1988 the country's informal sector grew 19.8 percent, while the formal sector only expanded 4.9 percent. Several university studies estimate that in 1988 the informal sector employed about 32 million people and accounted for 30 percent to 50 percent of the country's GDP.[24]

Tertiarization of the Brazilian economy and the growth of the informal sector during the 1980s mark a break with the labor practices characteristic of the modernization model of development dominant from the 1940s to the 1970s. As noted earlier, this model was fundamentally centralizing, based on industrial poles sustained by the activities of corporate actors such as the state, and foreign and national capital. This centralization of infrastructure, capital, and the labor force in self-contained poles created favorable conditions for the formation of a cohesive, highly organized working class. In economies of scale, the factory shop floor served as the privileged space for workers to interact and build unions and political parties such as the PTB during the 1940s and the PT and CUT (Central nica dos Trabalhadores) in the late 1970s.

The paradoxical formation of a unified, combative working class out of capitalist dynamics had already been foretold by Marx and Engels in *The Communist Manifesto*. They describe how, under capitalism, workers are extricated from the isolation and rigid bonds of feudalism, are "organized like soldiers" and "crowded into factories" to yield concentrated proletarian masses. Increased exploitation of these masses by the bourgeoisie leads them to organize in trade unions to defend their class interests. This development is "helped on by the improved means of communication that are created by modern industry and that place the

---

[23] Among the economic activities that have grown most rapidly within the informal sector are those connected to the illicit drug trade. As we have seen in Pedra Bonita's case, the growth of this trade has brought negative consequences to urban poor communities such as increasing levels of violence.

[24] See "O Brasil subterrâneo;" and The Economist Intelligence Unit, *Brazil*.

workers of different localities in contact with one another." In this fashion – out of Fordist and Taylorist managerial strategies to regiment the production site's spatio-temporal environment – capitalism begets its own "slayers."[25]

With the ascendancy of the service sector the spatio-temporal arrangements that promote a unified working class disappear.[26] The tertiary sector job market is inherently fluid and highly differentiated. There is no common workplace where workers can meet and build collective organizations and generate a class consciousness. Nor is there a single visible enemy against whom these organizations may mobilize to claim their demands, as was the case during the 1960s and 1970s when the country's industrial elites struck an alliance with an authoritarian-bureaucratic state to foster a developmentalist model. The informal sector, which is heavily concentrated around commerce and service, represents an extreme example of the tertiary sector's fluidity and disjointedness. In it, reliance on part-time, temporary, casual and sub-contracted workers reaches its zenith, producing an extremely high labor turnover and little job security.

More locally, the economic situation in Nova Iguaçu reflects closely the fragmentation and social insecurity at the national level. The configuration of Nova Iguaçu's labor responds to changes in Rio de Janeiro's economic base. Nova Iguaçu has been called Rio's "dormitory" city. People in the district normally work eight hours a day, six days a week.[27] To those eight hours a day one must add anywhere from three to four hours in commuting time, depending on traffic volume. A typical worker, thus, is forced to leave her/his home no later than 6.00 am, not to return until at least 6.00 pm. This consuming schedule leaves little time to engage in any extra-labor activities. In the case of women, this lack of time becomes even more severe, as they very often have to undertake unpaid domestic duties at home after a full day of paid work.

[25] K. Marx and F. Engels, *The Communist Manifesto* (New York: Russell and Russell, 1963), 65.
[26] See Lash and Urry, *The End of Organized Capitalism*, 5.
[27] Although the official workweek was reduced from 48 to 44 hours with the new constitution of 1988, IBASE found that 36 percent of those fully employed work more than 48 hours. Only 10 percent of the fully employed labor force works less than 40 hours a week. *O mercado de trabalho em Nova Iguaçu.*

As a dormitory city, Nova Iguaçu has been subject to Rio's widely fluctuating economic strength. Since the 1940s, when its industrial production constituted 25 percent of the country's total output, Rio de Janeiro has steadily lost its heavy industries to cities like São Paulo and Camaçari. By 1980, the city's industrial production amounted to barely 11 percent of the country's total industrial output.[28] Taking advantage of its natural beauty and its past as the nation's capital, Rio has based its economic fortunes on a strong tertiary sector, anchored upon tourism and public service, and on a relatively solid construction industry.

Although there are no empirical studies documenting changes in Nova Iguaçu's labor market during the 1980s, data collected in the mid-1980s demonstrate the level of tertiarization and informalization of the local economy. According to the IBASE (Brazilian Institute of Social and Economic Studies), 68.2 percent of the district's labor force is "fully employed." Of the fully employed more than 60 percent operate in the tertiary sector, with only 21 percent working in manufacturing industries.[29] For "free-lance" or self-employed workers (28.8 percent of the district's work force) the number of those working in the tertiary sector jumps to 83 percent. Although free lance workers are a diverse group, the great majority of them find jobs through a rapidly expanding informal sector. For 62.4 percent of male freelancers this means working in the construction industry as masons, carpenters and house-painters, or as street vendors. In the case of women, 73 percent offer domestic services. Besides having to operate under inherently unstable arrangements such as sub-contracting, free-lancers also receive exceedingly low wages despite their longer hours. Although 49.6 percent of free lancers work more than 48 hours per week, 88 percent earn less than two minimum wages, compared to 74 percent of the fully employed.

These numbers point to a highly fragmented and stratified

[28] See "O pesadelo de uma bela cidade," *Veja* (Rio de Janeiro), July 18, 1990, 26–33.

[29] "'Fully employed' are all those with a stable job or those who work for an employer, receiving in exchange a stipulated payment for a unit of executed labor." In Nova Iguaçu 60.4 percent of the fully employed work in the tertiary sector. IBASE, *O mercado de trabalho em Nova Iguaçu.*

labor force. At the top of the hierarchy is a minority of fully-employed wage laborers in the industrial sector – the proletariat in classical Marxist terms – followed by those fully employed in the tertiary sector, then free-lancers in the informal sector, and at the bottom a growing underclass (lumpen proletariat) struggling for mere survival. Although all segments of the working poor are vulnerable to changes in the country's economy, particularly as it becomes integrated in the global market through industrial restructuration, the lower the standing in the hierarchy the higher the insecurity and pressure for subsistence. In other words, different locations in the occupational structures yield different life conditions and needs and demand different strategies to meet those needs.

For instance, because workers in the informal sector lack collective agency to bargain with the state and other corporative actors, they must rely on protective networks of familial, friendship and clan-based connections sustained at the micro level (i.e., through everyday, localized face-to-face interaction). Because of this, the sector is not characterized by the concerted activity of collective actors (trade unions, political parties, a mobilized class, etc.) but by aggregate exchanges at the local level where self-help, barter, petty commodity production and commerce, and patron–client arrangements play a central role.

These particular spatio-temporal arrangements thus result in a heterogeneous, stratified, and fragmented working "class," exposed to the unpredictable oscillations of the tertiary and informal economic sectors. Such a fragmentation makes the formation of class consciousness difficult. It tends to render ineffective any appeal to an overarching proletariat, since life conditions (and therefore needs and interests) for workers in the tertiary and informal sectors differ markedly from those of traditional industrial workers. Efforts to reach the working poor through a traditional type of class-based appeal, in this context, are bound to meet serious difficulties.

In sum, during the 1980s, the period when the popular church began to experience a crisis of participation, a complex interplay of economic variables increased socio-economic insecurity for the working class in Brazil and in the metropolitan area of Rio de

Janeiro.[30] This situation forced many in the working class to abandon dreams of upward mobility and to concentrate all efforts on the daily struggle to avoid becoming an underclass.

Legitimation crisis and the persistence of patrimonial politics as a defensive maneuver

The sense of chaos generated by the protracted bout of stagflation is exacerbated by the public perception that collective and national actors are unable to control the situation, let alone transform it. The popular mass mobilizations of 1978, 1985, or even those that surrounded Collor's ousting in 1992 have not improved the lot of the Brazilian poor in any tangible way. Furthermore, attempts to deal with the economic crisis through democratic, electoral processes have thus far failed. Two successive civilian administrations, one elected by direct ballot, have proven unable to set the economy on a secure footing, despite a battery of economic packages.[31]

The failure of these packages points less to shortcomings in the adjustment plans than to the increasing inability of governments to regulate the terms of national growth and development in the face of world-wide economic dynamics (i.e., the internationalization of labor and the globalization of markets). Faced with these global processes, and saddled with a mounting debt, the Brazilian state has lost any legitimacy it derived from a relative redistribution of wealth through its welfare and corporatist policies. Moreover, as the recent Collor affair shows, the country's economic downturn has been accompanied by a severe political crisis. The influence-peddling apparatus set up by the Collor family and associates in the state of Alagoas is but the tip of a vast network of graft and corruption that has colonized virtually all state institutions, implicating various parties and even politicians with presidential ambitions.[32]

---

[30] In the metropolitan area of Rio de Janeiro the percentage of individuals below the poverty line increased from 27.2 percent in 1981 to 32.2 percent in 1990. See Oliveira, *O traço da desigualdade*, 35.

[31] The administration of Social Democrat Fernando Cardoso elected after Collor's impeachment has succeeded in controlling inflation but only at the cost of higher unemployment.

[32] See T. dos Santos, "Brazil's Controlled Purge: The Impeachment of Fernando Collor," *NACLA Report on the Americas*, 27, no. 3 (1993), 17–21.

Confronted by a political system laden with corruption, elitism and paternalism in its various guises,[33] the citizenry, and especially the poorest sectors, has fallen into a kind of tactical, detached, and often cynical individualist pragmatism. That is, for the most part people have accepted the baffling and intractable nature of the economic crisis. Cynicism toward and detachment from politics is only bracketed by ephemeral irruptions of public outrage at the most egregious corruption cases. Yet even those irruptions have become more sparse, as scandal after scandal comes to the surface.

Thus, at the political level, Brazilian society experienced during the 1980s what Habermas calls a legitimation crisis, which arises when all mechanisms for informed, effective political action are blocked and delegitimized. In such a situation citizens become disenfranchised – unable and unwilling to participate in the system. According to Habermas, this legitimation crisis may lead to anomic behaviors that further undermine the patterns of reciprocity and solidarity upon which democratic orders are based.[34]

In the case of Brazil, citizens have not surrendered by any means to a culture of despair and impotence. Rather, they have sought to develop their own "systems of defensive reciprocity"[35] drawing from Brazil's "settled" political culture to advance their own interests. In other words, they have gradually abandoned the utopian drive to change the system *tout court* which characterized the early stages of the democratic transition. Instead they have adopted localized strategies of survival within what has become a bewildering system, exploiting precisely those patterns that have vitiated it.

By creatively using traditional forms of solidarity more typical of agrarian societies, ranging from blood ties and godparenthood, to *coronelismo* (party bossism) and other patron-client relations, the urban poor have tried to secure access to resources which the weakened and corrupt state cannot provide. As in the informal economy, the clever utilization of kinship, friendship, and patron–

---

[33] For an analysis of the role patrimonial politics play in Brazilian politics, see M. Chauí, *Conformismo e resistência* (São Paulo: Brasiliense, 1986).

[34] See J. Habermas, *Legitimation Crisis*, trans. T. McCarthy (Boston: Beacon Press, 1975).

[35] The term is taken from E. Mingione, *Fragmented Societies: A Sociology of Economic Life Beyond the Market Paradigm* (London: T. J. Press, 1991).

client connections occurs at the interstices of the encroaching capitalist system.

Patron–client arrangements have played a central role in Brazilian society ever since the colonial period, as part of an enduring complex of patrimonial politics that also includes populism in the urban setting, millenarian movements in the countryside, and messianism at the national level.[36] In fact, some Brazilian political anthropologists see Collor's election as the latest reincarnation of these deeply ingrained cultural patterns. During the presidential election, Collor portrayed himself as something of a messiah – an energetic, innovative young leader who would singlehandedly deliver the government from the clutches of corruption, would slay the "tiger of inflation" with a single bullet, and usher Brazil into modernity.[37]

If it is true that systems of defensive reciprocity open the poor to manipulation by the country's political elites, as in the case of Collor's election, it would be wrong to impute reliance on them to the alienated, naive, or ideologically confused consciousness of the masses. In fact, it is because they know all too well the stakes and logic of the political game, in which special privileges, corruption, and lack of accountability are rampant that they have to resort to the clever use of political systems stacked heavily against them to achieve concrete gains. After all, even when the power imbalance is extreme, patron–client relations are always open to some manipulation on the part of the client. This is not true of national and international capitalist dynamics before which the individual is usually powerless.

It would also be wrong to brand these systems as *a priori* reproductive. They are above all strategic responses to the immediate needs and pressures generated by intransitive power asymmetries. They represent ingenious ways in which the poor make the best of a reality that appears ever more unyielding. These systems of

---

[36] On populism, see M. Conniff, *Urban Politics in Brazil and the Rise of Populism, 1925–1945* (Pittsburgh, University of Pittsburgh Press, 1981); on millenarianism, see P. Pessar, "Unmasking the Politics of Religion: The Case of Brazilian Millenarianism," *Journal of Latin American Lore* 7, no. 2 (1981), 255–278; on messianism, see M. P. de Queiróz, *Messianismo no Brasil e no Mundo* (São Paulo: Edusp, 1965).

[37] See G. Velho, "A vitória de Collor: Uma análise antropológica;" and L. Goldenstein "Rambo vem aí" *Novos Estudos CEBRAP*, no. 26 (1990), 39–47.

defensive reciprocity represent a prime example of what Bourdieu calls "invention within limits," transformative practice within the constraints of objective conditions.[38]

In some cases, patronage systems might even serve to resist outright exploitation and manipulation by the capitalist system or even the political patron himself. Clients may deploy parasitic and free-rider tactics, setting patrons against each other and feigning loyalty after receiving favors. Many roads have been paved, schools built and waterworks installed in poor neighborhoods in the greater metropolitan area of Rio through the astute utilization of competition among ward bosses for votes. Robert Gay, for instance, documents how the skillful use of clientelist politics by a neighborhood association's president in the western part of the city secured special benefits which other surrounding poor communities could not attain. According to Gay, "[d]evoid of economic resources and of the political power to obtain them, clientelist politics has offered and continues to offer the urban poor . . . a rare opportunity for material gain." He adds that, despite the on-going democratization process, clientelism will continue "to represent a relatively attractive and rational proposition" for the poor "until there is a fairly dramatic shift in the distribution of economic and political power in Brazil."[39]

Certainly, the recurring use of personal, local survival tactics and reliance of patron–client arrangements tends to weaken collective action toward structural change. Since these tactics issue from a (well-founded) perception that reality is in a state of crisis, that there exists a scarcity of resources, they foster a type of competitive individualism among the poor where each one is for him/herself. Each individual must use his/her own personal resources and connections (i.e. social capital) to survive regardless of the consequences for society as a whole.

Nancy Scheper-Hughes has observed this individualist retrenchment among the rural poor in northeastern Brazil. She depicts an attitude of rampant suspicion and mistrust among

[38] Bourdieu, *Outline of a Theory of Practice*, 96–158.
[39] R. Gay, "Community Organization and Clientelist Politics in Contemporary Brazil: A Case Study from Suburban Rio de Janeiro," *International Journal of Urban and Regional Research* 14, no. 4 (1990), 648–666.

community inhabitants, who adopt "defensive, individual, not aggressive, collective practices" that "may temporarily divert the more organized power plays of the *patrão* [boss] . . . [but] do not challenge the definition of the political economic situation." Yet she refuses to blame the poor for this response. In her view, "it is too much to expect the people of the Alto [the community she studied] to organize collectively when chronic scarcity makes individually negotiated relations of dependence on myriad political and personal bosses in town a necessary survival tactic."[40] Thus, while patrimonial politics can help the poor to survive under precarious conditions, it contributes to the further fragmentation of the working class by appealing to individual and local interests.

LIFE CONDITIONS SINCE THE 1980s: EXPLAINING PEDRA BONITA'S CASE

Having described life conditions in Brazil and Nova Iguaçu during the 1980s, we can now ask what obstacles these conditions create for the reception of progressive Catholicism's utopian message and for the application of the popular church's pastoral methodology among the poor. More specifically, how do they shed light on the decline of Pedra Bonita's CEB?

Restructuring everyday life

The first obstacle is the time constraint generated by the 48-hour work schedule. Participation in CEBs requires considerable free time for the lay person to undertake various religious activities (i.e., the preparation and execution of liturgical celebrations, baptisms, catechism classes and evangelization work) and to become involved in social and political activities in the neighborhood. The intensification of domestic work, the widespread practice of "moonlighting," and the increased percentage of women in the labor force during the 1980s, have made it increasingly difficult for the working poor to fulfill this requirement.

---

[40] Scheper-Hughes, *Death without Weeping*, 472.

The pastoral-pedagogic approach of the CEBs runs counter to the drastic reduction of leisure time for the working poor. It calls for a slow process of consciousness-raising, where the believers learn to draw the full implications of the faith-life link gradually, through sustained religio-political action and participation in study groups with members of their community, regional gatherings with other CEBs, retreats, seminars and conferences with pastoral agents. The transformation of CEB members into active social and religious actors, working to change societal conditions that distort relations with God, is ongoing. It requires an ascending spiral of engagement and critical reflection that, in the classical model of the CEB, takes the member from bread and butter issues in his/her immediate surroundings to full, informed involvement in larger organizations (i.e., political parties, trade unions, etc.) dealing with structural matters.

The long trajectory from the micro to the macro, from partial knowledge of immediate effects to a deeper understanding of the root causes of social sin, is what Brazilian Catholic activists call the *caminhada*. The successes and tribulations of the *caminhada* provide the inspiration and testing ground for the believers to renew their faith and strengthen their commitment. At a deeper level, the *caminhada* represents the defining metaphor of the Brazilian popular church's emancipatory efforts, for in the absence of an established revolutionary tradition as in the case of Nicaragua, the arduous process of self-empowerment among the poor becomes the central sign of transcendence, the only augur of things to come in the reign of God. Indeed, for Father José, a national assistant for the ACO, one of "the signs of the Kingdom" is "to see people grow and also hold steady and persevere, because the life of our suffering people is very difficult." The small victories in the *caminhada* (i.e., the roads paved, the bus service opened, the schools built) give the dispossessed an intimation of what a society built according Christian principles could be.

Reduction of working-class leisure time threatens to break the ascending spiral of praxis and reflection that drives the *caminhada* by limiting engagement in CEB and neighborhood activities. Pedra Bonita's Gerson remembers a time when more people participated in the popular movement. Now, he thinks that

People are getting discouraged and tired day by day. And that affects the community. It is unemployment I believe. Because they had more job opportunities years ago. Now there's more unemployment. The only thing there is underemployment, being a street vendor [*camelo*] and stuff like that. And street vendors don't have time because every day they have to go to Rio very early in the morning to be there before [commuting] workers arrive, because it is the worker who buys stuff from them. And then in the afternoon they have to stay there late, until all workers have returned from work. So they don't have time to come to a meeting of the neighborhood association. And they are also tired. So unemployment affects everything.

As thus explained, this problem is all the more serious for women, the backbone of base communities, for, in addition to time constraints generated by the work schedule and by commuting, worsening economic conditions in the district have forced them to enter the labor force in greater numbers, and to intensify domestic work in order to ensure the survival of their households. As we saw in Otília's case in Pedra Bonita, the responsibility for putting food on the table falls increasingly on women. They must also find ways to manage their households more creatively and efficiently, spending more time and energy mending and repairing their meager belongings and shopping for cheaper staples. The constant concern for making ends meet takes an emotional and psychological toll: at the end of the day there is little strength to undertake extra-household activities.[41] Otília describes the situation of women in her community thus:

Our community works slowly because we are the ones who work in it, we the suffering people of the neighborhood. The majority of women who participate in the community work, some are seamstresses, some are maids, things like that. That means that we have to work to help at home, because if only the husband works it doesn't cut it. So the community works to the extent that we can make it work. There are very few people who can take on a [community] task. It is difficult to find people available to work in the community.

[41] On the effects of the economic crisis and structural adjustment programs on women, see L. Benería and S. Feldman, *Unequal Burden: Economic Crisis, Persistent Poverty, and Women's Work* (Boulder, CO: Westview Press, 1992); J. Vickers, ed., *Women and the World Economic Crisis* (London: Zed Books, 1991); and C. Barroso and T. Amado, "The Impact of the Crisis upon Poor Women's Health: The Case of Brazil," in *The Invisible Adjustment: Poor Women and the Economic Crisis* (Santiago: UNICEF, 1989).

The case of Ana provides a good example of the plight of women as they are absorbed into the labor force, particularly through an export-oriented, putting-out system of production, the kind of hybrid of 'post-Fordist' and 'artisanal' forms of production that characterizes contemporary capitalism.

I am a seamstress, so I pick some work on Monday, let's say 50 pieces of clothing. I come home and work, work, work and the next Monday I have to have that lot ready to go there [the central factory] and hand it in. If I don't have it ready by that day they cut 20 percent [of my wage]. So if I pick up some homework on Monday and have a meeting of the [neighborhood] association on Wednesday, I have to put my work away. But since I'm not being paid a fixed salary every month, since I'm being paid by what I produce, I lose money.

Other households fare no better. Otília finds her situation at home very difficult:

Even with my daughter working, things are tight. She has to pay electricity, cooking gas, almost everything at home. We are not even buying any clothes. There are times when she owes already half of her next pay check. Naturally, everything I earn sewing goes to household expenses. I take 5,000 Cruzeiros and go to the market, and even looking for bargains [*rebuscando*] the money doesn't go too far. I buy rice, beans, cooking oil and maybe some other cooking item and the money is gone. But thank God we've always had food. I know a family with six children that lives in the next street. The wife is pregnant and the husband's salary is not enough to feed the children for a week! They starve! When I see that I even lose the desire to eat.

Under these precarious conditions the pastoral strategy of participation and consciousness-raising that aims at giving the poor the tools to challenge social injustice ends up unfortunately targeting only those households with enough economic stability and time flexibility to sustain the long *caminhada*. In Pedra Bonita, these households are in the minority, a fact that may explain the community's excessive reliance on a small nucleus of activists and the difficulty in generating new leadership when pastoral changes alienated that nucleus.

Fragmentation of the district's working class

A second obstacle to CEB growth arises from the transformations of the district's occupational structure and the resulting disarticulation of and stratification within the working class. To challenge social conditions that distort individuals' relations with God and their own humanity, the popular church seeks to train, through various consciousness-raising techniques, local organic intellectuals. These grassroots intellectuals, in turn, educate their neighbors and fellow workers, helping them to break the ideological bondage generated by an internalization of ruling-class values and interests. It is "the poor educating the poor," in Ernesto's words, to overcome the patterns that divide them and make them focus on egotistical and short-term gains. Once poor people understand themselves as a group with their own culture and interests, they will move from being a class-in-itself to a class-for-itself. Then, inspired by Judeo-Christian values of justice and equality, they will pursue singlemindedly their real interest: to transform the structures that generate social sin. This is why pastoral agents describe local leaders trained by the popular church as a "leaven": they are the ones who make the masses rise.

As we saw in chapter 1, this type of intervention in the political arena is informed by a (Marxist) conception of the poor as dormant collective social actor with a single set of interests and a unified worldview readily mobilizable as inequalities produced by the capitalist system escalate. This conception is central in the eschatology of the popular church and liberation theology. We have seen, however, that the economic crisis in the district has fragmented the working class, creating a hierarchy of fractions, each with its own life conditions, needs and expectations. Increased rates of unemployment and underemployment, together with the growth of the heterogeneous service and informal sectors, have imposed a multiplicity of spatio-temporal pressures and economic pressures for the district's working poor that preclude any appeal to a unified working class with a single collective interest.

The emerging configuration of the district's labor force, thus, poses a direct challenge to the popular church's strategy of connecting faith with collective political praxis, especially when the key element in making this link, the local, lay organic intellectuals, tends to come from households with relative economic stability and labor flexibility. Because of the economic crisis fewer and fewer households enjoy even this relative stability and flexibility.

According to Hewitt, the claim that "CEB are exclusively or even primarily lower-class," does not correspond with reality on the ground. This claim

suggests that the CEBs proliferate evenly throughout all sectors of the poor. Yet this is not the case. In actuality, they tend to find most fertile ground among the working poor – the working classes – as opposed to the poorest of the poor. They tend to grow, in other words, among those who are relatively, as opposed to absolutely deprived. Among the former, it would seem, there is a greater appreciation of the kinds of spiritual, and especially, material benefits that the CEBs can offer . . . Among the latter, group life, where it exists at all, is extremely fragile. This is because, as authors such as Barreiro and Ireland have pointed out, those who are already absolutely deprived have frequently lost all hope of ever removing themselves from their disadvantaged situation.[42]

Hewitt's observations in São Paulo are corroborated by Mariz's work in the outskirts of Recife, Burdick's in Duque de Caxias, and Brandão's in Itapira.[43] In the base communities he studied, Burdick, for example, found a tendency "not toward incorporation, but exclusion of the locally least well-off segments of the working class."[44]

In contrast, Francisco Rolim's analysis of CEBs in the greater metropolitan area of Vitória suggests that CEBs are not "homogeneous" or "exclusionary," for they include members with a multiplicity of socio-economic situations. Rolim even finds that most CEB members who are employed work in the service sector and not in industry.[45]

How then do we reconcile these two conflicting sets of data? The use of the metaphor of "polycentric web" to describe the community might help us overcome this contradiction. Rolim is correct in stressing the heterogeneity of CEB membership. In Pedra Bonita, the base community's periphery is loosely constituted by individuals and households with different levels of involvement and commitment to community life. This multiplicity of patterns of participation parallels a plurality of life conditions.

---

[42] Hewitt, *Base Christian Communities and Social Change in Brazil*, 66.
[43] See Mariz, *Coping with Poverty*, 42–50; Burdick, *Looking for God in Brazil*, 68–86; and C. R. Brandão, *Os deuses do povo* (São Paulo: Paulinas, 1980), 77–78.
[44] Burdick, *Looking for God in Brazil*, 69.
[45] F. C. Rolim, *Religião e classes populares* (Petrópolis: Vozes, 1980), 63–93.

Pedra Bonita shows that where Hewitt, Mariz, and Burdick may be right is in regard to the CEB nucleus, which does indeed tend to be more homogeneous and self-contained. All the households that formed the base community core in Pedra Bonita can be considered "poor, but with basic needs covered."[46] They all have at least one person employed full time for wages and several other members contributing to the pool. The men among those working full time either have been or are currently employed by industrial or construction firms. Women are either sub-contracted as seamstresses or work as maids in Nova Iguaçu's more affluent neighborhoods or in petty commodity production for community consumption. Due to the consciousness-raising efforts of pastoral agents, almost all those who work have their social security cards. Household incomes in the community nucleus range from two to five minimum wages, with an average of 2.6. This figure compares favorably with those in the district at large where the average income is 2.3, and where 69 percent of the population earn less than two minimum wages.[47]

We may conclude, therefore, that the nucleus of Pedra Bonita's CEB consists predominantly of individuals in the top two echelons of the occupational structure for the district's working poor (i.e., full-time employed in the manufacturing sector and full-time employed in the tertiary sector), with increasing numbers in the third rung (part-time free-lance workers) as the financial situation of households deteriorates.

Given this social differentiation, the CEB nucleus cannot but stand apart from the rest of the base community and the neighborhood as a relatively privileged group. The distance generated interferes with the pastoral work of the CEB leadership in the *bairro*, making it difficult to foster collective mobilization through an appeal to class solidarity.

The popular church's pastoral methodology unintentionally aggravates the distance between CEB organic intellectuals and the rest of the neighborhood. As we saw, the *caminhada* requires

[46] I borrow this category from Benería's work on Mexican households. See L. Benería, "The Mexican Debt Crisis: Restructuring the Economy and the Household," in Benería and Feldman, *Unequal Burden*.

[47] CEPEBA, *Dados Baixada Fluminense.*

extensive training. A typical popular education activity in Nova Iguaçu's retreat center costs 1/10 of the monthly minimum wage per day for lodging and food, with transportation not included. It is not unusual for retreats to take place over the weekend, so that, besides losing Saturday as a potential day of work, participants spend at least 0.3 minimum wages in the span of a few days. According to Leda, one of the pastoral agents in Nova Iguaçu's retreat center, with 68 percent of the population in the district earning less that 2 minimum wages, the retreat becomes "automatically inaccessible to the masses [*povão*]. Retreats are designed more for *liberados*."[48]

Cognizant that not all workers can spend 15 percent of their monthly income on a weekend retreat, movements within the popular church often pay travel and lodging expenses for participants. However, this practice is becoming more difficult as the movements themselves feel the pinch of the economic crisis. Ana, ACO's national treasurer, worries about the financial situation of the movement:

It concerns me because the main context in which we can bring activists together is the seminars: the national, regional and city-wide seminars. There is where ACO's work is developed [*se desdobra*], where you see your comrades from other places, where you exchange experiences with them. And at the moment we in the movement don't have the capacity to pay for the seminars. The workers – and people in general – don't have the financial resources to participate in the seminars. So, all that is forcing us to reduce the number of seminars. We have even reduced the length of some seminars. The regional, for example, used to be two-days long; now it's just one day. We didn't have money to pay for two days.

Those who can undergo leadership training and enter the ascending spiral of consciousness-raising will develop, through the various pedagogical tools of popular education, their own coherent

---

[48] *Liberados* are working-class persons hired by the various movements within the *igreja popular* to work full time for the cause. The goal is to allow members of the working poor to have the time and space to develop their leadership skills by attending study groups and training seminars and by supporting community initiatives throughout the region. In the case of the ACO, the movement normally employs between 3–5 *liberados* per year, each for a period no longer than 3 years. Pedra Bonita's Gerson served as one of those *liberados*.

worldview. They will gradually learn to view their immediate surroundings in more macro-structural terms, using newly acquired analytic categories to, as Paulo Freire says, "name their own reality." This small group turns into a "popular elite," as it were, with a language that is no longer the masses'. The latter, rather than articulating a time-consuming global critique of the system that oppresses them, focus their efforts on negotiating the more pressing effects of the economic crisis. Thus, a split emerges at the base between the leaven, which takes a more long-term, structural view of social problems, and the masses who are struggling to survive day-to-day. This gap limits the popular church's impact on the poor because it tends to isolate CEB nuclei, transforming them into closed groups with total responsibility for pastoral work among the poor by virtue of the CEB lay leaders' relatively more stable material conditions of existence.

Furthermore, the case of Pedra Bonita shows that class fragmentation has occurred not only within the neighborhood's working poor, but also in the parish as a whole. As the economic situation of the district has deteriorated, Nova Iguaçu's small middle class has also had to make adjustments. With the central, most urbanized part of the district becoming more expensive and crowded, many have had to move toward the periphery of the city where they can still enjoy relatively good services at lower costs. There they have introduced their quite distinctive lower middle class concerns, which stand in tension with those of the working poor with whom they share parish space and resources. This is why the shift in pastoral priorities brought by the Irish priests favoring Ocampo had such a detrimental effect on Pedra Bonita's CEB.

It is clear, then, that Nova Iguaçu's *igreja popular* cannot afford to continue "ontologizing" the poor as if they were a unified, homogeneous force and trying to reach "it" through a popular elite with its own particular perceptions, interests, and needs. Given the increasing fragmentation of and stratification within the working "class," the pastoral strategy of small "conscientized" groups threatens to widen the gap between the popular church and the variety of experiences that make up the world of the poor. To be able to understand these experiences and to design pastoral strategies that respond to them the popular church must contextualize its use of class analysis.

Immediatism and pragmatic individualism as favored survival strategies of the urban poor

One of the most common complaints CEB members in Pedra Bonita have of neighbors who are reluctant to participate in community activities is that their thinking is heavily colored by immediatism and accommodation (*comodismo*). According to Teresa, people are either "only thinking day to day; they don't think about tomorrow, what is going to happen to them in the future," or "settle themselves [*se acomodão*] at home, and they don't want to go out to meetings, to go to mass, to do a task in the community."

Although CEB members recognize the stranglehold that the economic situation has placed on the working poor, they tend to attribute this immediatism and *comodismo* to a *falta de consciência* (lack of consciousness). Otília asks rhetorically: "[If] I know that there is a group within the community, in the church, where I can achieve freedom, why is it that I don't go? Because I don't want to. [It is a] lack of consciousness. It is not good." Cléa is even more categorical:

There is a lot of poverty, and the poverty that we see more often is a poverty of ideas. Brazilians are too weak. It's only work, work and then stay at home. I believe that once a person becomes conscious [*toma consciência*], even if s/he comes tired from work s/he will find strength to look for something else. Her/his rights are going away! S/he is receiving a low wage. So s/he has to search. That's the difficulty in the neighborhood: to search together with people who are aware, who enter in an organization that belongs [*corresponde*] to the poor.

Pedra Bonita's base community activists are here, not only blaming the victim, but also inadvertently engaging in a bit of circular thinking. To achieve awareness, to awake to the real causes behind one's plight, one must participate in consciousness-raising activities in the CEB. But then, consciousness is also a precondition to show interest in CEB activities. So how can one break the never-ending cycle of immediatism and accommodation among the poor?

Community activists get trapped in this Catch-22 situation because they give too much weight to lack of consciousness as the cause for the paucity of collective action among the poor. I argue that the socio-economic insecurity created by stagflation and the restructuration of the Brazilian economy have forced the urban poor to focus on the present and to give priority to the specific demands of day-to-day survival. This leaves little breathing space for them to step back and analyze, let alone act effectively on, macro-processes. In the context of an uncontrollable inflationary spiral and the ever-present threat of job loss, it is not only rational and strategic to focus on the now; it almost becomes a necessity. Gerson understands this situation very well:

People complain that they have to struggle to survive. So they don't have time for anything else; they don't have time to think anymore. If you try, it doesn't do any good. People are tired, all tense [*nervosos*] about the situation. Instead of participating more in the movement, people get weaker and weaker. They get discouraged, they eat less. They think only about food, about securing a plate of food. Then they get weaker, discouraged, and begin to deny their comrades.

Still, he continues to think that people are complacent. "When there is an urgent need there is a lot of talk but very little action. When we call people for a meeting they don't have time. So that means that we [the community nucleus] are left with the responsibility." Thus, he is caught between empathy and contempt for his fellow neighbors, a tension that disrupts the effectiveness of his work as an organic intellectual.

In Nova Iguaçu insecurity is not restricted to the economic field; it assumes many forms. What all these forms have in common is that they pose a threat to the integrity of the body. Whether it is gang violence, the wear and tear of long working hours, disease or premature death, there is a constant assault on the bodies of the urban poor. To make matters worse, there are no adequate resources and mechanisms to deal with the debilitating effects of this brutal assault. The few medical facilities in the district are in deplorable conditions. The police are not only conspicuously absent from poor neighborhoods, but they have become just another vigilante group vying for power with local gangs and, in many cases, exploiting communities.

This insecurity may help explain the quest for miracle cures among the urban poor. It also sheds light on the persistence of practices common to popular Catholicism: prayers to insulate the body against disease and accidents and vows to saints. In the absence of this-worldly solutions to problems of health, hunger and violence, the poor have to turn to other-worldly answers. In my concluding chapter, I shall argue that the popular church needs to devise pastoral strategies to address the physical and spiritual needs – the pressures upon the body – created by the worsening life conditions during the 1980s.

CEB members tend to see excessive reliance on prayers, *promessas*, and miracle cures as an example either of *comodismo* or of alienation. It is part of a "pathological religion" that, as Father Mario, an assistant in the ACO pastoral team, says

[t]hrows problems up to the sky for God to solve them. [It is a religion] that diverts the person from the struggle and makes him think that just believing in God . . . will solve everything. But Jesus Christ showed very clearly that without participation from the person there is no solution to people's problems. Because waiting for everything to come from God is in a way to be presumptuous. "You jump down from the top of the temple because God has assured you that the angels will catch you down there. Get rid of your walking stick and your eyeglasses; God is going to cure you."

Instead of shifting the responsibility for one's fate to God, CEB members emphasize the power the poor have to transform reality when they act as a group, in community. In Cléa's words: "The richness of the community is there, in the fact that God is in everyone of us. It is like a clockwork that works slowly. And we see the combined force of each gear. It is not by becoming divided that one advances. If we lose unity we become poor again."

Transforming reality means knowing the root causes of the conditions that make the poor resort to divine help in the first place. It means changing the human institutions that have failed the poor. That is the logic behind Cléa's assertion that "what's important is not to give [the poor] a fish, but to teach them how to fish." This transformation involves, nevertheless, a long and arduous process of political involvement. In the meantime, the effects of the economic crises and the conditions of life in the district continue to demand urgent solutions, even if these are merely symbolic. With its emphasis on correcting the causes of the poor's plight, rather than addressing its immediate manifestations, the popular church loses sight of pressures, needs, and dreams as felt on the ground. According to Father José of the ACO, there is

a certain neglect from the [base] communities of certain concrete problems. That is, at the risk of being unfair to the communities by being too simplistic, I would say that they have up to now insisted on organizing to fight against the causes of evil and maybe other groups like the Pentecostals have taken care or have sought to deal with the consequences of evil. I believe we can't stop fighting against the causes, but at the same time it is necessary to follow [*acompanhar*] the consequences. But, maybe that is not too easy.

Father Patrício is even more blunt in his assessment of the shortcomings of the *igreja popular* in the diocese:

We, in recent years, have not dealt with the felt needs of the people. We have dealt or try to deal with what we think are the real needs. But the people don't know their real needs. And we are trying to tell them. We are telling them that they need to transform society, that they need to organize together and all that sort of stuff. And they are sort of saying: "yeah, yeah *padre*, you're a nice man." Their felt needs is what's down here [he points to his stomach] and we haven't been dealing with those. Their felt need is that their child is sick, they need a cure, when are they going to get it? They go to the *casa de benção*, there they have a cure for sick children. The husband is an alcoholic, they have to get a cure for that too. In the *Igreja Universal*, they have all their stuff out for the different needs, the felt needs of the people. We [Catholics] haven't got those.

As we saw in the case of Ana and Otília in Pedra Bonita, proper pastoral attention to the felt needs of the poor (i.e., sickness and premature death) are central to conversion to base community life. Vitória and Gabriela, the Pedra Bonita's new CEB leaders, understand this, but due to the ineffectiveness of the newly formed community council, which in turn resulted from a confluence of pastoral changes and economic factors, they have not been able to fill this gap. They have been unable to maintain the level of presence in the neighborhood achieved by evangelization groups established by the French priests.

In sum, the worsening situation of the urban poor has produced what Offe describes as "an interruption of the links between short- and long-term perspectives,"[49] with the root causes of social evil appearing ever more baffling and beyond control, while the conse- quences have thrust themselves into the forefront of the urban poor's field of experience. This interruption obstructs any appeal to the poor to transcend their "felt needs" to focus on their "real needs." Since this transcendence is central to the popular church's pastoral methodology of engagement and self-empowerment, it is not surprising to see CEBs and other progressive Catholic initiat- ives on the ground having difficulties connecting with the urban poor.

Perhaps the popular church's strategy of attacking the structural foundations of social evil would be successful in mobilizing the various segments of the impoverished masses if it were able to bring about radical changes in the precarious conditions under which they live. However, aside from specific gains like a paved road or running water for the neighborhood, achieved as we saw in Pedra Bonita after long and frustrating struggles with local and municipal authorities, it has not been able to eradicate the causes of injustice and economic inequality. In fact, the lot of the poor has worsened considerably. Even concrete gains are in constant danger of being coopted and have become increasingly difficult to wrest from a weakened state. It has now become easier to obtain these gains through the clever manipulation of systems of defens- ive reciprocity, and the exploitation of clientelist politics. With this we come to the fourth obstacle faced by the popular church in the district.

Dependence on and cooptation by clientelist politics

When Otília bemoans the fact that while the community has "awareness to help others" the "majority of the poor are egotisti- cal, they don't want to share with others," she is simply pointing to

---

[49] Offe, *Disorganized Capitalism*.

immediatism's twin: individualism. In his work on urban social movements, Manuel Castells contends that under the pressure of advanced capitalism, movements tend to retrench to the local arena. According to Castells,

> faced by an overpowered labour movement, an omnipresent one-way communication system indifferent to cultural identities, an all-powerful centralized state loosely governed by unreliable political parties, a structural economic crisis, cultural uncertainty, and the likelihood of nuclear war, people go home. Most withdraw individually, but the crucial, active minority, anxious to retaliate, organize themselves on their local turf. . . So when people find themselves unable to control the world, they simply shrink the world to the size of their community.[50]

In Brazil's "savage capitalism" of the 1980s, however, even that "crucial, active minority" experienced serious difficulties in mobilizing effectively, as time and economic resources necessary to undertake a sustained struggle at the local level became ever more scarce. During the last decade there was, then, a further retrenchment from the community-local to the household-local, with the individual becoming increasingly preoccupied about his/her own survival and that of his/her immediate kin.

Immediatism and individualism open the urban poor to manipulation and cooptation from local patrons and politicians. As Father José reckons, in the face of a fiscally-insolvent state and a corrupt and elitist political system "it is always easier to go for the individual solution than to search for one as a group. People say to themselves: 'Ah! Eu me viro com o meu santo.'"[51] Looking for individual solutions means putting to work creatively personal economic, political and cultural resources at hand to reach one's goals. Since those resources are very limited in the case of the urban poor, they must use them in such a way as to maximize their pay-off. This strategic use of resources is what lies behind communal self-help initiatives such as the proliferation of *comedores populares* or *ollas comunes* (soup kitchens) and *creches* (community childcare

---

[50] See M. Castells, *The City and the Grassroots* (Berkeley: University of California Press, 1983), 330–331.
[51] Literally, "I will stick with my own saint," which can be more idiomatically rendered as "I am looking out for number one."

centers).[52] It is also what lies behind the persistence of pragmatic and individualist reliance on clientelist politics to gain favors. Since clientelism is one of the few established and effective resources at hand in the "settled" culture, it must be used.

As Robert Gay argues, power inequalities in Brazilian society make reliance on patron-client relations a convenient, cost-effective option for the poor to extract some concrete benefits from the political elites. It is a cost-effective option in relation to the popular church's proposed model of political action because it does not demand engagement in an uncertain, long-term drive to raise consciousness among community members and to organize them to demand their rights.

Although Pedra Bonita's community leaders understand the need to deal with clientelism, as it is part of Brazil's political culture, they find that poor people's reliance on patronage is the product of short-sightedness, alienation, and "political illiteracy." They condemn clientelism because it leads to dependence, passivity, and division among the poor. For them, clientelism only reproduces the country's unjust power structure. Gerson and Ernesto provide an example of the CEB's ambivalence toward clientelism. Assessing the victory the community scored in bringing a bus service to the neighborhood by setting two opposing transportation companies against each other, Gerson believes that

[We] [the poor] have to play their politics a bit. There is no way around it. It's OK if we have to do it. If you want to get things for the people you can't reject their politics; you have to see what they offer. But our interest is with the needs of the people, not with their [the politicians'] politics, not with benefitting ourselves.

Yet, according to Ernesto, clientelism and assistentialism are the main reasons why the popular movement has not prospered in Brazil.

It is the politics of the dominant classes. When they perceive that popular movements are becoming a good means to take power, they invent their own strategies. They invent assistentialism ... milk

---

[52] See W. McFerren "The Politics of Bolivia's Economic Crisis: Survival Strategies of Displaced Tin-Mining Households," in Benería and Feldman, *Unequal Burden*.

vouchers, transportation vouchers coming from above. They create the image that the people have everything. So when we try to grow from below we can't because they are producing the image from above that they are giving us everything, that the people don't need to ask for anything else.

Ernesto's denunciation of the damage wrought by assistentialism and clientelism is justified. Nonetheless, the fact remains that given the desperate economic situation and the vitiated political culture in the country, the *igreja popular* cannot take an overly critical stance when the poor opt for these top-down strategies. A blanket rejection of direct aid to the urban poor on the basis of an elitist use of the concepts of class interest and alienation risks losing sight of the concreteness of individual suffering, of the human faces behind the crisis. So, as in the case of real versus felt needs, the popular church must strike a difficult balance: this time, between critique of and empathy for the use of patronage and individual strategies among the urban poor. This balance has so far proved elusive.

The troubles of the popular church go beyond the existence of strategic, utilitarian approach to politics among the urban poor. As Mainwaring has demonstrated, not all the consequences of the political transition in Brazil during the 1980s have been advantageous to the popular church and other grassroots movements.[53] In the confusing and fragmented world of Brazilian partisan politics, the church can no longer claim to be the privileged oppositional actor facing a clearly identifiable enemy. Confronted with a veritable menu of political options, many of the social activists that energized popular church initiatives during the military regime have moved on to other settings where they can pursue their goals more effectively, without having to contend with an increasingly conservative church hierarchy.

In addition to this membership drain and "secularization of the political arena," the transition to democracy has not changed the business of government in any substantial way. As the case of Collor shows, in the public mind politics continues to be synonymous with corruption and privilege for a small elite. Thus, the

---

[53] Mainwaring, "Grassroots Popular Movements and the Struggle for Democracy."

popular church's attempts to link faith with politics has met resistance, not because people oppose mixing the sacred with the secular, as if they were utterly separate (as the conservative wing of the Catholic Church claims), but because politics carries extremely negative connotations. As journalist Marcelo Coelho writes, Brazil is suffering an acute "crisis of belief [*um desespero de fé*]. It was easier when we believed in revolution, in a class movement capable of resolving Brazil's social problems by itself. [But] there is now a generalized disillusionment [*desencanto*] with all forms of political intervention in the strict sense."[54] This crisis is felt among grassroots activists and ordinary citizens alike. Gerson notes that "[p]eople don't believe in anything anymore." This vacuum weakens the evangelical and political appeal that lies behind the faith-life link.

The crisis of belief brings us to the last obstacle which life conditions in the neighborhood impose on the utopian vision of the *igreja popular*.

The erosion of this-worldly transcendence

As I showed in chapter 1 in my discussion of the ideological bases of the *igreja popular*, both liberation theology and CEBs preserve Thomistic voluntarism as reinterpreted by the modernist humanism of Vatican II and Medellín, stressing the effectiveness and relevance of human action in the scheme of things. The notion that divine law informs human *praxis* and that there is an underlying harmonious order dictated by God inspires liberationist critiques of the status quo. In the face of a broken human world full of contradictions, divine order remains a utopian horizon and an unfulfilled *telos*. Human actions that seek to redress injustices are simultaneously the signs and instruments of a latent fullness that will find a complete expression and fulfillment at the end of times. This is what Gutiérrez means by the affirmation that "there is only one history – a 'Christo-finalized' history"

. . . there are not two histories, one profane and one sacred, "juxtaposed" or "closely linked." Rather there is only one human destiny, irreversibly

---

[54] M. Coelho, "Desespero de fé fortalece campanha da fome," *Folha de São Paulo*, August 9, 1993.

assumed by Christ, the Lord of history. The history of salvation is the very heart of human history . . .

Temporal progress – or to avoid this aseptic term, the liberation of man [*sic*] – and the growth of the Kingdom both are directed toward complete communion of men with God, and of men among themselves. They have the same goal, but they do not follow parallel roads, not even convergent ones. The growth of the Kingdom is a process which occurs historically *in* liberation, insofar as liberation means a greater fulfillment of man.[55]

If "the historical, political liberating event *is* the growth of the Kingdom," then CEBs, struggling towards that liberating events are, "coparticipants in [their] own salvation." This is the heart of the popular church's re-enchantment of the world: placing human action within a meaning-giving eschatological horizon. By making struggles to achieve justice in the present a constitutive element of the march [*caminhada*] toward the reign of God, the popular church projects emancipatory human action onto a cosmic plane.

But what happens when that historical, political liberating event becomes an improbable dream? What happens when temporal progress appears to have been reversed, when the actions of the "coparticipants" in salvific work do not seem to be making any headway toward the creation of a "just society and a new man [*sic*]"? What happens when the "signs of the times" do not point to a Latin America "in the midst of a full-blown process of revolutionary ferment," but to one barely coping with the onerous effects of a savage, smugly triumphant capitalism? What happens when the poor – "the protagonists of liberation" – continue to lose control of their destiny as capitalism undergoes yet another cycle of globalization and deepening?

What one finds among the urban poor in Brazil, even among those active politically, is an increasing tendency to redefine the relationship between human and sacred history. As intra-historical transcendence becomes ever more difficult to sustain, people are increasingly forced to focus on day-to-day survival and to turn to other-worldly forms of transcendence. As human praxis appears less capable of addressing the problem of evil, more people place their desperate lives in the hands of God. Amélia's attitude is typical:

[55] Gutiérrez, *A Theology of Liberation*, 153 and 177.

I believe that the poor live because God protects them. I feel it inside myself. I have had some difficult spots in my life, but God helps. One continues along the same road and He gives one an easier spot. And that's how we walk the path of life. The poor live with God's protection, He gives them cunning for them to survive. There is a God in heaven and we have to have faith in Him.

Although liberation theology and the *igreja popular* do not claim that Christian salvation is reducible to socio-political emancipation, the erosion of intra-historical utopias poses a serious obstacle to liberationist Catholicism's work at the base. This erosion makes Catholic voluntarism and progressivism (i.e. the notion that works are effective and that history moves toward a *telos*) less plausible. Since for the popular church "our definitive eschatological salvation is mediated, anticipated and rendered concrete in the partial liberations that take place at every level of historical reality,"[56] any condition that results in the protracted negation of the effectiveness of these partial liberations on the road toward fullness cannot but lessen the plausibility of the liberationist message. This loss of plausibility problematizes the CEBs' re-enchantment of the world – the tight link between eschatology and socio-political liberation that grounds their spirituality and activism.

[56] Boff, *Jesus Christ Liberator*, 275.

PART IV

Reinterpreting the crisis

CHAPTER 8

The popular church and the crisis of modernity

> In spite of the criticism and denunciations that characterized
> Medellin, an enormous optimism is implicit. Without a
> doubt, it requires optimism regarding the possibility of
> changing society and achieving development to call for in-
> volvement as did the bishops at Medellin.
>
> The optimism was, without a doubt, a characteristic of the
> world in the 1960s . . . That state of mind contrasts markedly
> with the pessimism that prevails today with respect to the
> possibilities for growth and social change.[1]

Having examined the crisis of the *igreja popular* at the local level
through the case of Pedra Bonita's base community and having
linked this crisis to the interplay of institutional constraints within
the church and socio-economic variables, I will now explore the
implications of the case study for the Brazilian popular church as a
whole.

Before embarking on this exercise, I must acknowledge the risks
inherent in making generalizations about the popular church from a
single case study. As I have argued throughout the book, the *igreja
popular* is a highly differentiated set of institutions and pastoral strategies. There is also a great deal of variation across geographic
regions, especially close to the ground. Any reading of crisis based
on a single case runs the risk of not doing justice to this complexity
and diversity, particularly when the case study is urban and does not
take into account what is happening in the countryside. A statistical
study of Brazilian ecclesial communities found that only about
30 percent of them are located in cities and urban peripheries.[2]

---

[1] J. P. Arellano, "The 20 Years since Medellin," *Origins* 18, no. 44 (April 13, 1989), 755.

[2] Valle and Pitta, *Comunidades eclesiais católicas*, 26. Madeleine Adriance has rightly taken
researchers to task for focusing almost exclusively on urban CEBs.

Thus, Pedra Bonita is hardly a typical Brazilian base community.

Nevertheless, I believe that Pedra Bonita's CEB highlights the central issues surrounding the Brazilian popular church's difficulties in increasing participation and mobilization at the grassroots. In a predominantly urban country, the *igreja popular* must learn to address the emerging challenges of city life if it is indeed to become a church of the masses. In addition, since Pedra Bonita represents a mature CEB in a diocese known for its strong advocacy of the preferential option for the poor, the insights gained in the case study are important to our understanding of the crisis of the popular church in one of its most developed embodiments. Most importantly, the observations and conclusions I draw from Pedra Bonita are supported by the findings of other scholars studying the evolution of Catholicism and the rise of alternative religious traditions in Brazil. I will include some of this evidence as I lay out my argument. We shall also see that some of these conclusions resonate with the situation of progressive Catholicism in other Latin American countries such as Nicaragua and El Salvador.

I contend that one of the main sources of the crisis of the Brazilian popular church is the erosion of the utopian notion of intrahistorical transcendence brought about by recent socio-economic and cultural changes. This erosion is part of a larger crisis of modern emancipatory ideologies, particularly of their humanism and optimism about the possibility of a rational mastery of the world. As I argued in chapter 1, the *igreja popular* appropriated modernity's humanistic optimism in Vatican II and Medellín.

As a prelude to my argument, I want to present two "external" readings of the crisis of the popular church. In contrast to intraecclesial understandings of the crisis, these readings draw heavily upon the social sciences. To date, they represent the most coherent interpretations of the crisis by Latin Americanists. These readings serve as a good point of departure for my discussion of the crisis, although they are partial and sometimes flawed in their assumptions. Thus, my aim here will be to both criticize and complement these two readings, seeking to provide a more nuanced and global understanding of the popular church's plight.

TWO PARTIAL READINGS OF THE POPULAR CHURCH'S CRISIS

The misplaced charge of elitism

Among works which formulate unfounded generalizations about the crisis of the popular church are recent studies of the growth of Protestantism in Latin America by David Martin and David Stoll. Contrasting the success of Pentecostalism to the difficulties encountered by liberationist Catholic initiatives, Martin affirms that,

> However idealistic and decently concerned and shocked the leaders of 'liberationism' may be, they are not usually 'of the people.' Liberation theology has a decidedly middle class and radical intellectual accent alien to the localized needs of 'the poor.' It claims to be Latin American but it is, in fact, as 'foreign' as Pentecostalism, if not more so, with spokesmen – yes, spokesmen – who are part of the international circuit of theological lectures.[3]

According to Martin, the problem with progressive Catholicism is "its readiness to entertain radical social philosophies . . . [which] are put forward by radical middle-class Catholic intellectuals in concert with other social and political analysts in the middle class."[4] These radical philosophies, he claims, do not correspond with the reality or worldview of the poor. "A political theology rooted in the idea of liberation is inherently a product of the self-conscious and sophisticated political class, more particularly of the 'knowledge class,'"[5] Martin argues, than of the poor who are mostly illiterate and bound to folk Catholicism. In contrast, Pentecostalism is "a religion of the poor (rather than a religion *for* the poor)." It lacks "sophisticated structural views of society and of political change." According to Martin, "This is what you would expect from a movement that picks up the mute and strangled voices of those unheard throughout Latin American history."[6]

David Stoll makes a similar argument in his work on evangelical Protestantism in Latin America, although he focuses on political

---

[3] Martin, *Tongues of Fire*, 290.   [4] Ibid., 266.   [5] Ibid.
[6] Ibid., 108. Along the same lines, Mariz argues that the "Catholic church opts for the poor because it is not a church of the poor. Pentecostal churches do not opt for the poor because they are already a poor people's church. And that is why poor people are choosing them." *Coping with Poverty*, 80.

violence rather than economic hardship. Stoll argues that liberation theology may not work because, among other things, it is produced by "more or less safely situated intellectuals," "outsiders." While recognizing that liberation theology has striven "to build a grass-roots church," Stoll notes that "the prophets of the movement tend to be religious professionals with professional interests, a fact dramatized by their disputes with offended laities and anxious hierarchies."[7]

These "prophets" of liberation theology demanded, from their relatively safe position, "a life-and-death commitment from the people who were supposed to be liberated."[8] Although Stoll admits that "Christianity is about sacrifice," he argues that the revolutionary stance of progressive Catholicism has been "suicidal." By encouraging people to fight impossible battles, it has led them to risk violent repression by the region's military governments. Pentecostalism, on the other hand, with its mistrust of politics and its social conservatism, has provided a shelter for the poor in highly polarized societies.

The identification of the popular church with either liberation theology or with leftist, bourgeois intellectuals and "religious professionals" reflects reductionist thinking that obscures the institutional and pastoral diversity behind the liberationist efforts. As I described it in chapter 2, the popular church is constituted by a highly differentiated set of institutions, pastoral initiatives and scholarly practices, each with its own audience, products, range of action, and organizational structure. Although these different forms of intervention are interconnected by an underlying emancipatory ideology, they are not reducible to the activities of a particular group of individuals.

Such readings as Stoll's and Martin's often issue from a failure to do nuanced fieldwork and/or to take the complexity of the religious institutions seriously. As the case of Pedra Bonita shows, there is a plurality of voices and approaches within the church, even at its micro levels. If Pedra Bonita is any indication, the avowed tension between middle-class professional theologians

---

[7] D. Stoll, *Is Latin America Turning Protestant?* (Berkeley: University of California Press, 1990), 312.
[8] Ibid., 313.

who hold "sophisticated structural views of society and political change" and the people at the base, though present, has very little to do with the Brazilian popular church's crisis of participation on the ground.

The roots of the crisis are far more complex, stemming mainly from a combination of intra-ecclesial changes and the increasing heterogeneity and precariousness of life conditions for the urban poor. More specifically, the crisis of participation results from a dissonance between, on the one hand, the popular church's utopian project and pastoral-pedagogical method, and on the other, the emerging economic, political, and ecclesial contexts. This dissonance disrupts the work of the popular church's local "organic" intellectuals, that is, the lay leaders trained in CEBs and *círculos bíblicos* and charged with the construction of a church of the people. The dissonance generates, among other things, a gap between them and the rest of the poor masses.

As we saw in the case of Pedra Bonita, the *pastoral de grupos pequenos* model requires the grassroots Catholic activist to undergo a long process of formation which calls for participation in study groups, retreats, and seminars and for increasing involvement not only in intra-ecclesial activities, but also in political work in the community, neighborhood, union, and party. Such demands are hard to reconcile with the pressures of contemporary life at an urban periphery. These pressures have intensified radically in the 1980s as a result of the economic crisis and the government's restructuration policies, forcing poor households to "self-exploit more."[9] Poor households have had to stretch their meager resources and to intensify subsistence activities. These responsibilities have increasingly fallen on women, who play a key role in the implementation of liberationist initiatives on the ground. Under these conditions, it has become even more onerous for the poor to meet the educational and pastoral demands of the popular church. Only a dwindling minority among the poor are able to become part of the *fermento*. The leaven, then, rather than blending with and mobilizing the masses, has become increasingly small and isolated, turning into relatively closed

[9] Smith and Wallerstein, *Creating and Transforming Households*, 16.

nuclei of activists assuming all pastoral, ritual, and organizational responsibilities.

For those already participating in the *pastoral de grupos pequenos*, the constraints imposed by the crisis and restructuration of the Brazilian economy have severely limited their range of action. They have less time and resources to do community work, to visit households in the *bairro*, and to follow closely the daily vicissitudes in their neighbors' lives. All these activities are central to the evangelization process and to the incorporation of outsiders into CEB life.

Parallel to the reduction in leisure time for the poor and grass-roots Catholic activists, there has been a shift in the national church away from base communities and biblical circles. As we saw in Pedra Bonita, under the pretext of giving the CEB more independence, priests are becoming concerned with more tradi-tional pastoral activities, like saying mass and ministering to the spiritual needs of the population, leaving the consciousness-rais-ing, organizational and political activities to the lay leaders already produced by *pastoral de grupos pequenos*. This shift has its origins in the institutional transformation of the Brazilian Catholic Church in response to the Vatican restorationist drive. Furthermore, as part of this drive, the church has sought to sacramentalize and clericalize grassroots pastoral initiatives, with the aim of removing the church from partisan politics and controlling local religious practices. This effort has isolated politically militant leaders, who during the repressive years of the military regime, the period of popular church expansion, were the key protagonists of grassroots pastoral work. Isolated and without support from the priest, many of these lay leaders have become frustrated and abandoned their work.

An additional contradiction that has marred the *pastoral de grupos pequenos* is the fragmentation of the working class and the poor. The fragmentation of the urban occupational structure, the growth of the informal economy, and the pervasiveness of under-employment and other unstable work arrangements have created a multiplicity of local needs and pressures for the poor, making all appeals to unite behind a common set of interests difficult to sustain. The only commonality among these needs and pressures is that they require the poor to concentrate on personal and/or household survival. The demand to navigate economic chaos, as we saw, favors the adoption of pragmatic, short-term and individualistic (or at least household-based) strategies that seek to make do with the cultural resources of individuals or isolated households. Often these resources include patron–client, assistential arrangements, which popular church lay leaders reject categorically because they lead in the long-term to increased dependence.

The distance between the needs and aspirations of the CEB nucleus and those of the rest of the base community and the neighborhood in Pedra Bonita – a distance reinforced by differential levels of critical conscious and militancy – has turned the base community nucleus into a vanguard with the capacity and sole responsibility for organizing community life and for participating in the struggles to improve the *bairro*. This centralization of responsibilities has made the CEB vulnerable. When the Irish priests attempted to restructure the CEB to reallocate roles and emphasize more ecclesial issues such as the construction of a new church, they succeeded only in alienating the nucleus, which effectively unraveled the community web.

The tension, therefore, is not between middle-class, "safely situated" intellectuals and the poor, as Martin, Stoll, and Mariz would have it, but between core activists in the CEBs and the rest of the poor masses among whom they live. This tension became problematic for the *igreja popular* because it made the *pastoral de grupos pequenos* its central model for re-inventing the whole church and society. Its pastoral agents did not develop alternative strategies to work with the masses, assuming that the CEBs, *círculos bíblicos* and specialized outreach programs like the PO and the CPT would be sufficient to address their needs.

The elevation of the *pastoral de grupos pequenos* model to this status was prompted by its success during the years of the military dictatorship and the transition to democracy in the period between the late 1960s and the mid-1980s. Since the church was one of the few spaces open to oppose the regime, it was called to concentrate on supporting local political activists. The *pastoral de grupos pequenos* made sense at that time. People had the interest and, most importantly, the resources and time to become engaged in this pastoral approach. During the military regime it was still possible for significant sectors of the poor to engage in the spiral of training and *praxis* the popular church demands because the distance between relatively stable households (more likely to form the activist nuclei in CEBs) and those in the poorest fraction of the urban working class was not as sizable as today. Thus it was conceivable to think that a lay leadership drafted from among the more economically-stable segments of poor would be able to communicate with the rest of the disenfranchised and to mobilize them eventually. In the past decade, however, the poor people's reality has changed for the worse. The number of relatively stable households has decreased, and the gap between those dwindling households and the growing ranks of those at the brink has widened, making a single-minded reliance on the *pastoral de grupos pequenos* to reach the poor problematic. We see, thus, that Martin's and Stoll's charge of middle-class intellectual elitism against the popular church fails to capture the complexity of the crisis.

THE LIMITS OF MICRO-ANTHROPOLOGICAL ANALYSIS

The second partial reading of the crisis is exemplified by John Burdick's *Looking for God in Brazil.* Burdick avoids making the unfounded generalizations about the crisis of the popular church that characterize Martin's and Stoll's claims. In fact, Burdick's textured analysis is grounded on a thick description of "the poly-religious field" in a poor, urban neighborhood. Within the neighborhood he focuses on the worldviews, practices, everyday predicaments, and choices of "clusters of people" with particular social characteristics. This goes a long way to enriching our understanding of the micro-dynamics that constitute the life of the "poor." Rather than speaking of the poor in abstract and totalizing terms, Burdick writes,

Our analytic point of departure should be clusters of people as they enter into and interact with the whole panoply of religious discourses, practices and specialists. By "clusters," I mean people who share constructed identities, such as being a *negro* [black Brazilian], or important experiential commonalities discoverable through ethnography, such as domestic conflict. The empirical task then becomes to explore how these clusters of people cope, through the available religious acts and language, with their experiential predicaments. By examining how people in such clusters understand and move between the options in the religious arena, we may begin to grasp the reasons for the rise or fall of a particular religion within it.[10]

Burdick's point of departure allows him to convey the voices of real, embodied individuals, grappling with the demands of everyday life, the "dramas of conscience" and "searches for theodicy," as he terms them, which in one way or another condition the religious choices they make. I find his call to listen carefully to the broad and rich "range of voices"[11] on the ground as a way to understand the dynamics of the religious field fundamentally sound.

Despite this significant contribution, Burdick's efforts to operationalize his analytical insights do not yield an adequate reading of the main lines of force that have defined the dynamics of the religious field in urban Brazil since the mid-1980s, the period when the popular church's crisis took hold. More specifically, Burdick fails to offer a convincing explanation for the difficulties of the Catholic popular church in reaching the "poor," in comparison to Pentecostalism and African-based religions.

Burdick asks: "Why, in São Jorge [the neighborhood he studied], are [P]entecostalism and *umbanda* expanding, while the *comunidade* is not? What do the people of São Jorge find in other religions that they do not find in the *comunidade*?" In response, he offers a four-fold argument: (1) The base community model reinforces "the association between the institutional Catholic Church and relatively more stable, literate, and better-off segments of the local working class." Pentecostalism, in contrast, offers more flexible, less hierarchical forms of organization and practice that allow it to reach a more socio-economically diverse audience. (2) "Married women find it difficult to resolve domestic problems through progressive Catholicism, because the Church nurtures an atmosphere of gossip." Thus women turn to Pentecostalism and *umbanda*, both cults of affliction in which the participants do not pass

[10] Burdick, *Looking for God in Brazil*, 9.
[11] J. Burdick, "The Progressive Catholic Church in Latin America: Giving Voice or Listening to Voices?" *Latin American Research Review* 29, no. 1 (1994), 195.

any judgment on each other because they are all "in the same boat" or because they are just clients seeking advice on a particular matter. (3) "Unmarried youth, squeezed between the urban pressures of unemployment and heightened expectations for consumption and sexuality," find that CEBs do not permit them to break with the past, something that Pentecostalism does. (4) "One of the reasons so few *negros* are to be found in the CEB, and so many in *umbanda* and *crença* [Pentecostalism], is that the CEB has failed to forge an effective counterdiscourse to racism." In contrast, both *umbanda* and Pentecostalism provide the basis for a radical critique of racial hierarchies through spirit possession.[12]

It is clear that some of Burdick's arguments resonate with my own findings in Pedra Bonita, notably on the increasing isolation of the base community nucleus from the rest of the neighborhood. Burdick found that

the emphasis placed by the *comunidade* on reading, small-group interaction, and intense levels of participation have lowered the religious status of people who have relatively less literacy, are less well-off, and have relatively heavier and more inflexible work schedules. São Jorge's *comunidade* has thus reinforced a process of elitization, shoring up the institutional Church's rootedness in the stabler, better-off, more literate segments of the local working class, as well as pushing an increasing number of less stable or well-off segments on the margins of Church life.[13]

However, Burdick tells us that "economic differentiation is not the most important source of distinction in São Jorge's religious arena."[14] His reading of the popular church's crisis of participation rests primarily on the notion that Pentecostalism and *umbanda* are cults of affliction and transformation, whereas Catholicism, even in its CEB embodiment, is a cult of continuity. As cults of affliction, Pentecostalism and *umbanda* shift responsibility for evil and suffering away from the believer, attributing them to the work of supernatural forces. Burdick claims that this allows women, for example, to avoid blaming themselves for domestic problems and to articulate these problems without fear of gossip. As cults of transformation, both Pentecostalism and *umbanda* allow believers

---

[12] Burdick, *Looking for God in Brazil*, 15.   [13] Ibid., 224.   [14] Ibid.

to break with the past and to challenge exclusionary social practices such as those associated with racism and sexism.

The claim that CEBs are not a cult of transformation is problematic at best, as Mariz's comparative work on base communities and Pentecostal groups shows. According to Mariz, CEBs, like Pentecostalism, produce an experience of renewal for the believer. Base communities induce an experience of "discontinuity . . . in people's consciousness that involves a change in their ways of seeing the world."[15] Mariz goes even further, claiming that CEBs' break with folk Catholicism and tradition is deeper than that produced by Pentecostalism because it entails a cognitive rather than a purely normative rupture.

But this questionable claim is not the most troubling element in Burdick's reading of the crisis. The main flaw in his reading results from the fact that he relegates larger institutional and economic dynamics to a second plane and privileges micro-cultural processes such as the ideological aspects of domestic strife, gossip, and identity formation as the key to elucidate the dynamics of the religious field in urban Brazil in the 1980s. Burdick fails to take full account of the macro-social, structural, and systemic forces that constrain and enable the practices of local actors. This micro-reading of the religious field leads him to provide a decontextualized interpretation of the "process of elitization" that occurs within São Jorge. Thus, in Burdick's study, the formation of a community nucleus acting as a vanguard appears to issue solely from the elitist attitudes of local Catholic activists, from contradictions within the *pastoral de grupos pequenos* model, and from the latter's continuity with traditional forms of Catholicism. In fact, as my study in Pedra Bonita shows, the isolation of the CEB nucleus from the rest of the community and the neighborhood and the decline of the CEB is a more complex process. It is the unintended consequence of the interaction among intra- and extra-ecclesial factors, including a shift in the institutional direction of the national and universal church and a drastic transformation of life conditions for Brazil's urban poor.

Among the institutional, structural, and systemic obstacles that

---

[15] Mariz, "Religion and Poverty in Brazil," S64.

hinder the production, circulation, and reception of the liberation-ist messages on the ground are the conservative Vatican offensive, the persistence of clientelism and political corruption, the econ-omic crisis, the restructuring of the Brazilian work force, a legit-imation crisis that undermines the development of Brazilian civil society, the crisis of the Latin American left and, more broadly, of modern emancipatory discourses, the rise of a populist right, and the advent of a new phase of capitalist accumulation. All these elements affect the type of work that can be carried out at the base. They create specific problems for the various segments of the urban poor and they define people's access to economic, political, cultural, and religious tools to solve those problems, and the plausibility the tools have to address concrete needs. While some tools might appear ineffectual, costly, and implausible to deal with experiential needs at a point in time, others might appear effica-cious and more flexible, given the limits of the possible.

In contrast to Burdick's decontextualized reading, I contend that the source of the crisis for the *igreja popular* is a widening chasm between the logic and demands of the popular church's worldview and pastoral-pedagogical method, on the one hand, and the pre-carious life conditions on the ground for the urban poor, on the other. The crisis certainly includes questions of identity formation such as race and gender, but it cannot be explained solely or even primarily by them. Although Burdick might be correct in ident-ifying CEBs' inability to deal effectively with domestic conflict, transition to adulthood, and racism, my experience in the field leads me to propose that during the late 1980s and early 1990s, the time when CEBs began to show clear signs of decline, these factors did not play the determining role that Burdick assigns them. Rather, most of my informants, CEB members and non-members, pastoral agents and laypersons, agreed in pointing to the changes brought by the economic and political crisis as the main cause for the drop in participation in grassroots initiatives, including CEBs and other *pastorais populares* which thrived during the 1970s.

By bracketing discussion of the macro-sociological bases of the crisis, especially of its economic component, Burdick undermines his attempt to ground his analysis empirically by studying "clusters of people." He fails to identify the social processes that led him to choose the clusters that he studied. What criteria did he use to select, as clusters, "illiterates," married women, unmarried youth, and *negros*, the experiential predicaments of whom are not only relevant but key to our understanding of the crisis of the popular church in Brazil? More importantly, even granting that the experiences of these clusters are relevant to our understanding of the crisis of the popular church and the dynamics of the religious field in urban Brazil, how does Burdick justify the fact that he highlights some of these clusters' experiences at the expense of others of equal or perhaps greater significance? For example, why focus on married women's concern about gossip rather than on the predicaments resulting from their increasing responsibility for household survival? Why not focus on women's attempts to deal with the social violence and the health and educational problems that threaten their neighborhoods and homes? It is not enough – and, in fact, it is trivial – to say that the "identity and significance [of the clusters] should emerge from an ethnographic grasp of local social relations."

I submit that for the various segments of the poor in Nova Iguaçu the most salient and urgent drama they have faced since the early 1980s is the need to survive the perils of the economic crisis. Such a need has shaped their thoughts and actions, including their selective reliance on religious discourses and practices to solve everyday predicaments. It is in the context of this struggle for personal and household survival that the popular church's modernist project of intra-historical transcendence and hope for transformation via human institutions has lost plausibility for the poor.

Burdick's focus on the cultural dimensions of race and gender may stem from the strong interest in current scholarship on social movements on the matters surrounding the question of "identity formation."[16] This analytical focus helps open up our field of vision, eschewing the possibility of economic reductionism and monocausal explanations of the multiplicity of power relations in society. The researcher, however, must be self-reflexive, aware of the sources, limitations, and excesses of this micro bias.

To achieve a thick description of a social configuration it is

---

[16] See A. Escobar and S. Alvarez, eds., *The Making of Social Movements in Latin America: Identity, Strategy and Democracy* (Boulder, CO: Westview Press, 1992).

important to examine what Burdick elsewhere calls the "whole universe of [micro?] social processes" including those of

connecting, relating, and distancing people from movements; insidership and outsidership; boundary-making; access, socialization, and recruitment; rites of initiation; and the way in which all these processes articulate with local social differentiation along the lines of gender, race, class, age, literacy, and so forth.[17]

This, however, is insufficient. It is also necessary to see how these micro-processes interact with macro-social dynamics, serving simultaneously as their expression and the arena where they are contested and/or reproduced. As anthropologists George Marcus and Michael Fisher argue, in order to avoid the illusion of ahistorical, decontextualized local cultural units, the researcher must study the "embedding of richly described local cultural worlds in larger impersonal systems of political economy."[18]

In his study of popular Catholicism in Colombia and Venezuela, Levine makes a similar point. He explores the links between everyday life and what he calls "big structures," which include "institutional formations like church, state, or major economic groups." According to Levine, "The very notion of the 'popular' rests on relations between the everyday lives of poor people and the big structures of power and meaning that set parameters of change for the society as a whole." Thus, the task of the researcher is to elucidate how the ties between everyday life and big structures "are organized, legitimized, and put into practice, and then to figure out what difference this makes to the character of popular voices, to their viability, and to their impact."[19]

Levine's examination of ties between larger structures and everyday life leads him to discover two dynamics that constrain the popular church's development. First, at the intra-ecclesial level, "growing national and international pressures within the churches have begun to take their toll, cutting the ground from under the

[17] J. Burdick, "Rethinking the Study of Social Movements: The Case of Christian Base Communities in Urban Brazil," in Escobar and Alvarez, eds., *The Making of Social Movements in Latin America*, 183.

[18] G. Marcus and M. Fisher, *Anthropology as Cultural Critique* (Chicago: University of Chicago Press, 1986), 77.

[19] Levine, *Popular Voices*, 317.

most activist groups. Leaders are transferred, resources withdrawn, and legitimate tasks and roles are redefined. As a result, popular groups find that the road gets harder and its direction more and more uncertain." Secondly, the pressures stemming from the Vatican's drive to affirm "authority and unity in the church" have been "magnified by the notable economic and political decay that the 1980s brought to Latin America. Accelerated economic crisis in the context of weak and ineffective government reduces the survivability of social movements inspired by religion and cuts the ground from under their potential for sustaining and enriching democracy."[20]

In sum, Burdick's micro-reductionism leads him to produce a one-sided reading of the crisis of the popular church and of the relative success of Pentecostalism and *umbanda*. Religious options on the ground in urban Brazil appear to be competing against each other only within the analytical soap bubble that Burdick has created. This micro bias dovetails with the postmodernist aversion towards totalizing visions of reality and a concomitant sensitivity towards local discourses and readings of the social world that emphasize its fragmentarity, fluidity, and indeterminacy. David Harvey considers this approach "dangerous for it avoids confronting the realities of political economy and the circumstances of global power."[21] According to Harvey, by stressing the fragmentary and multiple nature of local power dynamics and discourses, postmodernism fails to "grasp the political-economic processes (money flows, international division of labour, financial markets and the like) that are becoming ever more universal in their depth, intensity, reach and power over daily life." Furthermore, Harvey argues, while postmodernism

opens up a radical prospect by acknowledging the authenticity of other voices ... [it] immediately shuts off those other voices from access to more universal sources of power by ghettoizing them within an opaque otherness, the specificity of this or that language game. It thereby disempowers peoples those voices (of women, ethnic and rational minorities, colonized people, the unemployed, the youth, etc.) in a world of lop-sided power relations.[22]

The discussion of Burdick's postmodern sensibilities brings us to

---

[20] Ibid., 369.   [21] Harvey, *The Condition of Postmodernity*, 117.   [22] Ibid.

the deeper claim I wish to make concerning the crisis of the popular church: the crisis is ultimately connected to the loss of plausibility of modernist emancipatory projects, particularly at the grassroots level, among the poor.

MODERNITY, THE PROBLEM OF EVIL, AND THE POPULAR CHURCH

In recent years there has been a profusion of works proclaiming the demise of modernity and the advent of postmodernity. What is behind this "rage against humanism and the Enlightenment legacy," as philosopher Richard Bernstein describes it?[23] Although the crisis of modernity is a complex event, we can characterize it as the problematization of the concept of representation. The crisis of modernity is linked to a crisis of the correspondence theory of truth, which in its extreme forms, claims that, given the right epistemological moves, beliefs correspond directly, in a one-to-one ratio, to phenomena. The mind, in this view, mirrors the world, reflecting reality without distortions through language.[24]

Kant, arguably the defining philosophical figure in Enlightenment modernity, did not subscribe to this extreme version of the correspondence theory of truth. For Kant, the mind is not a *tabula rasa* that simply registers the impact of outside stimuli. The mind has a universal, *a priori* structure that allows it to grasp reality in a systematic and critical fashion. Despite this difference, Kant shares with the correspondence theory of truth a strong version of foundationalism, that is, the belief that there exists an Archimedean point from which reason can produce an accurate picture of reality and capture the totality of the world. For Kant, this Archimedean point is the transcendental ego, a unified, self-evident subjectivity, which operating with the right consciousness can unmask illusions, rectify distortions, and apprehend ultimately the essence of reality as it appears to us.

As I discussed in chapter 1, the notion of right consciousness, which is connected with the instrumentalism of the emerging

---

[23] R. J. Bernstein, "Introduction," in *Habermas and Modernity*, ed. Richard J. Bernstein (Cambridge, MA: MIT Press, 1985), 25.

[24] See R. Rorty, *Philosophy and the Mirror of Nature* (Oxford: Blackwell, 1980).

scientific worldview, leads post-Enlightenment modernity to dream of a fully transparent nature, society, and self, totally pliable to human activity. Philosopher Jacques Derrida associates this dream with a "metaphysics of presence."[25] Presumably, the possibility of a wholly transparent nature, society, and self should lead to a fully rationalized world: a "humanized" world whose ordering principles are cultural and historical products, not the dicta of a supernatural force. Then, the quest for a fully rationalized world should in theory be an emancipatory one. However, as critics of this quest, beginning with Nietzsche, have noted, the Enlightenment rationality, though presenting itself as the impartial, authoritative adjudicator of all claims, is driven by a surreptitious will to power. This will to power came to the surface conspicuously in the rise of Nazism and the Holocaust with its "rational" treatment of the "Jewish question." The atrocities committed during that period have seriously questioned modernity's naive view of history as progress: rather than leading to us to full emancipation, modern rationality has produced self-domination.[26]

The intertwining of post-Enlightenment rationality and power is not limited to cataclysmic events such as the world wars and the Holocaust, but as Foucault has shown, it is connected with the rise of the social space and modern subjectivity through applications of discursive and non-discursive practices developed in prisons, asylums, schools, factories, and armies to regiment the body. Feminist and post-colonial analyses establish a similar connection, showing the effects of domination of a rationality construed as both male and Western.

If reason is defined by a will to power, it can no longer claim to be pristine and to have privileged access to reality, as if it were a sovereign eye standing above the contingency of history and capable of grasping essences and producing a total perspective. The fact that reason is implicated with power, thus, leads to a crisis of modern representation. All totalizing representations of reality become suspect, linked to a will to dominate. According to Norbert Lechner, one of the interpreters of postmodernism in the

---

[25] J. Derrida, *Writing and Difference*, trans. A. Bass (London: Routledge, 1978).
[26] M. Horkheimer and T. Adorno, *Dialectic of the Enlightenment* (New York: Seabury Press, 1969).

Latin American context, "a primary dimension of postmodern disenchantment is the loss of faith in the possibility of a theory that possesses the key to understanding the social process in its entirety." Later on, he argues that "the break with modernity . . . consists in rejecting the reference to totality."[27]

The crisis of post-Enlightenment totalizing rationality, in turn, shatters all hopes of progress, all hopes that humanity can eventually achieve control of its fate and vanish all forms of tyranny and prejudice through Reason. For all of its pretensions to neutrality and to the capacity to overcome distortions, modern reason is based on a non-rational, interested drive to dominate which ultimately undermines its quest for human emancipation. Thus the crisis of modernity is ultimately a crisis of utopias, utopias "understood as images of an ideal social order that possess an orienting force for decision-making in the present and that provide a unified directionality toward the future."[28] According to cultural theorist Dick Hebdige, postmodernism marks the demise of

divine revelation, the unfolding of the Word, the shadowing of history by the Logos, the Enlightenment project, the belief in progress, the belief in Reason, the belief in Science, modernisation, development, salvation, redemption, the perfectibility of man [sic], the transcendence of history through divine intervention, the transcendence of history through class struggle, Utopia subtitled End of History . . .[29]

The suspicion against totalizing rationality is the source of postmodernism's emphasis on alterity, heterogeneity, plurality, and localism. Postmodernism enjoins us to eschew fixed, totalizing, and essentialist conceptions of the world and to privilege the indeterminacy and fluidity of the event. Against the fully transparent and rationalized world of post-Enlightenment modernity, postmodernism offers a fragmented, protean reality resistant to any reductive reading. In lieu of the orderly progress towards full rationality, postmodernism posits a disjointed history, where past, present, and future come together in a collage.

---

[27] N. Lechner, "A Disenchantment Called Postmodernism," *Boundary 2* 20, no. 3 (1993), 127, 128.

[28] M. Hopenhayn, "Postmodernism and Neoliberalism in Latin America," *Boundary 2* 20, no. 3 (1993), 97.

[29] Quoted in N. Wakefield, *Postmodernism: The Twilight of the Real* (London: Pluto Press, 1990), 22.

Some critics attribute postmodernism's emphasis on difference and impermanence to the new capitalist configuration which, as I argued in the previous chapter, is characterized by heterogeneity and instant flows of capital across sectors and national borders.[30] On the one hand, the penetration of this capitalism to all spheres of life has prompted the emergence of new oppositional subjects (such as women, minorities, and colonized people) which modernity's male and Western rationality has not only ignored but often silenced. On the other hand, postmodernism's penchant for diversity and enjoyment of the moment goes hand in hand with the neoliberal project of unregulated markets. As Martín Hopenhayn has observed,

[P]ostmodernist rhetoric has been profitably capitalized on by neoliberalism in order to update its longed-for project of cultural hegemony. This project, the dream of liberalism in its formative stages, was frustrated by the universalist ethic of modern humanism, by political mobilization, and/or social pressures. What many neoliberals saw, especially in the industrialized countries, is the possibility that reculturization, via a seductive postmodern narrative, could serve to legitimize the market offensive of the eighties, in other words, could make the desires of the public coincide with the promotion of pro-market policies and with the consolidation of a transnational capitalist system. It is no accident that the elements of ... the postmodern narrative have been disseminated, at least in good measure, by neoliberals and disenchanted leftists seduced by anarcho-capitalism.[31]

It is in this latter sense that an unreflexive celebration of the micro, such as Burdick's, might end up inadvertently reinforcing global power dynamics rather than allowing us to "listen to the voices of people." Uncritical micro-empiricism is ultimately based on the assumption that the neutral ear of the social scientist can capture the multiplicity of voices as they are, unmediated by larger sociopolitical processes.

Postmodern politics, in any case, translates into a rejection of "master emancipatory narratives" which present a global, teleo-

---

[30] See F. Jameson, "Postmodernism, or the Cultural Logic of Late Capitalism," *New Left Review*, no. 146 (1984), 53–93. For a similar argument in the case of Latin America, see G. Yúdice, "Postmodernity and Transnational Capitalism in Latin America," in G. Yúdice, J. Franco, and J. Flores, eds., *On Edge: The Crisis of Contemporary Latin American Culture* (Minneapolis: University of Minnesota Press, 1992).

[31] Hopenhayn, "Postmodernism and Neoliberalism in Latin America," 98.

logical, and progressivist vision of history. I shall address the
lessons of the postmodern critique for emancipatory movements,
particularly for religious movements that stress intra-historical
transcendence, and for the possibility of reconstructing the notion
of utopia in the next chapter. I shall argue that when stripped of
their more polemical tone and its neoliberal connections, postmodernist critiques can help reformulate modernist utopian projects to respond more effectively to the challenges of contemporary
capitalism. For the moment, I want to explore the consequences of
the crisis of post-Enlightenment emancipatory rationality for liberation theology and the Latin American popular church.

As we saw in our discussion of the ideological bases of the *igreja
popular*, the latter's utopian ideology of this-worldly transcendence
was influenced by a modern understanding of history, agency, and
society, particularly in its Hegelian-Marxist version. In fact, the
popular church and liberation theology cosmicize the quest for
human self-realization envisioned by Hegel and Marx, connecting
it with the coming of the Kingdom. Thus, when modern discourses enter into crisis, both the popular church and liberation
theology necessarily suffer the consequences. Their vision of history and salvation becomes tainted with the will to power that
informs modern rationality and its utopian projects.

As post-modern critiques highlight, modern rationality is connected with a will to power that ends up distorting its original
intention. This distortion makes its way into liberation theology
and the ideology of the popular church. By making "man the lord
of this creation,"[32] liberation theology becomes implicated in the
drive to dominate nature which has turned the Enlightenment
from a quest for self-transcendence into an iron cage of self-
domination. Since "the work of man, the transformation of nature, continues [divine] creation," dominion of nature by science
and technology is not only inherently positive, but divinely sanctioned. The only way this work may become a vehicle for domination is if it is not a truly "human act," that is, if it is carried by
individuals "alienated by unjust socio-economic structures."[33]
The possibility that the rationality deployed to control nature may

[32] Gutiérrez, *A Theology of Liberation*, 67.   [33] Ibid., 178.

lie behind the creation of unjust socio-economic structures is not explicitly explored by liberation theology.

Although the popular church's ideology is very critical of instrumental rationality, particularly as it is embodied in bourgeois science and capitalism, it does not challenge the metaphysics of presence informing post-Enlightenment thinking. In fact, the popular church's ideology ends up cosmicizing this metaphysics. Both the popular church and liberation theology assume that they can grasp history from its foundations (which ultimately point to God) through the right consciousness provided by eschatological faith. The essence of history is already-given and fully transparent: it is the unfolding of the eschatological promise. The salvific dynamics of history "mirrored" through the eyes of faith and advanced through human works then blend with the Enlightenment's progressivist *hubris* and teleological essentialism as Catholicism opens up to modernity. In this way, despite the fact that for both liberation theology and the popular church salvation is not reducible to liberation, human emancipatory action comes to be conceived as a divinely sanctioned progressive mastery over nature and self. The conviction that salvation is ultimately an act of divine grace thus does not preclude liberation theology and the popular church from espousing an instrumental, totalizing, and evolutionary approach to history that has been discredited by postmodern analyses.

However, the crisis of modernity and of the popular church's project does not remain at this abstract level. While in Europe the crisis of modernity is marked by existential events like the Holocaust and the two world wars, in Latin America the challenge comes from the failure of modernist projects to empower vast sectors of the population. Modernity, in fact, has benefited mostly the urban elites, exacerbating social exclusion and stratification. Developmentalism in both its export-driven or import-substitution modes, socialism, neoliberalism, and even representative democracy have not altered the appalling life conditions of most Latin Americans. As we saw in Brazil, despite undeniable gains in terms of the articulation of a representative democracy in the last decade, poor people have had to contend with worsening life conditions and the deepening of social inequalities.

The shocking situation of the poor, which in theological terms we can call the "problem of evil," challenges the assumption of all modernist projects, particularly the notions that history is a gradual process of emancipation and that it is possible to construct a fully rationalized society; that is, a society in which every individual attains "maturity" in the Kantian sense, being subject only to the rational rules s/he constructs. This is the reason why Lechner finds that in Latin America postmodernism has taken the form of a disenchantment, "a *loss of faith in progress*," that threatens the region's precarious process of democratization by "weakening its political roots."[34]

Because they make the "non-person," those at the margins of society, the locus of reflection, prophetic inspiration, and pastoral action, both liberation theology and the *igreja popular* must confront head on the problem of evil and the failure of modern emancipatory projects. They must deal with the plausibility of the Christian message of liberation in the midst of a world full of injustice, suffering, and brokenness. This is why, in his reflections on Job's plight, Gutiérrez asks:

How are we to talk about a God who is revealed as love in a situation characterized by poverty and oppression? How are we to proclaim the God of life to men and women who die prematurely and unjustly? How are we to acknowledge that God makes us a free gift of love and justice when we have before us the suffering of the innocent? What words are we to use in telling those who are not even regarded as persons that they are daughters and sons of God?[35]

These questions gained urgency in the 1980s, when Latin America's poor began to suffer the pernicious effects of economic crisis and restructuration. Rather than bringing to fruition the "revolutionary ferment" that characterized the Latin American in 1960s and 1970s, which Gutiérrez saw as one of the most important and hopeful "signs of the times" in the region, modernity has brought the poor increasing hardship and loss of control over their lives. Modernity has not liberated the disenfranchised from economic alienation, political subjugation, and cultural domination, but

[34] Lechner, "A Disenchantment Called Postmodernism," 134.
[35] G. Gutiérrez, *On Job: God-Talk and the Suffering of the Innocent* (Maryknoll, NY: Orbis Books, 1987), xiv.

rather has led to sophisticated global, and insidious exclusionary power dynamics.

How then can liberation theology and the popular church proclaim a God of life who sides with the poor in their quest for emancipation, who is working with them and through them to build the reign of God, when their life conditions deteriorate day-by-day, when they continue to lose control over their fate in a world subjected to the twin forces of globalization and disintegration? How can liberation theology and the popular church ask the poor to take the reins of their lives, fashioning a new society from below through grassroots organizations such as the CEBs, in the face of tremendous pressure to focus on survival and to make do with the predominantly authoritarian and clientelist cultural resources at hand? How can the *igreja popular* and liberation theology continue preaching the God of the life and intra-historical transcendence in a "situation of exile," similar to the Babylonian captivity that generated a "profound crisis of faith in the Jewish people"? In the Babylonian captivity, the Jewish people,

[f]inding themselves once more in servitude . . . began to wonder about the God who had liberated them from Egypt. The situation was now even worse than it had been before, worse than in Egypt. The oppression was more cruel now. Their homeland had been destroyed, their temple leveled. Their national consciousness of being a free people had been humiliated. How could Yahweh permit this? Was he a God of liberation or was he not? Why was he allowing them to fall into slavery all over again?[36]

The urban poor in Brazil and throughout Latin America are experiencing a situation similar to the Babylonian captivity. This situation contradicts the popular church's utopian view of history as the "fulfillment of the [eschatological] Promise." This contradiction not only generates a crisis of faith and identity among theologians and pastoral agents, but also weakens the appeal of the liberationist message for the poor. Under these conditions, the *igreja popular*'s quest for intra-historical transcendence rings hollow, just another modernist fantasy in a long lineage of projects that stretches back to the republic's founding motto: "order and progress."

---

[36] Gutiérrez, *The Power of the Poor in History*, 10.

In the new context of "captivity," the quest for intra-historical transcendence gives way to the day-to-day struggle for personal and family survival. In his most recent work on Nicaragua, Roger Lancaster documents how the precarious life conditions generated by the Contra War and the US embargo during the mid-1980s undermined popular confidence in the Sandinista revolution, weakening the utopian vision that had inspired the movement. In this context, he found that political activism and involvement in the popular church decreased as people's attention was "turned increasingly away from public, political, and social issues ... toward domestic, immediate, and personal concerns. The problems that most affected ordinary people were simple: how to obtain enough cash to feed oneself and one's family; how to weather the crisis with one's family intact."[37]

In an insightful essay assessing the consequences of postmodernity for Brazilian society and the popular church, theologian Paulo Carneiro de Andrade observes that

[t]he situation of persistent and progressive economic crisis together with the continuous frustrations in politics, where successive gains always show themselves a posteriori insufficient to resolve the country's structural problems, has generated a profound crisis of hope, that expresses itself in a generalized sense of impotence and disbelief in the future. Popular imagination appears to have lost its capacity to formulate plausible representations of the future, which may orient and give meaning to political actions in the now, leading to a crisis of utopias . . .[38]

Thus, the predicament of the popular church is how to rekindle the utopian drive in the context of a dystopia; it is how to reconnect intra-historical transcendence with everyday life, with a reality that is ever more resistant to transformative action from the grassroots. It is how to "sing the praises of a God of liberation in the midst of a situation of oppression" brought by transformations in the capitalist world system, which have radically altered the life and composition of the poor as a "class," limiting their capacity to act upon the world.

---

[37] R. Lancaster, *Life is Hard: Machismo, Danger, and the Intimacy of Power in Nicaragua* (Berkeley: University of California Press, 1993), 7.

[38] P. F. C. de Andrade, "A condição pósmoderna como desafio à pastoral popular," *Revista Eclesiástica Brasileira* 53, no. 209 (March 1993), 108–109.

PENTECOSTALISM AND THE CRISIS OF MODERNITY:
SOME HYPOTHESES

As I argued in chapter 4, the crisis of the popular church has an external, background component defined by the increasing fragmentation of the religious field, especially by the growth of Pentecostalism. In this section, I want to suggest some hypotheses for further empirical investigation that might help explain the growth of Pentecostalism among the urban poor in the light of the crisis of modern utopian projects. I contend that Pentecostalism offers urban poor people alternative forms of organization and practice that are more adapted to recent socio-economic and religious changes. More importantly, Pentecostalism provides a viable utopian ideology that is able to explain and address specific existential problems in the now, while producing a radical break with the unjust and iniquitous social order through its apocalypticism. The tension between present and future makes Pentecostal ideology more flexible than the popular church's, given the recent socio-economic and cultural transformations. This flexibility allows Pentecostal ideology, on the one hand, to respond better to the multiple needs of the "poor" than the base ecclesial communities, and on the other, to survive, and even thrive, in the context of a crisis of the notion of intra-historical transcendence.

My first hypothesis is that Pentecostalism's decentered organizational structures allow more space and time flexibility to the believer. In contrast to the highly hierarchical and rigid parish-priest centered Catholic approach which, as we saw in Pedra Bonita's case, CEBs have not been able to transcend, Pentecostalism offers an autonomous and participatory form of practice and organization. Pentecostalism, even when it does not obviate the need to re-energize faith through continual communal ritual activity, demands of the believer reaffirmation of her/his justification in Christ mainly in her/his *individual* daily activities. The distinguishing mark of those who have been saved by the blood of Christ resides in the righteous way each of them conducts herself/himself *vis-à-vis* God and her/his immediate environment. Individual faith provides justification before God. By placing the emphasis on individual faith rather than on large-scale collective action, Pentecostalism provides a more flexible way to live one's religiosity. This is particularly important for persons with a heavy work schedule and for those households in which all family members must work to make ends meet.[39]

This is not to say that Pentecostal practice is not time-intensive. In fact, the core leadership of more established Pentecostal churches such as the Assemblies of God also undergoes extensive training in the form of Bible and evangelization courses. In addition, established churches offer an array of religious activities including services, prayer and youth groups, and choir practices that can easily take 2–3 hours everyday. Nevertheless, since Pentecostal practice is fundamentally a matter of personal faith, the believer need not engage in all these group activities to lead a truly religious life. At least potentially, Pentecostalism does not necessitate that the faithful engage in collective exercises or in consciousness-raising activities to learn to read the Bible and to link faith and life. For Pentecostals the main source of guidance is the Holy Spirit, which may inspire anyone at any moment, even those who are illiterate. This is part of the Lutheran legacy of the "priesthood of all believers" and the egalitarian spirit of early Methodism. For Pentecostals, moreover, there is no need for a critical-hermeneutical approach to the Bible, such as CEBs use, since the Scriptures speak for themselves. The principle of *sola scriptura* stands in opposition to Catholicism's use of church tradition in making sense of Christianity. While it is true that the pastor often plays an important role in shaping local beliefs and practices, the principle of *sola scriptura* and the rejection of church tradition makes it possible for Pentecostals to attenuate the contradictions generated by the concentration of religious goods in the hands of a corps of specialists (i.e., the clergy). Within the Catholic church this concentration affects even traditional practices such as those of folk Catholicism, pushing them to the margins and/or coopting them through official liturgies.

Along the same lines, to carry out their proselytizing work effectively, Pentecostals need not receive evangelization courses. Conversion, a once-and-for-all event, makes the believer one of

---

[39] See Burdick, *Looking for God in Brazil*, 82.

God's soldiers, charged with the responsibility of fighting Satan and of spreading the Gospel. While this fact may help account for the constant splintering within Pentecostalism, it also guarantees independence of practice and organization on the ground. In comparison to Catholics in base communities, Pentecostals are not as vulnerable to changes within a hierarchical, global institution, such as the Vatican restoration. Although Pentecostal groups depend on charismatic pastors for their cohesiveness in much the same way that CEBs rely heavily on supportive priests and bishops, the distribution of power tends to be local and open to contestation. This is not so in the case of the Catholic church in which the power structure is highly bureaucratized and reified. Thus, organizationally, Pentecostalism is far more flexible than the institutional framework in which CEBs must operate. This flexibility allows it to respond better to the differentiated needs of the local population.[40]

My second hypothesis is that Pentecostalism, though stressing eschatology, never forsakes the present. Even when it sees salvation as occurring outside human history, Pentecostalism addresses present, everyday issues in the believer's life such as domestic problems, alcoholism, unemployment, and illnesses through the disciplined ethos that stems from its moral asceticism, through the practice of miracle cures and exorcism of demons and through the formation of self-help networks. This "presentism" responds to the urban poor's felt needs, that is, to their concern for immediate and concrete solutions to their pressing problems. Although CEBs deal with these felt needs, they often subordinate immediate personal problems such as alcoholism and illness to the search for more long-term community solutions.

A third hypothesis points to Pentecostalism's conception of the limits of human agency. Contrary to the Catholic notion that works are an essential component of the quest for salvation, Pentecostalism adheres to the Lutheran doctrine of "justification by grace through faith only." As we saw in chapter 4, the doctrine of the Fall renders all human efforts, including those that have a socio-political dimension, not only ineffectual but perilous

---

[40] For a similar point see David Stoll, "Introduction: Rethinking Protestantism in Latin America," in Garrard-Burnett and Stoll, *Rethinking Protestantism*, 5–6.

because they might make the believer too proud, leading her/
him to think that s/he can bring her/his own salvation. In addition, excessive concern with works may lead the believer to become too invested in this world and to forget that her/his real
interest is with the reign of God, a qualitatively different order of
existence.

In contrast to works, faith is fundamentally an individual dynamic, a matter between God and the believer. The emphasis on
faith, thus, effectively sidesteps (though it does not disqualify) any
need for collective action to justify one's election. There is no
need to appeal to a class interest to target the believer. The
appeal must be made to his/her personal interest for salvation.
Naturally, the individual will be interested in saving his/her loved
ones from eternal damnation and will act vigorously to convert
them. However, this social action is local, directed toward the
micro level, seeking to change individual behavior, not to transform the macro, structural level. In this fashion, the focus on the
individual and the local allows Pentecostalism to eschew the effects of the urban poor's fragmentation. This focus, in fact, resonates with the move among the urban poor from community-local
to household-local survival strategies as the socio-economic situation deteriorates.

As a corollary of Pentecostalism's rejection of works as the key
element in the salvific process, the believer is insulated from the
potential belief vacuum that is generated when sustained human
action fails to point to and usher in the reign of God. Since the
coming of the Kingdom is God's will, and humans do not know
and understand God's ways, failure to progress towards liberation
does not shake the believer's faith. If, as in the case of the popular
church, salvation is inextricably linked to historical and political
liberation, any setback on the road to the latter represents a direct
challenge to the believer's faith. As the obstacles and setbacks
mount, the possibility for a crisis of motivation and hope increases.
Pentecostals are "immunized" against this crisis: this fleeting life is
nothing more than a testing ground. The harder it becomes, the
greater the opportunity to affirm one's faith and election. In fact,
read through the prism of Pentecostal apocalyticism, the deterioration of everyday life becomes part of a biblical prophecy that

points to the end of times: things will get much worse before the Second Coming.[41]

Finally, we may hypothesize that Pentecostalism offers a viable other-worldly utopia. By radically decoupling human and divine history, and by positing the latter, not as the fulfillment of the former, but as its total suspension, Pentecostalism avoids the problems posed by the erosion of intra-historical transcendence. In contrast to CEBs, which as part of a church stand in a relation of continuity with the secular order that forces them to seek the latter's redemption, Pentecostalism, with its sectarian orientation, is not invested with the idea of saving the social world. In a country such as Brazil, where all social and political institutions appear to be sullied by corruption and impotence, CEBs' intercourse with the secular order runs the risk of implicating them "in the *massa perditionis.*"[42]

The doctrine of two dominions allows Pentecostalism to provide the believer with: (1) a plausible theodicy that renders meaningful, and thus more bearable, the existence of evil and injustice, tracing it to a divinely-planned cosmic struggle in which evil seeks to prevail over good, and (2) a totalizing critique of the shortcomings of human history. Human institutions are inherently flawed; that is why there is so much injustice and suffering. Yet, for the suffering righteous there will be ultimate redemption when, at the end of times, Christ will return to upend this world of injustice and to punish the wicked.

Pentecostal theodicy, however, does not preclude participation in human institutions. After all, human history is the testing ground where each believer must reaffirm his/her faith by battling evil in all its manifestations. To carry out this fight one might have to resort to human institutions, to politics, the media, etc. Nevertheless, this participation is merely instrumental. It does not define

---

[41] Political scientist Philip Williams found that Evangelical churches were successful in El Salvador during the 1970s in part because they "offered both a *reason* and a *solution* for the crisis afflicting Salvadoran society. The suffering of the Salvadoran people followed biblical prophecy. The war and economic crisis was a sign that the second coming was imminent. Salvadorans must repent, stop sinning, give up their vices and accept Christ as their savior." P. J. Williams, "The Tambourines are Banging: The Politics of Evangelical Growth in El Salvador," in Cleary and Stewart-Gambino, *Power, Politics and Pentecostals*, 186.

[42] Martin, *Tongues of Fire*, 286.

the identity of the believer, which continues to be grounded in the beyond. This is the meaning of the injunction: "be in this world, but not of this world."

In sum, we may theorize that at its most effective Pentecostalism offers an alternative type of "reality-transcendence,"[43] which gives intra-historical activity a more modest role (i.e., individual and local action with moral aims rather than collective and structural struggles to usher in the divine reign). This form of transcendence achieves a balance between the short and long term. In the long term it offers a radical critique of the status quo, a complete undoing of distortions and contradictions of human history with the end of times and the coming of Christ. In the short term, it deals with the specific evils of this world as they appear to embodied individuals (i.e., ailments, unemployment, family disintegration, etc.) through the gifts of the Holy Spirit (i.e., cures, miracles, etc.) which are the signs of the times to come, the ethos it instills, and the grassroots self-help networks it establishes. Here, rather that serving as a break from the status quo, Pentecostalism provides ritual, psycho-cognitive, and material elements that help the survival and re-articulation of selfhood within an increasingly baffling and threatening world. Pentecostalism offers, then, a balance between rupture and continuity, between now and the thereafter, that the popular Catholic Church, in its impatience to erase the present and usher a better future in human history, fails to provide. Far from being a purely escapist and alienating ideology, as some popular church activists claim, Pentecostalism is also, like liberation theology, a utopian project, perhaps better suited to deal with the effects of the crisis of modernity at the grassroots.

The impact of Pentecostal conceptions of history, action, and salvation on the construction of a participatory democracy in Brazil, and Latin America more generally, is not clear. Some, like David Martin, see in them the perfect vehicle to articulate an autonomous, vibrant civil society from below, as the monolithic Catholic world disintegrates. Others see Pentecostalism as a desperate response to postmodernity's "hypersecularization." According to political scientist Daniel García Delgado, in an increasingly disenchanted, fragmented, and baffling world, one "observes

---

[43] Mannheim, *Ideology and Utopia*, 262.

a search for certainty, affirmation, and identity . . . and a resacral-
ization starting from the micro and from a religious sensibility
devoid of political and social [components] in the context of
intimate and expressive communities."[44] In García Delgado's
reading, the growth of Pentecostalism is part of a "passage from a
holistic to a neo-individualistic [cultural] model," in which a
fragile subjectivity is constantly struggling to survive and assert
itself in the micro-political field. In the neo-individualistic model,
the self "internalizes history as it is given. Very little can be done to
change this history or to become a protagonist in it. What is central
is to adapt, survive, and in any case, to leave the obligation to
change the world to others . . ."[45] This loss of agency is reflected in
the Pentecostal reliance on "magical" conceptions of the world
(i.e., the belief in sacred forces, such as the Holy Spirit, that act on
nature and society and transcend human control).[46]

Obviously, not having focused on Pentecostalism in an actual
setting, this study cannot confirm or disprove this bleak (totalizing)
vision. I believe, however, that Pedra Bonita's case offers sufficient
evidence to demonstrate that the erosion of progressive Catholicism's notion of intra-historical transcendence, like the crisis
of modern emancipatory ideologies, poses a serious threat to
grassroots transformative activities: it is both a sign and the source
of further political disempowerment of those at the margins of
society. While recent socio-economic and cultural changes might
have helped us rethink the concept of politics to understand and
value the strategies people use as they seek to gain some control of
their immediate surroundings, personal, familial, and local praxis
appears increasingly vulnerable to ever encroaching macro-processes.

The hypotheses about Pentecostalism I have proposed are
meant to serve as a point of departure to explore the connection at
the local level between the growth of Pentecostalism among the
urban poor and the current socio-economic and cultural changes
in Latin America. We must keep in mind that, while Pentecostal

[44] D. García Delgado, "Modernidad y postmodernidad en América Latina: una perspectiva desde la ciencia política," in Michelini, San Martín, and Lagrave, eds., *Modernidad y
postmodernidad*, 47.
[45] Ibid., 52.
[46] R. Prandi, "Perto da magia, longe da política," *Novos Estudos CEBRAP*, no. 34 (November
1992), 81–91.

ideology has a strong influence on local practices and forms of organization, there is a great deal of heterogeneity at the grass-roots. As Ireland argues in *Kingdoms Come*, Pentecostal ideology does not determine action on a one-to-one basis; it only provides a bounded repertoire of courses of action (a "settled culture," as it were) from which the individual believer can creatively choose in response to the challenges and needs at hand.

We must also avoid falling in the trap of understanding the rise and development of Pentecostalism only as the product of a social pathology, as Lalive D'Epinay's and Willems's early studies of anomie and Protestantism did. This type of reductive understanding continues to dominate Catholic readings of the growth of Pentecostalism. Some pastoral agents in the *igreja popular* see a direct connection between the poor's worsening economic situation and Pentecostalism's rapid expansion. Comblin, for example, argues that

[t]he decline of the so-called historical churches – both Catholic and Reformed – and the growth of Pentecostal sects can be seen as the consequence of the disillusionment of urban Brazilians who do not find in them where and how to compensate spiritually for the bitterness of their daily lives. Disillusionment largely explains why five churches from "new denominations" appear in Rio de Janeiro every week ... The more dehumanizing that life becomes in urban spaces it would seem that the less space there is for the acceptance of historical religions. The poorer the population of Rio becomes, the less Catholic it is.[47]

Along the same line Frei Betto affirms that "sects grow because of the utter misery that exists among forty million Brazilians. People in misery need solutions yesterday, not today! People will go to that pastor who promises healing to a person without any access to medical care."[48] Readings such as Comblin's and Betto's, while pointing to the importance of recent socio-economic changes in the growth of Pentecostalism, run the danger of immunizing the popular church against any serious examination of shortcomings and contradictions in its worldview and methods.

---

[47] J. Comblin, "A religião que passa," *O Estado de São Paulo*, 02/21/93, quoted in Cook, "Santo Domingo through Protestant Eyes," 196.

[48] M. Puleo, *The Struggle is One: Voices and Visions of Liberation* (Albany: State University of New York Press, 1994), 95–96.

Their critiques see the crisis of participation in the *igreja popular vis-à-vis* Pentecostal groups as the result of factors external to the religious/ideological field. Against Comblin and Betto, we must recognize that religious allegiance and conversion are complex processes that cannot be reduced to simple utilitarian calculation or to socio-economic determinants. Socio-economic factors merely provide a context in which individuals make certain choices. These factors may indeed make some religious ideologies, practices, and forms of organization more attractive than others, depending on the psycho-cognitive, material, and spiritual resources to deal with the "existential dramas" of everyday life. That a person finds certain religious options more effective than others to cope with the world does not mean that s/he will automatically convert. Religious motivations are never that transparent.

Keeping these caveats in mind does not entail that we forsake the study of the role of external forces in shaping religious choices and practices. Even those who warn us against sociological functionalism and reductionism acknowledge that the restructuration and crisis of everyday life during the 1980s in Latin America is an important variable in the growth of Pentecostalism. According to Paul Freston,

[t]here would seem to be a case for linking economic crises with Pentecostal growth. The "lost decade" of the 1980s (stagnation, mounting foreign debt, falling per capita income) saw an acceleration of Protestant growth in many countries [in Latin America]. Economic desperation, and especially *impoverishment* (loss of access to services previously within reach) rather than poverty (which is endemic), are supposedly causing large numbers to seek solutions in miracle-working churches. The "health and wealth gospel" offers a "religion of results." In the context of "savage capitalism," it proclaims the "survival of the most faithful." This explanation is plausible.[49]

The crisis of the popular church, the fragmentation of the religious field, and the growth of Pentecostalism thus call for nuanced, non-reductive sociological approaches that take into account the relative weight of various factors in shaping religious practices and choices in a particular situation.

---

[49] Freston, "Pentecostalism in Latin America," 19.

CHAPTER 9

Rethinking the popular church's project: lessons for this-worldly religious utopias

Having located the predicament of the popular church in the context of a crisis of modern emancipatory projects brought about by a new capitalist configuration and by postmodern discourses, I want to explore in this chapter ways in which the *igreja popular* might transcend its current predicament. On a more general level, this exploration will help us redeploy the notion of utopia, and particularly the idea of intra-historical transcendence, which has come under challenge by postmodernism and the new capitalist configuration.

To avoid engaging in an overly abstract reflection, I will begin by presenting two alternative, seemingly contrasting, pastoral strategies to overcome the crisis already operative at the grassroots. I present these strategies through the voices of two pastoral agents with long histories of involvement in various popular church initiatives in Nova Iguaçu. I do this because, as I have been arguing, the core of the popular church's crisis lies at the grassroots, in a lack of popular mobilization. Thus, for any solution to work, it must address the crisis in its local dimensions. Further, many of the issues raised by the two pastoral agents I introduce here are echoed in debates by Brazilian and Latin American theologians on the future of the popular church. In a way, the confrontation between these two ecclesial visions mirrors more wide-ranging discussions within the institution on the popular church's proper role in society and on its place within Catholicism as we approach the twenty-first century.

The two alternative proposals offered by the pastoral agents are not necessarily mutually exclusive or even incompatible. In fact, I contend that the creative tension between the two proposals might help to maintain a self-critical dynamism within the popular church. Each of the perspectives relativizes the other, making it possible to construct more flexible and context-sensitive pastoral approaches. To demonstrate the fruitfulness of the creative tension I propose, I offer in the third section of this chapter a synthesis that incorporates elements from the two perspectives and my own suggestions.

It should be noted that the two visions of the popular church I present here do not by any means exhaust the multiplicity of voices in the on-going dialogue about the future. Rather they represent two points at different ends of the basism-vanguardism continuum that defines popular church praxis.[1]

The tension between basism and vanguardism crystallizes around the notion of *conscientização*. According Sergio Haddad, in the vanguard tendency, "it is necessary to undertake a work of unconcealment [*desvelamento*] of people's culture, through the inter-vening action of intellectuals and vanguards, with the aim of replacing naive popular consciousness with a critical consciousness striving towards social transformation." The basist tendency, on the other hand, departs from the idea that popular culture has "its own forms of production and reproduction of its social structure and of symbolic resistance and submission." Thus, basists argue that "popular education would work with the popular groups to value authentic forms of struggle, making explicit their organicity with the movement."[2]

The perspectives that follow are articulate expressions of the basist and the vanguardist positions. A careful consideration of the complexities, pitfalls and potentials of these positions is necessary for the *igreja popular* to address its current crisis of identity and participation.

LEDA: "A CHURCH AT THE SERVICE OF LOCAL
COMMUNITIES"

Born in Minas Gerais, Leda spent the early years of her life imbib-ing the deep spirituality that characterizes the state's traditional

---

[1] For a good general discussion of basism and vanguardism within the popular church see Mainwaring, *The Catholic Church and Politics in Brazil*, especially chapters 8 and 9.
[2] S. Haddad "Educação popular e cultura popular." *Tempo e Presença*, no. 220 (1987), 16.

Catholicism. This background gave her a special sensibility for the affective component of religious practice: the power of ritual, devotion and personal commitment to one's tradition. In the 1970s she brought this sensibility to Rio de Janeiro, enrolling at the city's prestigious Jesuit university to study theology. At the university she was introduced to the social sciences and became familiar with liberation theology's formative debates. At the same time, she started to work in *favelas* in the western part of the city. She saw this dual training as an essential part of her plan to become a nun working primarily with the poor.

The 1970s, however, were difficult years for the nascent popular church, especially in Rio, where conservative archbishop Eugênio Sales sought to rein in radical impulses within the archdiocese. In an effort to smooth relations between the local church and the military, Dom Eugênio expelled or withdrew his support for Catholic activists involved in grassroots organizing. Faced with an unsupportive archbishop and a repressive government, Leda decided to leave the university and abandon her plans to become a nun. She concluded that she could better reach her ideal of serving the poor as a lay pastoral agent in north-eastern Brazil.

In the north-east, she worked with Dom Antônio Fragoso, the progressive bishop of Crateús, Ceará, one of the poorest dioceses in the region. In Crateús Leda became more acquainted with Carlos Mesters's pioneering method of biblical exegesis from the standpoint of the poor. Using Freirian techniques of popular education, Mesters brought together poor farmers in the informal, intimate setting of *círculos* (small groups) to reflect on the Scriptures. In these groups the poor came together to select and elaborate their own understanding of Biblical stories and images that helped them make sense of the struggles of daily life in the countryside. Leda also experienced first-hand the tenacious faith of poor people in the north-east, who, faced with abject poverty and the ever-present threat of drought and starvation, continue trusting in God's plan for them. She witnessed moving displays of collective faith such as *romarias*, solemn pilgrimages to regional sacred places. Despite the considerable expenses of the long journey, many poor farmers were ready to sacrifice all their meager resources to pay vows made to their patron saints.

The stubbornness and intensity of faith among the poor in the Northeast only deepened Leda's empathy for the spiritual dimensions of popular religiosity. This sharpened sensibility, which she brought to Nova Iguaçu in the late 1980s, informs her critique of the popular church's present *modus operandi*. For Leda the current crisis of CEBs is due to what she calls the "hegemony of the urban and southeastern model of pastoral activity." Just as the south-east is the center of economic, political and cultural life in the country, so has the region imposed its particular experience and interests in liturgical and pastoral matters within the national church. In the south-east, particularly in São Paulo and Rio de Janeiro, CEBs are connected with the rise of a combative popular movement that includes such well-organized instances as the Workers's Party (PT). This connection has drawn CEBs into a political activism that requires the training of a grassroots leadership capable of joining Christian inspiration with analysis of Brazil's unjust social structures and strategic knowledge of politics. This is why the faith-life link has taken a more politically militant tenor for south-eastern CEBs.

In Leda's view, this tenor was entirely appropriate for the south-east given the socio-political climate of the late 1970s and early 1980s. Nevertheless, she believes that the success of south-eastern urban CEBs in sustaining and re-energizing the popular movement during the military regime elevated this tenor to national and international prominence, firmly establishing the *fermento de massa* conception of base communities as the dominant model for linking religion and politics in the *igreja popular*. In an excessively triumphalistic mode that precluded dialogue with other visions of the pastoral role of base communities, CEBs came to be seen as the architects not only of a new church, but of a new, more just and equitable society. Given the obstacles to organizing, the emergence of alternative channels for effective political action with the *abertura*, and the pressures exerted by the conservative Vatican restoration, this view placed too much weight on CEBs, inflating expectations beyond the limits of the possible. This inflation in turn set the stage for a rapid deflation as the new society failed to materialize and as life conditions worsened in the late 1980s.

Jether Pereira Ramalho, advisor to base communities, concurs with Leda on the deleterious effects of inflated expectations for CEBs. Reflecting on the seventh interecclesial meeting of CEBs in 1989, he writes:

During a certain period some church sectors, especially CEBs, became the privileged space for popular mobilization and resistance to the military dictatorship. That fact created the idea in some [pastoral] agents that [base] communities would become the main actors in the process of construction of a new society. The political game and the communities' maturation have shown that things are more complicated and that many other popular actors are partners in the same struggle [*caminhada*], and that possibly these actors could even have a more prominent role in the process.[3]

Leda's reading of the crisis is also echoed by pastoral agent and feminist theologian Ivone Gebara. According to Gebara,

[P]opular movement theorists had great expectations for the CEBs. They believed they were a *fermento* for a bottom-up transformation within the church. And what happened? Socialism, a word much used in popular struggles, became obsolete. We [the popular church] stressed a utopian discourse that didn't have a chance of becoming a reality ... I don't believe anymore that CEBs are the only road [*caminho*] toward liberation.[4]

Leda, like Gebara, criticizes a vanguardist conception of CEBs, where base communities represent a political group charged with directing the moral and social transformation of Brazilian society. This conception leads to a separation between a trained, enlightened *cadre* of CEB activists and the *massa* which continues to operate with the categories of traditional popular religiosity.

To avoid this gap, the *igreja popular* must, according to theologian José Comblin, go through a true process of "inculturation" (*inculturação*), immersing itself in "the symbolic world that provides the poor with their own understanding of the world and life." For Comblin, "We are no longer in a time when it was possible to think that an enlightened elite could free the masses, or could be

[3] J. P. Ramalho, "Avanços e questões na caminhada das CEBs (reflexões sobre o VII encontro)," *Revista Eclesiástica Brasileira* 49, no. 195 (1989), 573–577.
[4] I. Gebara, "Aborto não é pecado," interview by K. Nanne and M. Bergamo, *Veja* (Rio de Janeiro), October 6, 1993, 10.

identified by them as their vanguard, without passing through a true inculturation."[5] Inculturation demands that CEBs "turn outward" (*CEBs voltadas para fora*), abandon their condition of "isolated islands," and come into contact with the poor's life-world.

Leda offers a solution which parallels Comblin's in many ways. To revitalize CEBs, she would move them closer to the northeastern pastoral model, in which liturgical, affective, symbolic, and ritual aspects have always played a more central role than political praxis because of the region's popular religiosity. In addition, she favors a separation of CEBs from the popular political movement to avoid the danger of religious methods, goals, and activities becoming overwhelmed by more politically savvy segments of the movement. The separation would also protect CEBs against the popular movement's fluctuating fortunes.

Leda is quick to point out that this separation, however, does not entail a withdrawal of CEBs from the society. They do not have to turn themselves inward and become concerned only with purely religious, other-worldly matters, as many church conservatives suggest. For Leda, CEBs must continue working to change society; nonetheless, they must do it not by seeking an immediate, total transformation of unjust structures but by "serving their local communities." In other words, CEBs should focus their activities at the micro level, listening attentively to the needs and aspirations of the neighborhoods in which they are located. These needs and aspirations have to set the agenda for CEB action. The radical transformation of Brazil's unjust social order continues to be the underlying objective of base community praxis, but it now functions as a utopian horizon that CEBs can only gradually approximate through the accumulated weight of small victories from below. Here Leda's position comes close to Dulce's modest vision of CEB life in Pedra Bonita: base communities are extended families, self-support networks for those at the margins.

According to Leda, a focus on the micro, on addressing the concrete life conditions of the poor, would enable base communities to avoid imposing visions of the social world which separate them from their target constituency. The renewed emphasis on the

---

[5] J. Comblin, "Inculturação e libertação," *Convergência*, no. 235 (1990), 428.

affective, symbolic, and liturgical components of religious practice
will also resonate with the urban poor's deeply rooted religiosity,
with their sense of wonderment and their tenacious hope for
transcendence in the face of so much suffering. After all, a great
majority of the urban poor have migrated from the north-east,
bringing their traditional religiosity with them to the big cities in
the south-east.

In addition to appealing to the north-eastern CEB model, Leda
considers that base communities could learn a great deal from
Mesters's *círculos bíblicos*. In the circles poor people do not have to
confront popular educational materials that introduce categories
of social analysis and require a certain level of academic sophistication. Nor do they have to attend training seminars on politics. In
their "purest form," Bible circles merely open a space for the poor
to come into dialogue with a single text, the Bible, which they
approach with their own cultural resources and concerns. The
circles' participants collectively, bit by bit, construct interpretations of biblical passages that make sense of their everyday existence. The pastoral agent is not the main actor in this process; s/he
only plays a supportive role whenever s/he is called by the people
in the group. Even when a member of the *círculo* offers a reading
that is discriminatory, that flies in the face of the group's communal spirit, it is not the pastoral agent who corrects him/her, or
leads him/her to a more emancipatory interpretation. Rather, the
group confronts him/her and calls into question his/her reading.
The group acts, in Leda's words, as a "mirror" where the poor
come to regard themselves as people with rights. As such, it is truly
the "poor teaching the poor," not a vanguard carrying the poor on
its back.

Consciousness-raising should continue to be the aim of CEBs
and the *círculos*. Yet, the logic of the process must not be dictated by
the need to teach the poor a method to grasp the underlying causes
of social injustice and to change the system. *Conscientização* is above
all an exercise through which the person comes to gain a sense of
self-worth, of personal dignity. *Conscientização*'s point of departure
and arrival is, in Leda's view, not social scientific knowledge or
political know-how, but the facts of everyday life, the existence of
each of the CEB participants.

Leda recognizes the limitations of her proposal. She realizes that the worldview and group solidarity that have sustained *nordestino* religiosity have been challenged by the dislocation of small farmers as large-scale agribusinesses and cattle-raisers penetrate deeper into the region. These capitalist forms of agrarian production have uprooted people, forcing them to look for land elsewhere or to become itinerant workers in search for seasonal/occasional employment. Such economic change might force CEBs to divert their attention from liturgical and ecclesial matters and to focus on socio-economic issues. Furthermore, she has seen enough contradictions within *círculos bíblicos* to understand that her reading of their dynamics points more to an ideal-type than a reality. *Círculos* are also subject to excessive episcopal control and increasing bureaucratization. And finally, why assume that importing a different pastoral approach to urban CEBs might solve the crisis when it is clear that part of the problem is due to the hegemony, at the national level, of a single model of base community praxis? Still, Leda thinks that the northeastern pastoral model teaches the popular church an important lesson that should serve as its guiding principle: "the people always know better."

Leda, thus, presents fundamentally a "basist" vision of the future of CEBs and of the popular church in general. This vision is challenged by Helena, for whom the church now more than ever must be *fermento*.

HELENA: "YOU CANNOT ACHIEVE A NEW SOCIETY ONLY BY SAYING 'OUR FATHERS' AND 'HAIL MARYS'"

Although Helena's parents were born in the countryside, her mother in Minas Gerais and her father in the north-eastern state of Paraíba, she is a product of the Baixada Fluminense. An activist since her student days in high school, Helena grew up in the shade of the emerging popular church during the 1970s. Her initial involvement in the *igreja popular* was through *grupos de perseverança*, groups organized to support Catholic youth after their first communion. Gradually, Helena moved to more advanced groups organized by the diocese's *pastoral da juventude* (youth outreach). There she came into contact with "people who had a different vision of reality, who did a different type of political work." These people began to introduce her to the situation of the poor throughout the country. New insights spurred her to continue reading sociological and political materials and to get involved in study groups in her neighborhood and diocese. Increased social involvement and political awareness paved the way for her to become a member of the directorate of the Friends of the Neighborhood Movement (MAB). From 1981 to 1984 she was the movement's secretary, planning and executing strategies for about 100 neighborhoods throughout the district of Nova Iguaçu.

Helena's involvement with MAB, besides allowing her to intervene effectively in local politics, gave her a good sense of the national political scene. Around that time, she also began to participate in several groups that later would become the various currents within the PT in the state of Rio de Janeiro. According to Helena, this period of her life was "fundamental in [her political] growth. A period to sit, discuss and debate ideas, to participate in electoral processes, to form alliances with people, to defend my theoretical arguments against those that challenged me." It seemed to her that she had "almost everything in her hands, that [she] had the possibility of having a considerable impact on the popular movement. But then things came apart [*se desmoronaram*]."

As her commitment with the more secular segments of the popular movement deepened, Helena felt the pull of two opposing forces. On the one hand, she began to experience tensions with the pastoral agents in her parish who did not approve of her involvement with radical extra-ecclesial groups.

[Our pastoral agents] were Belgian priests who were willing to discuss whatever was connected with the preferential option for the poor and the youth. Only that the option could only be taken within the church. That is, one should not become, for example, a member of the directorate of a neighborhood federation ... or of a political party. In other words, everything was tied closely to popular education, to reflection: What a certain thing had do with the Bible and God's word. So there was a contradiction, because [base] communities encourage [Catholic] activists to become involved, but when they begin to participate, communities start to reject them. Communities believe that everything comes from themselves, that everything is born out of and ends with faith ... that change is going to come just by transforming one's consciousness . . . by educating the people.

On the other hand, Helena was openly challenged by colleagues within the popular movement who felt she was too religious. "I was very confused at the time. While I was very critical in relation to the church, I reacted defensively when a predominantly atheistic group challenged my views. [So] within the church I was a communist, and in leftist circles I was a right-winger."

The tension between religion and politics in Helena's work came to a head in 1982 when the parish priest tried to expel her from her base community:

He didn't want me to participate anymore in the community. He said that all we did was organize PT meetings and that I was ruining [*estragando*] the community. Then I told him that I would stay as an independent, even if the community did not want to accept me, that I would remain and that I thought that he didn't have the right to order me out.

Helena's plight is not uncommon among Catholic activists. Sociologist and CEB advisor Pedro Ribeiro de Oliveira has argued recently that the popular church has failed to develop a coherent pastoral approach to the *militantes*. He observes that

[t]here are innumerable cases of people coming from Christian communities who occupy a leadership position in popular politics . . . who feel distant from the church, despite their Christian faith. After assuming positions of political responsibility these men and women become distant from their base communities. The motives are diverse: on the one hand, the new commitments take time, leaving little time for community and religious activities; on the other, the community seeks to protect itself against a political-partisan instrumentalization and creates obstacles for the participation of politically-marked people.[6]

To address this problem, Oliveira suggests that the popular church design a non-partisan, pluralistic and inclusive pastoral strategy to accompany Catholics in their political *caminhada*. This pastoral accompaniment is critical since members of CEBs and *círculos bíblicos* are perhaps the most important building blocks for popular

[6] P. R. de Oliveira, "A igreja dos pobres e a atividade político-partidária," *Cadernos Fé e Política*, no. 2 (1989), 41.

organizations such as the PT and CUT because of their work at the grassroots. Despite this activism, Oliveira notes that

[t]he participation of people connected with Christian communities in leadership positions [*as cúpulas*] within popular organizations is minimal. Christians perceive that they execute their work at the base but that they exert very little influence in setting the party's or the trade-union's direction. They see other groups, which generally do little work at the base, having more influence . . . precisely because the focus on internal work, vying for different positions in the party leadership. This fact . . . generates dissatisfaction among Christians and often leads them to become discouraged with party politics, to deny the legitimacy of these other groups and to oppose the party's leadership.[7]

Why do *igreja popular* activists have so little influence on popular organizations? According to Oliveira, the answer lies in the popular church's *modus operandi*. Christian communities "refuse to manipulate the bases and reject any vanguardism. [They] prefer to err on the side of basism." This position is essentially correct because it affirms "that it is the people itself who must be the subject of their history." Nevertheless, basism leaves popular church activists unable to challenge other, much more savvy popular elites which have a more vanguardist, even authoritarian, approach. To address this problem Oliveira argues that Christian activists must receive the politico-theoretical education necessary to navigate the dangerous waters of the party system and to be able to articulate long-term proposals for the movement. Acceptance of this proposal, however, would mean giving up the popular church's purist basism.

Oliveira, thus, offers a corrective to the basist approach in CEBs and *círculos bíblicos* in relation to the link between faith and politics. Helena, on her part, goes further in her critique of *basismo*:

Let's return to what the people in the *igreja popular* are saying. They think that society exists within a make-believe world. They believe that transformation will happen just as Christ opened the skies. But we are not going to have a transformation only from the theological point of view. You can't propose a project of social transformation by saying "Our Fathers" and "Hail Mary's." "Our Father" is a beautiful prayer, but so what? You can't transform society by organizing a procession with

---

[7] Ibid., 35.

prayers to the Guanabara palace [the Governor's house]. At some point that's not going to work.

According to Helena, significant changes in Brazilian society and politics can only happen when people with emancipatory ideals, people who "have a clear vision of reality, who can mobilize the base, who can establish objectives and can present and defend a long-term plan," come to have influence within the popular movement. Even within the church Helena rejects a basist appeal to spirituality. Responding to Leda's proposal, Helena argues that even when there is sometimes "an exacerbated militancy" in the south, this region offers "better chances for transformation":

People in the north-east vote for the Right. Many of them vote in exchange for a kilogram of beans, of salt. It is because conditions are so disgraceful that people lose even the will to live, let alone fight. People end up, let's say, crawling [*se restrejando*] to get a certain thing. So I feel that people in the cities can organize themselves better, can risk more, perhaps because conditions are more favorable, perhaps because of their more wide-ranging view of the world.

Further, Helena considers that the renewal of the popular church calls for more than a purely spiritual and liturgical change. Even if it is true that people in the north-east have a "stronger spirituality" because they need to "continue having hope to give them enough motivation to go on living in a situation of great injustice and suffering," transplanting their spirituality will not have an impact at the institutional level, where the fate of the popular church is being decided.

The process of intervention in society does not happen through those more poetic and ritual aspects. The church's agenda is not defined by the great *romarias* of the north-east. These *romarias* are great, they are beautiful, they give you chills. But they do not intervene in the relations within the CNBB. And as I said the other day, bishops have great power. They have the power to decide, to name, a power that surpasses any local movement. Those processes of spirituality and prayer do [not] build the new church. They enrich the new church. You need to have people in the pastoral commission. You need to have people inside the church battling to become coordinators at the regional level. You need to make sure that the coordinator is not a priest because it is the coordinator who is going to decide what's going to happen in the region.

Helena aims at the heart of Leda's basist proposal when she states that: "Not all that comes from the people is good." Popular culture contains racist, sexist, and jingoistic elements that hinder the process of liberation. Someone has to confront and criticize these elements, and what better person than the "organic" intellectual who understands, by personal experience, the inner workings of popular culture?

You don't have to be paternalistic with the people. Yet, you have to bring new facts to them. I know people who say that you can't use difficult words when speaking with the poor. But you have to make sure that people learn new words so that they can say: "It's great that I've learned difficult words! It's great that I've learned that the world doesn't end in Santa Marta [a neighborhood in the Baixada]."

Helena's position *vis-à-vis* popular culture corresponds to what Father José of the ACO understands to be the Catholic activist's role concerning popular religiosity. According to Father José, the critically conscious Catholic activist must "evangelize and purify popular religiosity, taking the best from it, that which orients life toward the reign of God." He believes that "just like any human reality, popular religion is not an absolute in itself. Popular religion, like any religion, may sometimes lead to enslavement [*escravatura*], dependence, and fear." He bases this belief in the Gospel and Jesus' example:

Jesus had to confront many ideologies of His time. For instance, let's say the bourgeois ideology of the Pharisees and the Scribes, and also the ideology of the Zealots, the guerrillas, as it were. Jesus never left the people's religiosity as intact. He always took its essential values and elaborated them further. He spoke in parables, the language of the people, to challenge, taking care to explain the message behind.

Both Helena and José are defending a vanguardist strategy to work with popular religiosity, since they stress the need to uncover and correct impurities within it. When questioned about the possibility that she is espousing an elitist position that privileges the vanguard's more specialized knowledge over that of the people,

Helena responds that she does not believe that the former is the only or even the best kind of learning:

I think that when one works with the people one brings certain things and receives others. Now there is a current of thought that wants to make people the subject of their own history, but at the same time keeps them ignorant. If one does not introduce new elements, reality is going to stay the same. People continue doing the same thing over and over. To value the people does not mean that you're going to deny them access to certain things that are important for them to know. Giving them access to those things and saying that they don't know them yet is not devaluing what they already know. I can't say that child trapped in abject poverty in Santa Marta has consciousness of the world at large! It is important that s/he learn that the world is bigger than that. Do rich kids not have computers at home? They have access to so much information. So too I think the people should have this access. People have to learn to do a bank transaction, how to pick up a phone, how to sign a document. This is important in today's world.

In contrast to Leda's injunction that "the people always know better," and that the "organic" intellectual minimize its role in the consciousness-raising process, Helena argues that "there is no neutral formation."

Everybody has a project. Even if I say: "I'm going to use popular education. Let's see what words are the ones that you think are most common in your lives, the words that you want to say to me." And then people tell you. In the simple act of selecting words, I'm already introducing my ideas. There is no one who is free of prejudices. Even the fact of defending a popular pedagogy is already a political project. I think, on the contrary, that the best guarantee that the people be the subject of their own formation, is for the pastoral agent to be honest about his/her proposal and project. People then will decide which project they find more acceptable.

Thus, for Helena "there is no way of saying that everybody is going to walk together. Some people are going to advance more rapidly. There is no denying that you'll always have a vanguard." And given the institutional obstacles that the popular church faces and the fragmentation of the popular movement, it is necessary that a vanguard "make things advance. The process is long and you have to help people grow politically." The solution of the popular church crisis, then, lies in the intensification of the *pastoral de grupos pequenos*, of which the CEBs are a central manifestation. Moreover, within that pastoral approach the south-eastern model of linking faith and politics has to become the guiding paradigm.

Helena appears to be presenting a classical vanguardist line. Yet, despite her outright rejection of Leda's basist project, she recognizes dangers in her approach:

I believe that when one speaks of work at the popular level one must really operate at the popular level. Work at the popular level is not really putting together half-a-dozen enlightened characters who are going to remain reflecting on the country's future. Rather it is to work concretely so that the population have access to democracy, to basic conditions for living.

Her awareness of these dangers is heightened by the current crisis in the popular movement and her recent experiences as an activist. After spending five years working with the *pastoral operária* (workers' Catholic outreach), which took her to São Paulo for some time, she grew tired of "endless, repetitive meetings" and the petty intrigues of partisan politics:

I had discovered so much reality that I didn't have hope any more, I didn't have anything that could tell me why I should get up everyday, why I should smile. We used to say that people were alienated but it was us who were alienated. Because everyone goes to parties, and we used to say that going to a party was alienating. We just talked about politics; we couldn't talk about anything else. We couldn't speak with people who were different from us. We couldn't go to a movie that we thought was stupid. We only heard revolutionary music. All our lives were like that. As much as we were immersed in the process of analyzing reality, the present historical situation [*conjuntura*], collectively and personally there was a process of separation from the reality that the common person lived.

This separation resulted in some of the impasses the popular movement and the church is experiencing presently:

We worked with a process of formation and of regaining our rights that was gradually becoming exhausted. And in the end what happened? A small group of people remained that could not haul the totality of the population. We began to defend a project, a dream that was ours, that wasn't the dream of the masses. In other words, we worked with wrong strategies that were not conducive to the reception and formation of new leaders. On the contrary, they produced the hardening of those who were already there. We started to have a hunger for power, to occupy power positions, to perpetuate ourselves in directorates.

Helena has become an independent grassroots activist now and has turned to what she calls "a project to recover the life of the population." She realizes that she must deal with "things of life: education, health, which are worsening for the poor." Her focus is now on "concrete reality . . . [which] involves perceiving if your comrade is unemployed, if his/her mother is sick, if his/her father died . . . things that have to do with everyday life." In addition, she has sought to recover values that were lost during her arduous *caminhada*. She has begun to "value life and people: the relationships I build, the time I have to reflect on the meaning of life." This recovery has led her to form a group where the poorest children in her neighborhood come to play, do hand-crafts and talk about their experiences at home. Thus, for all her vanguardist rhetoric, Helena is sensitive to the need to amend pastoral and pedagogical strategies that have hitherto proved unproductive.

The tension between vanguardist and basist tendencies in Helena already points the way to a possible solution to *aporias* the popular church is currently suffering: a relativization of the *pastoral de grupos pequenos* and the redeployment of a new brand of basism more in accordance with the life conditions of the urban poor.

PASTORAL PLURALISM AND BASIST REALISM

Anthropologist Carlos Rodrigues Brandão identifies two approaches to CEB pedagogy and pastoral practice which resonate with Leda's and Helena's positions:

The first one: If the church wants to commit itself to the liberation of its people, its mission is to organize small groups of popular leaders who will act as *fermento na massa*. That is, small popular elites . . . which represent a fraction of the overall [Catholic] community . . . with little direct involvement in the life of the common person, even in his/her religiosity . . . would make the popular classes rise and would conduct all liberation work. The other: all work must reflect a commitment by the church with the totality of the [Catholic] community, even if that means a less advanced pastoral practice than the one that attracts activists.[8]

He goes on to say that in reality there is no contradiction between the two pastoral approaches because popular religiosity as experienced on the ground exists at the margins of both institutional, official religion and of society. Popular religiosity is an expression of the culture of the oppressed classes. Therefore, Brandão argues, "reinforcing the popular elements of religion," as Leda has suggested, "means reinforcing the identity of these oppressed classes, [and] consequently means reinforcing their solidarity and their capacity to fight oppression."[9]

Brandão makes two unwarranted assumptions: (i) that popular culture/religion is of one piece (a sort of anthropological holism), and (ii) that because it exists at the margins of official and sanctioned modes of action and thinking it is inherently liberatory. Recent work in anthropology and critical theory has shown that rather than forming a single fabric with an underlying structuring principle, culture is a shifting terrain formed by discursive and non-discursive clusters, each with its own history and range of application. Furthermore, practices and worldviews more emblematic of the life-style of dominant groups in society are incorporated in the formation of the subcultures that accompany groups at the margins. This incorporation reproduces at the symbolic level the institutional and structural conditions that have marginalized these groups.

Brandão's resolution of the tension between a pastoral approach directed to a small popular elite and one addressed to the masses is, therefore, theoretically inadequate. More importantly, at the practical level, Brandão's optimism notwithstanding, pastoral agents continue to experience this tension in their everyday practice despite their best efforts to balance the opposing strategies.

Claúdio Perani, another pastoral agent with experience in northeastern Brazil, offers a more plausible alternative. In re-

---

[8] C. R. Brandão, "Elite e massa na religiosidade do povo," in *A Religiosidade do Povo*, Lísias Negrão et al. (São Paulo: Paulinas, 1984), 179–180.
[9] Ibid., 181.

sponse to the question of whether the *igreja popular* should emphasize pastoral approaches directed toward a popular elite or "favor
the capacity to open itself to the masses (opening not in the
numerical sense but in the sense of being able to relate to the
language and day-to-day problems of the working masses),"
Perani proposes a "pastoral pluralism."[10] Rather than denying
that there is a tension between faith and politics, between a *pastoral
de grupos pequenos* and *pastoral de massa*, he calls for the recognition
that "there are, within the popular [church], differing viewpoints
and lines of action . . . differing forms of intervening in the historical process." For Perani,

One cannot deny the difference between faith and politics . . . they
operate under two different logics. The logic of politics is a logic of power,
of efficacy, of clear identity and definition of projects and programs. The
logic of faith is the logic of meekness, of error and sin [*escândalo*], of loss of
identity and gratuitous surrender. The Christian lives an inevitable
tension between identity and involvement. S/he must *affirm* her/his life
and at the same time *surrender* it . . .[11]

Pastoral pluralism needs to be accompanied by an ecumenical
attitude to allow enhanced dialogue with the poor, not from a
preconceived vision of how the world is and should be, but from a
position of openness and willingness to learn. In this model "the
community of the faithful is more a space to exchange [experien-
ces] than [one] to make political decision and to play the political
games." Such openness should help avoid the "risk of deducting a
historical project from faith."[12] The process of automatically de-
riving a historical project from faith has legitimized the existence
of a popular vanguard which claims a privileged access to that
project.

Perani's proposal for a more diversified and participatory pastoral approach, thus, echoes Leda's concern about politics imposing its own rhythm, methods and goals to transformative religious
practice. After arguing that the popular church should give more
space to the poor, "spaces where they can think and reinforce their
own *caminhada*," Parani concludes his article with a plea:

---

[10] C. Perani, "Novos rumos da pastoral popular." *Cadernos do CEAS*, no. 107 (1987), 39, 44.
[11] Ibid., 43. [12] Ibid., 44.

To strengthen the signs of change that have appeared in the recent years, it seems to me that it is important not to give too much weight to the traditional political channels, which may generate elitism and with that weaken the growth of the popular movement. Without rejecting them, it is a matter of maintaining a broader perspective, and because of that, one that is necessarily more gradual.[13]

Perani's idea of pastoral pluralism certainly represents an improvement over Brandão's uneasy reconciliation of pastoral work directed toward small groups and toward the masses. However, Perani's mistrust of "traditional political channels," leaves Catholic activists like Helena, who must deal with such channels to advance the liberationist message, out in the cold. How can the popular church accompany them in their perilous journey in a world dominated by the "logic of power and efficacy," as Perani himself states?

Given the obstacles that confront grassroots activists (i.e., the political system's rampant corruption and elitism, the ever-present danger of manipulation and co-optation through relations of patronage), it is imperative that the popular church continue training individuals capable of exercising their rights as citizens, and in the process, expands the reaches of what hitherto has been a shallow civil society. The case of Pedra Bonita shows how the base community core exerted strategic pressure on reluctant and paternalistic politicians, holding them accountable for their promises, showing the duplicity of their moves, and securing better life conditions for the neighborhood. It was the CEB core's tenacity, clearsightedness and dedication that brought significant improvements to Pedra Bonita.[14]

The imperative for the popular church to help train informed citizens capable of entering the debate about the future configuration of Brazilian society is all the more urgent in view of the elitist nature and deplorable state of the educational system in

---

[13] Ibid., 46.

[14] According to Mariz, "the data show that political struggles supported by CEBs have been successful in the areas researched. The neighborhoods obtained some material improvements. CEBs used political tools for the material improvement of the poor community, and people from different religious groups benefited from these improvements. CEBs intend to eliminate clientele political behavior and individual abuse of power." *Coping with Poverty*, 119.

the country. Furthermore, with collective and national actors weakened by the legitimation crisis, the Catholic Church continues in poll after poll to top the list of institutions the public still trusts. Because of this legitimacy, the church's pastoral-pedagogical strategy has the potential for reaching a wide audience and achieving success in its efforts to re-enfranchise the marginalized. This does not mean that the church should supplant the state in matters of education. It just means that the popular church should continue to play an active role in the process of democratization from below, by providing the context and resources for the formation of critical consciousness and informed participation.

Father José of the ACO understands the unavoidable need to work with small groups, the best pastoral strategy to train local organic intellectuals because it provides concentrated attention to their gradual political, religious and cultural development. Confronted with a "system that is not interested in developing the culture of its people because they might become dangerous to it," he thinks that it is "essential, obligatory for the church to train leaders. They are a central part of our utopia: to see people experiencing the power of self-organization."

The centrality of the *pastoral de grupos pequenos*, nonetheless, does not make it the only strategy to reach and serve the poor, the once-and-for-all pastoral panacea. CEBs and *círculos bíblicos* represent an approach to a particular audience within the poor. As Leda argues, they should not bear the whole weight of the liberationist project; they are not the ones that are going to single handedly "re-invent" society, or even the church. They are not going to fulfill all the pastoral needs of the increasingly differentiated poor. The hope that a small vanguard can lead the masses towards a total critique of the system is based on the notion of right consciousness, which as we saw in the previous chapter has been challenged with the crisis of representation.

Small groups such as CEBs have a more limited range of action and a circumscribed domain of effectiveness. Their pay-off lies in (1) fostering the process of democratization within the church and in society from below, gradually opening spaces for greater participation; (2) helping, as both Daniel Levine and Paulo Krischke argue,[15] in the formation (through the see-judge-act conscious-ness-raising spiral) of committed and critical citizens engaged in a long-term project of transformation in accordance with the church's social teaching; and (3) the proclamation of the possibility of this-worldly transcendence.

The popular church, therefore, need not jettison the *pastoral de grupos pequenos*; it just needs to relativize it. Here the postmodern call to reject the totalizing drive of modernity may help the popular church redeploy its project. We can take as a point of departure Ernesto Laclau's claim that postmodernism is not a rejection of modernity, as some of the most polemical critics have claimed, but rather "a modulation of its themes and categories."[16] Postmodernism represents a critique and a "weakening" of the "absolutist pretensions" of modern discourses: the idea that there is only one correct way to relate to the world. As we saw in the previous chapter, modernity's epistemology is based on a version of the correspondence theory of cognition, which posits that given the right consciousness the world becomes fully transparent.

The popular church absorbs these "absolutist pretensions" by incorporating and cosmizing modernity's understanding of hu-man action and progress. To weaken the absolutist character of these modernist themes in the popular church requires a critique of its "ontologization" of the poor – its conception of the poor as a unified social class with a single culture and set of interests.[17]

The case of Pedra Bonita has shown how the increasing frag-mentation of the urban poor and the adoption of household-based strategies to cope with worsening life conditions has made the appeal to a unified class difficult. Under these conditions the *igreja popular*'s eschatological teleology, the transformation of the "poor"

---

[15] See Levine, *Popular Voices*; and P. J. Krischke, "Church Base Communities and Demo-cratic Change in Brazilian Society," *Comparative Political Studies* 24, no. 2 (1991), 186–210.

[16] E. Laclau, "Politics and the Limits of Modernity," in *Postmodernism: A Reader*, ed. T. Docherty (New York: Columbia University Press, 1993).

[17] According to Brazilian theologian and CEB advisor Frei Betto, among the new chal-lenges that liberation theology must face up to is the construction of a "new epistemol-ogy." As part of this epistemology, liberation theology "in its analytical work . . . must take care not to remain in thrall to the concept of social classes. There are realities like women, children, blacks, indigenous peoples which require a different approach. One can no longer talk of evangelization without carefully tackling the question of incultura-tion." Betto, "Did Liberation Theology Collapse?" 38.

into a spiritual collective agent whose actions are leading towards salvation is in danger of committing what Bourdieu calls the "theoreticist error," which consists in "treating classes on paper as real classes, in concluding from the objective homogeneity of conditions, of conditioning . . . which all come from the identity of position in the social space, that the people involved exist as a unified group, as a class."[18] Júlio de Santa Ana expresses this danger in more religious terms:

The [base] community people believe that the poor are the messianic subject . . . But [to say that] the poor are intrinsically the messianic subject is to engage in a sociological sacralization. The poor are supporting Collor and Menem [Argentina's populist president]. [There is] no perception of the ambiguities that exist within the poor – ambiguities that are common to all human beings – and as a result a collective subject is sacralized.[19]

The classes that intellectuals identify through their sociological analysis are constructed classes, the product of a heuristic explanatory scheme to render the social space meaningful. As Bourdieu argues, they are in reality not "actual class[es], in the sense of group[s] mobilized for struggle, at most, [they] might be called probable class[es], inasmuch as they are set[s] of agents which will present fewer hindrances to efforts of mobilization than any other set of agents."[20] Classes are not given in "social reality" as finished, naked facts as the metaphysics of presence would have it. Rather, they are, in the words of E. P. Thompson, "events," "historical phenomena," "made" by real people who share "common experiences . . . feel and articulate the identity of their interests as between themselves, and as against other men [sic] whose interests are different from (usually opposed to) theirs."[21]

The formation of a class with common interests will depend on its various members coming to share a perception of the conditions that affect them and the needs these create. Structural location in

[18] Bourdieu, "Social Space and Symbolic Power," 129.
[19] Santa Ana, "Lecture to the National Team of Advisors," 43.
[20] Bourdieu, "The Social Space and the Genesis of Groups." *Social Science Information* 24, no. 2 (1985), 198.
[21] E.P. Thompson, *The Making of the English Working Class* (New York: Vintage Books, 1963), 9.

the mode of production is not enough to guarantee class formation, as class members must come to see and feel the world in a
similar fashion. They must share, as Thompson calls it, a "lived"
or "human experience."[22] Thompson's concept of experience
bridges the gap between structure and process, between determination and agency. Through this concept,

[m]en and women also return as subjects . . . not as autonomous subjects,
"free individuals," but as persons experiencing their determinate productive situations and relationships, as needs and interests and as antagon-
isms, and then "handling" this experience within their consciousness and
their culture . . . in the most complex (yes! "relatively autonomous")
ways, and then (often but not always through the ensuing structures of
class) acting upon their determinate situations in their turn.[23]

I would go further than Thompson and say that sharing a lived
experience is not enough for a group to form a class. To constitute
a class, members must grasp this experience through its economic
determinants. It is possible that a group of individuals confronting
the same life conditions may organize and apprehend these conditions through cultural frameworks built upon race, gender, ethnic-
ity, religious differences, etc. Identifying economic determinants as
primary in a particular situation makes it possible for the group to
construct shared economic interests which stand in opposition to
others.

The understanding that classes are articulated historically by
the actions of human actors who, operating under certain social
constraints, choose to cast their lots together should forestall overly
mechanistic and teleological readings of class formation and
struggle. The "working class" is not an already-made, homogeneous, inherently revolutionary collective subject predestined to slay
capitalism.

In the case of the "urban poor" in Brazil there appears to be
neither a "homogeneity of conditions," nor the same "lived experiences" for the various segments contained in this term. The
popular church must understand this heterogeneity of objective
and subjective conditions, for this understanding will result in not
treating the urban poor as a unified class which just needs to be

---

[22] Thompson, "The Poverty of Theory."   [23] Ibid., 164.

directed, "made to rise" by a vanguard: the CEBs. Without the burden of carrying a whole class, which now appears inert, on their backs, CEBs can concentrate on the grassroots activities, promoting democracy, participation, and self-governance at the local and intra-ecclesial levels. Such activities do not preclude alliances with other groups to search for more structural and long-term solutions to social ills. CEBs, however, will not be placed in the role of having to awaken an alienated, resigned, oppressed class, and thus will not have to resort to elitist condemnations of popular culture and religiosity. CEBs can then better engage the multiple elements of popular culture and religiosity in "a give and take," as Helena calls it.

The foregoing discussion dovetails with debates on post-Marxism and the intellectuals' retreat from the concept of class.[24] In my view, the relativization of the concept of class does not imply that the latter should be rejected as an invalid or outmoded analytical tool. Neither does it call for the adoption of an idealist, or an "anything-goes" understanding of history. As we saw in Brazil, a lopsided distribution of wealth was aggravated by economic changes during the 1980s. The worsening of economic conditions during the past decade has, paradoxically, not only produced a fragmentation of the working poor, but also created an opposite "levelling" pull which is increasingly eroding the position of the middle class and threatening to divide Brazilian society into two camps: a vast majority of have-nots and a dwindling minority of haves. Under these conditions it would be unwise to abandon class analysis altogether, since the potential for group formation and mobilization in direct response to economic pressures is high.

Thus, while conservative Catholics criticize the use of Marxist categories because they ideologize faith and divide the church, I propose that the popular church refine its materialist socio-analytical tools to enhance its pastoral reach. The relativization of the concept of class aims to "lower its ontological pretensions," so that it is not seen as "the ground of History," or part of an emancipatory metanarrative, but as a "pragmatic and limited [and yet important] synthesis of a historical reality that subverts and surpasses"

---

[24] See E. Laclau and C. Mouffe, *Hegemony and Socialist Strategy* (London: Verso, 1985); N. Geras, "Post-Marxism?" *New Left Review* 163 (May/June 1987), 40–82.

it.[25] The relativization of class is a reformulation of a particular understanding of materialism, or what Ivone Gebara calls "a revision of inflexible positions that distance the church from the life and the real needs of the poor."[26]

To understand the situation of the poor better, it is necessary to examine the totality of conditions that shape and enable their activities, or as Raymond Williams puts it, "the production and reproduction of real life."[27] One can only understand the behaviors and worldviews of particular individuals, households, and communities by focusing on the life conditions in which and through which they act. Even when some of these life conditions are more specifically cultural (i.e., ideologies, patterns of political activity, religious discourses and practices), they carry a structuring density that both enables and forecloses certain courses of actions. In other words, they are no less "material" and "real" than the economic dynamics that ensure the individual's physical reproduction. In this context, the old base–superstructure dichotomy that has disabled historical materialism gives way to a model of the social space in which practices in the economic, political and cultural fields of action enter into complex and historically contingent relations of reciprocal determination.

The relativization of the concept of class, thus, leads to a non-reductive materialism, which rejects dualism and essentialism. This materialism focuses on the plurality of human practices, all of which carry concrete, material consequences for our existence, and seeks to elucidate the interplay of conditions that shape lived experience. The non-reductive nature of the approach does not imply, however, that the social space is indeterminate or only open to local readings, as certain postmodern discourses would have it. Rather, there are often salient phenomena, which at a given time, play a determining role in the social configuration

---

[25] Laclau, "Politics and the Limits of Modernity," 340. Marxist theorist Erik Olin Wright suggests a reconstruction of class analysis involving "a shift from an a priori belief in the primacy of class in social explanations to a more open stance in exploring the causal importance of class," which is likely to continue to be "powerful." E. O. Wright, "Class Analysis, History and Emancipation," *New Left Review* no. 202 (November/December 1993), 27.

[26] Gebara, "Aborto não é pecado," 10.

[27] R. Williams, *Marxism and Literature* (Oxford: Oxford University Press, 1977), 91.

under study. These "saliences" allow for the formulation of analytical generalizations that go beyond pure micro-descriptivism.

A non-reductive materialist focus on lived experience would
help the popular church to understand conditions on the ground
better. It would make the church sensitive to the multiplicity of
pressures and needs that various sectors of urban poor confront
and to their meager resources to cope. This increased sensitivity
would help the church to avoid labelling as alienated and
acomodados the poor who choose to engage in pragmatic, individualist and immediatist strategies or to rely on patron-client exchanges. Such labeling ends up being a self-fulfilling prophecy, as
CEB members often strike a vanguardist attitude of condescension
which isolates them further from their neighbors.

Perhaps CEBs are not the most appropriate pastoral strategy to
redirect the popular church's focus toward the lived experiences
of the urban poor. CEBs' range of action and effectiveness
touches only some aspects of the urban poor's field of experience.
To penetrate the urban poor's lived experience more fully, the
popular church needs a strategy that goes beyond the training of
local organic intellectuals; it needs to create new forms of basist
realism.[28] The aim of this realism is to understand and respond
adequately to alterity of and within the poor. To accomplish this,
basist realism should contain at least four elements: (1) a recognition of the centrality of the body as the instance that both receives
the impact of life conditions and mediates world-transforming
action; (2) a better understanding of the evolving life conditions for
poor women, the main participants in CEBs and *círculos*; (3) institutional support for local, community and household-based defensive initiatives among the poor; and (4) a recovery and
strengthening of the plausibility of immanent transcendence at the
local level.

Sociologist of religion Meredith McGuire recently urged theorists and researchers to "take seriously the fact that humans are
embodied . . . that believers (and non-believers) are not merely
disembodied spirits, but that they experience a material world in

---

[28] For an alternative, though related, proposal see D. Lehmann, *Democracy and Development in Latin America: Economics, Politics and Religion in the Postwar Period* (Philadelphia: Temple University Press, 1990). Lehmann calls for a "*basismo* as if reality really mattered."

and through their bodies."[29] McGuire's call is relevant for our intent and purposes in view of the precarious life conditions experienced by the urban poor. As we saw in the case of Nova Iguaçu, and more specifically in Pedra Bonita, the bodies of the poor are under constant attack by illness, hunger, heavy work-schedules, long bus rides, violence, and premature death. Bodies cannot bear the brunt of pain, suffering, and illness indefinitely; they have to find a physical and symbolic release, even if it is only a temporary one. Otherwise there is a risk of total disintegration.

This need for release lies behind the quest for immediate solutions, for miracle cures in religious traditions such as Pentecostalism, Umbanda, and folk Catholicism, which provide coherent and often effective therapeutic systems to deal with illness, particularly that connected to mental and nervous problems. Conditions for the urban poor have become so desperate that it becomes increasingly difficult to postpone release until the structural causes of injustice and suffering have been removed. The urgency of this need for release calls the popular church to learn from other forms of popular religiosity rather than trying only to correct and purify them. The *igreja popular* is also called to construct a pastoral approach that accepts and even contains practices that hitherto the popular church has considered wrong, i.e., programs that provide temporary solutions to the effects of economic inequalities without changing the underlying causes. Progressives in the church have argued correctly that such practices generate dependence among the poor and reproduce the system. However, a critique of assistentialism should not ignore the fact that the poor have immediate, urgent needs, which cannot wait for structural change.

The same goes for "other-worldly" strategies to deal with precarious life conditions. While there cannot be a return to an "other-worldly mysticism" that legitimizes the poor's increasing loss of control over their lives, the *igreja popular* has to take care not to advocate a stern "this-worldly asceticism" that overemphasizes effectiveness of human actions and disenchants the world through critical thinking. It must not let its particular re-enchantment of the world (predicated on the close connection between this worldly

---

[29] M. B. McGuire, "Religion and the Body: Rematerializing the Human Body in the Social Sciences of Religion," *Journal for the Scientific Study of Religion* 29, no. 3 (1990), 283.

transcendence and eschatology) stifle other forms of transcendence, especially other-worldly ones. The popular church must not let its work for intra-historical transcendence obscure the eschatological dimension of the Christian message. It must also respect the ludic, performative and symbolic aspects of human practice, which in Brazilian culture find such powerful expressions as the carnival, soccer, and popular religiosity. We saw how in Helena's case, the identification of religion with politics conceived in a narrow, instrumental sense (attaining power) led to frustration and exhaustion.

Criticizing "clinical stances" *vis-à-vis* popular religiosity, anthropologist Rubem Fernandes calls for an understanding of the "polyphonic composition" of Brazilian religiosity, an understanding that may lead the popular church to a greater respect for the logic of other-worldly religious expressions. The appeal to the "extraordinary" is not primarily "an illusory form to confront crisis situations,"[30] a mere "symptom of a social crisis . . . anomie and absolute poverty," as some pastoral agents claim. The cult of the saints is an instructive example in this regard. According to Fernandes,

[saints] are beings that express earthly limitations in contrast to superior powers. More than "instruments" for the resolution of problems, they are epiphanies that structure [human] consciousness in the broadest sense. [They] are characters in a dramatization of finitude which present mortality in the form of dependence. They expose the precariousness of our being, demonstrating at the same time the visceral need we have to be protected.[31]

In pointing to our "finitude" and the "precariousness of our being," the cult of the saints also signifies the limits and vulnerability of any intra-historical utopia. Although life requires hope, there can be no place for an unreflective triumphalism. The ever-present danger behind this triumphalism is in elevating any emancipatory strategy, be it CEBs or a social movement based on identity, to a Promethean status – as the sole redeemer of humanity – and in the process creating a rigid, totalizing category that fails to capture the dynamism and complexity of social reality and blurs distinc-

---

[30] Fernandes, "Santos e agentes," 6.   [31] Ibid., 7–8.

tions between the "ought" and the "is." Something along these lines appears to have happened to progressive Catholicism in Nicaragua, according to pastoral agent María López Vigil. Reflecting on the electoral defeat of the Sandinistas, with whom progressive Catholics had forged a close alliance, she writes:

It is evident that the triumph of the Sandinista popular revolution made the church of the poor bigger that what in reality it was. [This triumph] distorted it beyond the dimensions it really had. It also gave the church a continental, universal, historic responsibility which far surpassed the church's true strength.

I believe that what weakened us the most was our certainty that in Nicaragua the ultimate synthesis between faith and politics had been reached. We even came to think that we had achieved the ultimate synthesis between Marxism and Christianity! We did not take into consideration the slowness of the consciousness raising process. We used to shout: "Between Christianity and revolution there is no contradiction." This, however, blocked us from seeing that contradictions existed in reality.[32]

Respect for the need for other-worldly transcendence and for the existential aspects of religion does not mean, however, that the popular church should remain confined to the spiritual realm. It has to maintain also this-worldly approaches that operate at the medium-term to address injustice if it is to work for the coming of the reign of God. CEBs can continue to fulfill this role.

The popular church will have to develop a liturgy that pays attention to the ever more common moments of loss and pain the urban poor are experiencing. The sacraments – the quintessential pastoral strategies to deal with boundary situations in the life-cycle – will have to be revitalized in ways that overcome the impersonality and rigidity of the parish structure, and the monopoly of legitimate religious goods by a small elite of pastoral agents. On the social front, even Helena, who defends a more vanguardist line, admits that

[m]any times in the [popular movement] one has priorities that are not the ones of the great mass of the population. We had a grand project of how society should be, but at the same time, we could not take care of a

---

[32] M. López Vigil, "Los cristianos y la iglesia ante el colapso del comunismo y la derrota del Sandinismo," *Amanecer*, no. 69 (1990), 33.

hungry person nearby because we had to go to a [popular group] meeting. But if people don't eat they go to a party meeting to do what? We are going to be talking about the same thing over and over and they are going to say: "I'm tired of hearing the same thing; this is not going to fill my gut." You know, I once saw a billboard that said: "People don't have a party, what they have is hunger."

The realization of the precarious plight of the poor is what has driven some sectors of the popular church to collaborate with assistential initiatives such as *a campanha da fome* (campaign against hunger), which collects funds and goods from various social sectors of the Brazilian society, including middle class and well-to-do families, to deliver to the destitute.[33] Nova Iguaçu's Adriano Hipólito became a major player in this campaign.

As I argued in chapter 7, the economic crisis and the adjustment measures adopted to resolve it have increasingly placed the burden on women for the physical reproduction and wellbeing of their households. The new pressures have restructured daily life for women, generating constraints and new needs that must be addressed with the resources at hand. In Brazilian society religion has been traditionally one of the central cultural resources available to women. The popular church must then identify the emerging constraints and needs for women and fashion adequate pastoral responses. It may be difficult for an institution that is dominated by patriarchal relations to take a woman-centric view of reality, but given conditions on the ground, the adoption of this standpoint is necessary for the popular church to become a more inclusive project.

Basist realism is not only realistic, in the sense of providing a more nuanced diagnosis of social conditions and the prospects for changing and coping with them; it is also basist. In other words, it seeks to strengthen communal strategies, fashioned by the poor themselves, which are already operating successfully in the crevices of the system. Although many times defensive strategies carry a strong self-interested, individualistic undercurrent

[33] Initially drafted under the name *ação da cidadania contra a miséria e pela vida* (Citizens' Action against Poverty and for Life), the campaign has been extremely successful, drawing wide support and spreading rapidly throughout the country. To date there are 3,346 local committees in twenty-seven states collecting and distributing food. See "A fome adquire rosto e move o Brasil comum," *Veja* (Rio de Janeiro), December 29, 1993, 86–97.

that tends to divide communities, neighborhoods and even households, there are grassroots maneuvers characterized by a high element of reciprocity and an incipient level of organization.[34] I have already mentioned the example of *ollas comunes* or *comedores populares* (community soup kitchens) in which several households pool resources to be able to provide better sustenance for their members. There is also the example of community day-care centers (*crèches*), where the various women in the neighborhood take turns at supervising community children. These centers are bound to become more important as work and domestic responsibilities for women increase.

In other words, despite Brazil's authoritarian and corrupt political culture, and despite the tremendous economic pressures the poor face, grassroots survival strategies need not reproduce the system. They do not have to fall under the sway of patrimonial politics oriented by purely individualist interests. The popular church must identify and strengthen participatory, solidarity-building initiatives among the poor, providing logistical and institutional support and helping in the gradual articulation of extended self-help networks. This is of vital importance given the radical fragmentation of the public sphere brought about by contemporary capitalism. The role of the popular church here is to help rebuild the conditions for sociality which have been severely damaged by Brazil's savage capitalism during the 1980s.

In encouraging grassroots communitarian action, the *igreja popular* must be careful not to establish the agenda for the poor or to determine their real interests from above, on the basis of a particular model of social reality, or of a fixed conception of what the poor must be in order to be a true emancipatory subject. It must support cooperative projects and initiatives created by the poor themselves to address their needs and aspirations. It is here that Leda's and Dulce's basist vision of community life applies.

---

[34] Some authors even envision the creation of an empowering, alternative "popular" economy at the margins of technocratic capitalism. This economy would include practices that "combine diverse functions, such as the administration of scarcity, the mobilization of dispersed social energies, the de-hierarchization of production relations, the construction of collective identity, the socialized provision of basic necessities, the promotion of community participation, and the search for democracy in small spaces (or democracy in daily life)." Hopenhayn, "Postmodernism and Neoliberalism," 106–107.

A note of caution should accompany this basist strategy, however. Anthropologist Helen Safa has argued that the informal economy, which "originally served primarily the needs of the poor," has increasingly become subordinated to the capitalist production system, providing more flexible ways to extract surplus. The growth of the informal sector not only reduces the overall cost of capitalist production by forcing the poor to pay for their own reproduction, but favors firms in the formal, modern sector. These firms "have found a way of retarding or bypassing wage gains and state-enforced labor legislation" simply "by subcontracting goods and services to small enterprises and casual laborers."[35] There is a danger too that subsistence initiatives at the local level will be accepted as the natural mechanism for the urban poor to secure their reproduction and survival in the new international division of labor. Local, short-term responses to the economic crisis might come to be seen as the only solution to the poor's plight in this new order.[36]

To avoid letting self-help strategies set the limits of the possible for the poor, it is necessary to continue fighting for improvement, through bread-and-butter struggles and through concerted attempts to modify the system. In addition, there has to be a critique of the economic logics that have forced the poor to fall back on household-local survival strategies in the first place. Such a critique is necessary to show that the status quo is a result of human actions and not of supra-social forces (i.e., God's will). It is at these intermediary and structural levels that the work of socially conscious (*conscientizado*) CEB activists continues to be central. As Levine claims, CEBs provide potential and necessary "linkages between everyday life and big structures." Helena is, thus, right in pointing at the limits of Leda's basist approach.

Thus, basist realism needs to be relativized. The suggestion to

---

[35] H. I. Safa, "Urbanization, the Informal Economy and State Policy in Latin America," in M. P. Smith and J. R. Feagin, eds., *The Capitalist City* (Oxford: Basil Blackwell, 1987), 259.

[36] Thus, the basist realism I am proposing should not be confused with the type of neo-conservative basism that Hernando de Soto advocates. I do not see the informal economy as the cradle of a new sort of grassroots entrepreneurship that calls for a minimization of state intervention. Rather, its primary role is defensive: to help the poor survive the pressures of capitalism. See H. de Soto, *The Other Path* (London: I. B. Tauris, 1989).

support grassroots initiatives, rather than encouraging passive acceptance of the inevitability of the status quo and of the impossibility of change beyond micro-defensive maneuvers, is intended to recover the plausibility of the notion of immanent transcendence for the poor. In the face of worsening life conditions and an economic system that appears ever more baffling and intractable, the poor must begin to regain a sense that they can take control of at least some aspects of their lives. They must come to realize that their actions make a difference, that they are effective in alleviating the most urgent pressures they experience. While it is important to have a utopian vision to rally people, it is also key for people to see some of the fruits of this vision in their everyday lives. People need to be able to connect their actions, their struggles for survival, with this vision. This link makes change plausible and motivates the individual to seek this-worldly transcendence. As Frei Betto recognizes, the liberationist utopia "needs to translate itself into feasible 'topias,' realisable in the world of the poor as a condition for new roads to social transformation. In reality, nothing indicates that revolutions, understood as the violent destruction of the state, are going to occur with the same frequency as in the past."[37]

Helena understands the importance of linking concrete needs and aspirations in everyday life and utopia:

I believe that the [popular] movement is going through a delicate phase. It is a phase in which many have fallen out of the initial euphoria and have realized that in reality things were not as simple as we thought they were. Many are discouraged in relation to the movement . . .

There is a need for the [activist] to achieve things that can make people believe that change is possible. But for people to believe that it's necessary that people have the minimal conditions to live . . . to exist.

The popular church's task is to re-energize transcendence within history at the local level, building up trust in the efficacy of the poor's communal, "Catholic works." Only after this efficacy has been restored can the popular church help to articulate more global forms of action. It is a matter of "nurturing the embryos of tomorrow's social movements within . . . local Utopias."[38]

---

[37] Betto, "Did Liberation Theology Collapse?" 37.
[38] Castells, *The City and the Grassroots*, 331.

Conclusion

> What remains of the option for the poor, of everything which
> we have proclaimed and lived with such passion and fervor,
> of all the hopes for which many brothers and sister have
> given their lives? Are there any utopias? Or is what's left just
> a lie, the awakening from a dream, or the bitter taste of the
> resigned flight to the "every man for himself" [attitude] of
> this new empire of individualism and neoliberal exclusion?[1]

One of the central aims of this study has been to demonstrate the
complexity of the Brazilian popular church's crisis. I have sought
to do this by elucidating obstacles to the production, circulation,
and reception of the *igreja popular's* message and practice. In particular, I have concentrated on the negative effects of large-scale
transformations in the economic, political, cultural, and religious
fields on grassroots work.

In focusing on macro-dynamics such as the capitalist world-
system, the Vatican restoration offensive, and the crisis of modernity, I have not intended to reconstruct totalizing logics that determine local praxis in an abstract, mechanical, and reductive
fashion. Rather, I have tried to show the ways in which macro-
processes simultaneously encompass and are embodied in everyday life. Thus, I have documented the concrete consequences of
ecclesial changes (mediated by diocesan pastoral shifts and the
replacement of pastoral agents) and socio-economic transformations (resulting in a restructuring of everyday life) on a particular
base community.

If it is true that macro-processes are not given facts whose brute
force establishes every aspect of a social order, as people on the

---

[1] J. M. Vigil, "O que fica da opção pelos pobres?" *Perspectiva Teológica* 26 (1994), 187.

ground appropriate, resist, negotiate, and adapt to them in diverse ways drawing from socio-cultural tools at hand, it is equally certain that they delimit the field of experience at the local level. In the words of political scientist Adam Przeworski, larger social logics define "realms of possibility and impossibility."[2] This is clear in Brazil since the 1980s, when larger social changes redefined the limits of the possible for the poor and eroded the potential for collective mobilization from below to effect structural transformations.

The focus on the macro-micro link takes us back to our discussion in the Introduction of dichotomies that have disabled the study of social phenomena. Thus, at a deeper level, this book has sought to develop an approach to the study of the relation between society and religion that takes into account the interplay between the local and the global, structure and agency, the "material" and the "mental," and the intra- and extra- ecclesial.

Beyond that, the case of Pedra Bonita and the Brazilian popular church's plight in the context of the crisis of modernity and the emerging capitalist configuration raise important lessons. Latin American cultural theorist Nestor García Canclini argues that, in the face of the fragmentation and hybridization produced by contemporary capitalism, it is necessary to move "from a vertical and bipolar conception of socio-political relations to one that is decentered and multidetermined."[3] The development of such a perspective is crucial for the *igreja popular*, if it is to gain a more nuanced understanding of the needs and aspirations of poor people and to construct context-sensitive pastoral-pedagogical approaches. I have suggested that a critical non-reductive materialism may help make sense of the simultaneous fragmentation and globalization of our present age.

At the ideological level, it has become no longer tenable to ground transcendence in teleological and totalizing frameworks. This-worldly utopias must work with the ambiguity and heterogeneity of the present. To be able to inspire and mobilize an

[2] A. Przeworski, *Capitalism and Social Democracy* (Cambridge: Cambridge University Press, 1985).
[3] N. García Canclini, *Hybrid Culture: Strategies for Entering and Leaving Modernity* (Minneapolis: University of Minnesota Press, 1995), 258.

increasingly fragmented and complex society, they must address local and personal predicaments rather than formulating abstract and finished models of progress and salvation.

Today, utopian thinking is only viable as pure futurity, as an open-ended historicity that admits no closure.[4] The "metaphysics of progress,"[5] which construes history as inexorably moving, through the work of the *Geist*, the proletariat, or a unified poor to its closure, must give way to an open-ended, uncertain exercise of self-critique. This exercise of self-critique is all the more vital when human efforts are cosmicized, as in the case of liberation theology and the popular church. Religious utopias must resist the temptation of "onto-theologizing" their eschatologies, hitching them on essences which can be recovered in a single fashion, given the right consciousness. There can be no fixed view of salvation and transcendence determined *a priori*. As Mardones recognizes, postmodernity marks the "loss of the conditions for the possibility of history" conceived in a metaphysical sense. Mardones finds in postmodernity "an emptying out of the Christian salvific conception," under which "linear history as a history of salvation became the quest for this-worldly perfection and later on the history of progress."[6] Such an "emptying out" challenges not only the popular church's project, but more sharply the Vatican's restorationist drive to construct once more a Catholic hegemony based on "universal" values.[7]

Despite loud proclamations of the end of history and the eternal return of the same (i.e., neoliberalism), I believe that it is possible to preserve the notion of intra-historical transcendence. Yet, it can be done only in a relativized fashion. The divine reign must be

---

[4] In the words of a CEB advisor, "There is now the clear conviction that CEB history is fluid and open-ended. There is no longer a place for idealistic reifications. It is time for a new sensitivity towards new roads." F. Texeira, "CEBs: cidadania em processo," *Revista Eclesiástica Brasileira* 53 (September 1993), 605.

[5] F. Hinkelammert, *La fé de Abraham y el edipo occidental* (San José, Costa Rica: DEI, 1989), 81ff.

[6] J. M. Mardones, *Modernidad y Postmodernidad* (i). Posmodernidad y Cristianismo (ii). Un Debate Sobre la Sociedad Actual (Montevideo, Uruguay: CLAEH, 1987), 24.

[7] In a skillful appropriation of the crisis of modernity, the Vatican under John Paul II has sought to present Catholicism as the Archimedean point for a moral regeneration and ontological re-foundation of the disintegrated and threatening world left behind by the failure of modern projects. In this sense, the Vatican's restoration offensive has a conservative, anti-modernist thrust.

defined as the horizon of the possible, perhaps of the desirable, but not of the ineluctable. There are always limits and contradictions in any attempt at self-transcendence. A clear understanding of these limits and contradictions might help us to design strategies more attuned to the possibilities at hand and to maintain an attitude of constant vigilance, lest those strategies become reified and fail to address reality as we experience it.

Utopian thinking's new referent must be, to draw from philosopher Emmanuel Levinas, "infinity," not totality.[8] Transcendence, like the "Other" (i.e., the "poor") is "a surplus always exterior to totality," always resistant to Western metaphysics which seeks a "reduction of the other to the same."[9] And it is this surplus that bids us to continue dreaming, to continue searching even in the midst of a chaotic world.

Reference to "infinity" does not entail a retreat to a de-politicized and ahistorical other-worldly mysticism. Spirituality must continue to enter everyday life, just as the popular church has sought to do with its particular re-enchantment of secular emancipatory projects. However, this interaction should not take the form of a quest to uncover a hidden divine plan in daily life. Rather, spirituality must be based on the recognition that life, even in its more mundane expressions, is a mystery that can never be grasped once and for all. The struggle for liberation becomes, then, a struggle to defend and expand the openness of this mystery, and more specifically of the human capacity for intra-historical transcendence, in the face of forms of power that seek to eliminate, contain, and/or reify it.

There are current efforts in constructive theology within the popular church that seek to incorporate a de-ontologized notion of transcendence as surplus. Enrique Dussel, for example, speaks of an "analectical" philosophy of liberation that goes beyond ("ana-") the dialectics of totality.[10] It is a philosophy that "affirms the 'reason of the other'," that while recognizing its inexhaustible

---

[8] E. Levinas, *Totality and Infinity: An Essay on Exteriority* (Pittsburgh: Duquesne University Press, 1969). I would warn against Levinas' identification of Infinity with God. This identification runs the risk of re-introducing ontology, as God is often associated with perfection and full presence.

[9] Ibid., 43.   [10] E. Dussel, *Philosophy of Liberation* (Maryknoll, NY: Orbis, 1985).

mystery proposes an "incorporative solidarity."[11] "Ontology," Dussel writes, "the thinking that expresses Being – the Being of the reigning and central system – is the ideology of ideologies, the foundation of the ideologies of the empire, of the center."[12] Against classical ontology Dussel stresses the exteriority of the Other, a flesh and blood person, "an imploring, revealing, and provoking face."[13]

On a more concrete level, prominent progressive theologians have turned from explicitly political concerns to popular culture and religion, anthropology and psychology of religion, biblical studies, and spirituality, including a strong feminist dimension, all in an effort to capture the richness of the lived experiences of various subaltern groups.[14] In addition, currents within Latin American liberation theology have begun to interact with post-colonial discourses, postmodern perspectives, and an emerging, multifaceted US Latino/Hispanic theology, laying the ground-work for potentially more nuanced emancipatory approaches.

All this leads one to think that reports about the death of liberation theology may prove exaggerated. The future of the Brazilian popular church is another matter. Given the pastoral shifts within the global church this future looks uncertain.[15] In the 1995–1998 pastoral plan, the Brazilian Bishops reaffirm the cen-trality of the preferential option for the poor. They praise CEBs for "representing a rich ecclesial experience whether it be for lay participation [in them], or for their efforts to bring social trans-formation."[16] The CNBB, however, challenges CEBs not only to

[11] Dussel, "Eurocentrism and Modernity," 76.   [12] Dussel, *Philosophy of Liberation*, 5.
[13] See also J. C. Scannone, "Modernidad, posmodernidad y formas de racionalidad en América Latina," in Michelini, San Martín, and Lagrave, *Modernidad y Posmodernidad en América Latina*. Dussel's approach is not without its contradictions. Ofelia Schutte has challenged its absolutist understanding of the notion of the Other in *Cultural Identity and Social Liberation in Latin American Social Thought* (Albany, NY: State University of New York Press, 1993).
[14] See L. Boff, *A nova evangelização: Perspectiva dos oprimidos* (Fortaleza: Vozes, 1990); J. Comblin, *Retrieving the Human: A Christian Anthropology* (Maryknoll, NY: Orbis Books, 1990); G. Gutiérrez, *The God of Life* (Maryknoll, NY: Orbis Books, 1991); I. Gebara and M. C. Bingemer, *Mary: Mother of God, Mother of the Poor* (Maryknoll, NY: Orbis Books, 1989).
[15] In Nova Iguaçu it is still too early to assess the impact of recently appointed Bishop Werner Seibenbrock on grassroots pastoral work.
[16] CNBB, *Diretrizes gerais da ação evangelizadora da Igreja no Brasil 1995–1998* (São Paulo: Paulinas, 1995), 148.

"work more with the masses and not to close themselves into small groups and to be more welcoming of popular religiosity and more respectful of its symbolic universe but, more importantly, to always search for communion with the church as a whole."[17] We have seen in Pedra Bonita how this call for communion might create problems for progressive grassroots pastoral work in the context of a hierarchical institution.

Furthermore, discerning the signs of the times, the Brazilian bishops devote a whole section of the plan to discussing the challenges posed by neoliberalism and postmodernism. Nevertheless, aside from an affirmation of the "incomparable value of the person and human life" – an abstract principle that tends to receive a conservative, pro-life interpretation in the new evangelization – the plan does not offer any specific strategies to undertake emancipatory pastoral work in the new setting. Yet not all is lost for the popular church. Currently, there are attempts within the popular church to appropriate elements of the new evangelization extolled by the Vatican in ways that can legitimize the utopian interest behind the preferential option for the poor. One example of this potential for emancipatory appropriation surrounds John Paul II's call for inculturation of the Catholic faith. Taking this call seriously, without a pre-established proselytizing agenda, may lead the church to an even greater immersion in the plurality of lived experiences of people at margins.

Postmodernity and contemporary capitalism, in sum, need not spell the end of utopian ideologies. Rather, when deployed strategically, postmodernist categories may help us make sense of and respond to the simultaneous fragmentation and globalization produced by contemporary capitalism. The postmodernist critique of Enlightenment thinking, particularly of the totalitarian aspects of master narratives it inspired, represents in its most productive versions a radicalization of the modern emancipatory impetus. It is an attempt to recover the radical openness that characterizes our quest to express our creative capacities. As I argued in chapter 2, for all its distortions in post-Enlightenment thinking, the quality of transgressive, open-ended critique lies at the heart of the modern

---

[17] Ibid.

emancipatory impulse. As Foucault writes, modernity's most enduring legacy is the "principle of critique and permanent creation of ourselves in autonomy." Only this painstaking, modest, and constant "work carried out by ourselves upon ourselves as free beings,"[18] can help us advance, however precariously, the ideal of self-consciousness, self-determination, and self-realization that informs liberation theology, the *igreja popular*, and other this-worldly utopias. Notwithstanding claims to the contrary, intra-historical transcendence is more than ever the central task of our age, when socio-economic and cultural changes threaten to impose the atomized logic of the market on everyday life and to continue disempowering large segments of the world's population.

[18] Foucault, "What is Enlightenment?," 47.

Bibliography

Adriance, M., "Agents of Change: The Role of Priests, Sisters and Lay Workers in the Grassroots Catholic Church in Brazil," *Journal for the Scientific Study of Religion* 30, no. 3 (1991), 292–305.

"A fé que move multidões avança no país," *Veja* (Rio de Janeiro), May 16, 1990, 46–52.

"A fome adquire rosto e move o Brasil comum," *Veja* (Rio de Janeiro), December 29, 1993, 86–97.

Andrade, P. F. C. de, "A condição pósmoderna como desafio à pastoral popular," *Revista Eclesiástica Brasileira* 53, no. 209 (1993), 99–113.

Antoniazzi, A., "O catolicismo no Brasil," in *Sinais dos tempos: Tradições religiosas no Brasil*, ed. L. Landim et al., Rio de Janeiro: ISER, 1989.

Antonio, R. J., "The Decline of the Grand Narrative of Emancipatory Modernity: Crisis or Renewal in Neo-Marxist Theory," in *Frontiers of Social Theory: New Syntheses*, ed. G. Ritzer, New York: Columbia University Press, 1990.

Archdiocese of São Paulo, *Brasil nunca mais*, Petrópolis: Vozes, 1985.

Arellano, J. P., "The 20 Years since Medellin," *Origins* 18, no. 44 (April 1989), 754–756.

Azevedo, M., *Basic Ecclesial Communities in Brazil: The Challenge of a New Way of Being Church*, Washington, DC: Georgetown University Press, 1987.

Bamat, T., "Political Change and the Catholic Church in Brazil and Nicaragua," in *New Perspectives on Social Class and Socioeconomic Development in the Periphery*, ed. N. W. Keith and N. Z. Keith, New York: Greenwood Press, 1988.

Barbé, D., *Grace and Power: Base Communities and Nonviolence in Brazil*, Maryknoll, NY: Orbis Books, 1987.

Barroso, C. and T. Amado, "The Impact of the Crisis upon Poor Women's Health: The Case of Brazil," in Barroso and Amado, eds., *The Invisible Adjustment: Poor Women and the Economic Crisis*, Santiago: UNICEF, 1989.

Bastian, J. P., *Breve historia del Protestantismo en América Latina*, México: Casa Unida de Publicaciones, 1986.

"The Metamorphosis of Latin American Protestant Groups: A Sociohistorical Perspective," *Latin American Research Review* 28, no. 2 (1993), 33–61.

Bastide, R., *The African Religions of Brazil*, Baltimore: Johns Hopkins University Press, 1978.

Bastos, I. V., "Experiência de Nízia Floresta," *Revista Eclesiástica Brasileira* 24, no. 2 (1964), 497–498.

Becker, B. and C. Engler, *Brazil: A New Regional Power in the World-Economy*, Cambridge: Cambridge University Press, 1992.

Bedoyere, M. de la, *The Cardijn Story*, London: Longman, Green and Co., 1958.

Bell, D., *The Coming of the Post-Industrial Society*, New York: Basic Books, 1973.

Benería, L., "The Mexican Debt Crisis: Restructuring the Economy and the Household," in *Unequal Burden: Economic Crises, Persistent Poverty, and Women's Work*, eds. L. Benería and S. Feldman, Boulder, CO: Westview Press, 1992.

Benería, L. and S. Feldman, eds., *Unequal Burden: Economic Crises, Persistent Poverty, and Women's Work*, Boulder, CO: Westview Press, 1992.

Berger, P., *The Sacred Canopy: Elements of a Sociological Theory of Religion*, New York: Anchor Books, 1967.

Bernstein, R. J., "Introduction," in *Habermas and Modernity*, ed. R. J. Bernstein, Cambridge, MA: MIT Press, 1985.

Betto, F. [C. A. Libânio Cristo], *O que é comunidade eclesial de base*, São Paulo: Brasiliense, 1981.

"Did Liberation Theology Collapse with the Berlin Wall?" *Religion, State and Society* 21, no. 1 (1993), 33–38.

Blumenberg, H., *The Legitimacy of the Modern Age*, trans. R. Wallace Cambridge: MIT Press, 1983.

Boff, C., "CEBs e práticas de libertação," *Revista Eclesiástica Brasileira* 40, no. 160 (1980), 595–625.

"Desafios atuais da pastoral popular," *Tempo e Presença*, no. 232 (1988), 30-32.

"Entrevista com Clodovis Boff," *Políticas Governamentais* 7, no. 68 (1991), 15–19.

Boff, L., *Jesus Christ Liberator: A Critical Christology for Our Time*, Maryknoll, NY: Orbis Books, 1978.

Ecclesiogenesis: The Base Communities Reinvent the Church, Maryknoll, NY: Orbis Books, 1986.

A nova evangelizacão: Perspectiva dos oprimidos, Fortaleza: Vozes, 1990.

"Implosão do socialismo e teologia da libertação," *Tempo e Presença*, no. 252 (1991), 32–36.

Boff, L. and C. Boff, *Introducing Liberation Theology*, Maryknoll, NY: Orbis Books, 1987.

Bourdieu, P., "Genèse et structure du champ religieux," *Revue Française de Sociologie* 12 (1971), 295–334.

Outline of a Theory of Practice, Cambridge: Cambridge University Press, 1977.

Distinction: A Social Critique of the Judgement of Taste, Cambridge, MA: Harvard University Press, 1984.

"The Social Space and the Genesis of Groups," *Social Science Information* 24, no. 2 (1985), 195–220.

"Social Space and Symbolic Power," in *In Other Words: Essays Towards a Reflexive Sociology*, Stanford: Stanford University Press, 1990.

Braer, W., *The Brazilian Economy: Growth and Development*, New York: Praeger Publishers, 1989.

Brandão, C. R., *Os deuses do povo*, São Paulo: Paulinas, 1980.

"Elite e massa na religiosidade do povo," in *A religiosidade do povo*, orgs. Lísias Negrão et al., São Paulo: Paulinas, 1984.

"O festim dos bruxos," *Religião e Sociedade* 13, no. 3(1986), 128–156.

Brown, D. *Umbanda: Religion and Politics in Urban Brazil*, Ann Arbor, MI: UMI Research Press, 1986.

Brown, R. M., *Gustavo Gutiérrez: An Introduction to Liberation Theology*, Maryknoll, NY: Orbis Books, 1990.

Bruneau, T., *The Political Transformation of the Brazilian Catholic Church*, New York: Cambridge University Press, 1974.

The Catholic Church in Brazil: The Politics of Religion, Austin: University of Texas Press, 1982.

"Brazil: The Catholic Church and Basic Christian Communities," in *Religion and Political Conflict in Latin America*, ed. D. H. Levine, Chapel Hill: University of North Carolina Press, 1986.

Bruneau, T. and W. E. Hewitt, "Patterns of Church Influence in Brazil's Political Transition," *Comparative Politics* 22, no. 1 (1989), 39–61.

"Catholicism and Political Action in Brazil: Limitations and Prospects," in *Conflict and Competition: The Latin American Church in a Changing Environment*, ed. E. L. Cleary and H. Stewart-Gambino, Boulder, CO: Lynne Rienner Publishers, 1992.

Brusco, E., "Reformation of Machismo: Asceticism and Masculinity among Colombian Evangelicals," in *Rethinking Protestantism in Latin America*, ed. V. Garrard-Burnett and D. Stoll, Philadelphia: Temple University Press, 1993.

Burdick, J., "Rethinking the Study of Social Movements: The Case of Christian Base Communities in Urban Brazil," in *The Making of Social Movements in Latin America: Identity, Strategy and Democracy*, ed. A. Escobar and S. Alvarez, Boulder, CO: Westview Press, 1992.

Looking for God in Brazil: The Progressive Catholic Church in Urban Brazil's Religious Arena, Berkeley: University of California Press, 1993.

"Struggling against the Devil: Pentecostalism and Social Movements in Urban Brazil," in *Rethinking Protestantism in Latin America*, ed. V. Garrard-Burnett and D. Stoll, Philadelphia: Temple University Press, 1993.

"The Progressive Catholic Church in Latin America: Giving Voice or Listening to Voices?" *Latin American Research Review* 29, no. 1 (1994), 184–197.

Camacho, D., "A Society in Motion," in *New Social Movements in the South: Empowering the People*, ed. P. Wignaraja. London: Zed Books, 1993.

Cardoso, F. H., "Associated-Dependent Development: Theoretical and Practical Implications," in *Authoritarian Brazil*, ed. A. Stepan, New Haven: Yale University Press, 1973.

Castañeda, J. G., *Utopia Unarmed: The Latin American Left After the Cold War*, New York: Alfred A. Knopf, 1993.

Castanho, A., *Caminhos das CEBs no Brasil: Reflexão crítica*, Rio de Janeiro: Marques Saraiva, 1988.

Castells, M., *The City and the Grassroots*, Berkeley: University of California Press, 1983.

CELAM (Conference of Latin American Bishops), *The Church in the Present-Day Transformation of Latin America in the Light of the Council: Medellín Conclusions*, Washington, DC: National Conference of Catholic Bishops, Secretariat for Latin America, 1979.

CEPEBA (Center for Study and Research in the Baixada Fluminense), *Dados estatísticos Baixada Fluminense*, Duque de Caxias, RJ: CEPEBA, 1988.

CERIS (Center for Religious Statistics and Social Research), *Anuário Católico de 1985*, Rio de Janeiro: CERIS, 1985.

Chauí, M., *Conformismo e resistência*, São Paulo: Brasiliense, 1986.

Cleary, E. L., "Conclusion: Politics and Religion – Crisis, Constraints and Restructuring," in *Conflict and Competition: The Latin American Church in a Changing Environment*, ed. E. L. Cleary and H. Stewart-Gambino, Boulder, CO: Lynne Rienner Publishers, 1992.

CNBB (National Conference of the Brazilian Bishops), *Comunidades: Igreja na base*, São Paulo: Paulinas, 1977.

Comunidades eclesiais de base no Brasil: Experiências e perspectivas, CNBB Studies no. 23, São Paulo: Paulinas, 1979.

Comunidades eclesiais de base na base na Igreja no Brasil, CNBB Document no. 25, São Paulo: Paulinas, 1982.

Diretrizes gerais da ação pastoral, 1983–1986, São Paulo: Paulinas, 1983.

Diretrizes gerais de açao pastoral de Igreja no Brasil, 1995–1998, São Paulo: Paulinas, 1995.

Coelho, M., "Desespero da fé fortalece campanha da fome," *Folha de São Paulo*, September 8, 1993.

Collins, D., *Paulo Freire: His Life, Work and Thought*, New York: Paulist Press, 1978.

Comblin, J., *The Church and the National Security State*, Maryknoll, NY: Orbis Books, 1979.

"Algumas questões a partir da prática das comunidades eclesiais de base no nordeste," *Revista Eclesiástica Brasileira* 50, no. 198 (1990), 335–381.

"O ressurgimento do tradicionalismo na teologia latino-americana," *Revista Eclesiástica Brasileira* 50, no. 197 (1990), 44–75.

"Inculturação e libertação," *Convergência*, no. 235 (1990), 423–432.

Retrieving the Human: A Christian Anthropology, Maryknoll, NY: Orbis Books, 1990.

Committee of Santa Fe, *A New Inter-American Policy for the Eighties*, Santa Fe, NM: n.p., 1980.

Conniff, M., *Urban Politics in Brazil and the Rise of Populism, 1925–1945*, Pittsburgh: University of Pittsburgh Press, 1981.

Cook, G., "Santo Domingo Through Protestant Eyes," in *Santo Domingo and Beyond*, ed. A. Hennelly, Maryknoll, NY: Orbis Books, 1993.

Cox, H., *The Silencing of Leonardo Boff. The Vatican and the Future of World Christianity*, Oak Park, IL: Meyer Stone, 1988.

Da Matta, R., *O que faz o Brasil, Brasil?* Rio de Janeiro: Rocco, 1989.

Daudelin, J., 'L'Eglise progressite brésilienne: la fin d'un mythe?' in *L'Amérique et les Amériques*, ed. J. Zylberberg and F. Damers, Sainte Foy, Quebec: Les Presses de l'Université de Laval, 1992.

Daudelin, J. and W. E. Hewitt, "Latin American Politics: Exit the Catholic Church?" paper delivered at the conference on "Church, State, and Society in Latin America: Socio-political and Economic Restructuring since 1960," Villanova University, Villanova, PA, March 18–19, 1993.

Dayton, D. W., *Theological Roots of Pentecostalism*, Metuchen, NJ: The Scarecrow Press, 1987.

Della Cava, R., *Miracle at Joaseiro*, New York: Columbia University Press, 1970.

"The 'People's Church,' the Vatican and the Abertura," in *Democratizing Brazil*, ed. A. Stepan, New York: Oxford University Press, 1989.

"Vatican Policy, 1978–1990: An Updated Overview," *Social Research* 59, no. 1 (1992), 171–199.

"Financing the Faith: The Case of Roman Catholicism," *Journal of Church and State* 35, no. 1 (1993), 49–52.

Derrida, J., *Writing and Difference*, trans. A. Bass, London: Routledge & Kegan Paul, 1978.

De Theije, M., " 'Brotherhoods Throw more Weight around than the Pope': Catholic Traditionalism and the Lay Brotherhoods of Brazil," *Sociological Analysis* 51, no. 2 (1990), 189–204.

Diocese of Nova Iguaçu, *O povo de Deus assume a caminhada*, Petrópolis: Vozes, 1983.

Domínguez, E. and D. Huntington, "The Salvation Brokers: Conservative Evangelicals in Central America," *NACLA: Report on the Americas* 18, no. 1 (1984), 2–36.

Dos Santos, T., "Brazil's Controlled Purge: The Impeachment of Fernando Collor," *NACLA: Report on the Americas* 27, no. 3 (1993), 17–21.

Drogus, C. A., "Popular Movements and the Limits of Political Mobilization at the Grassroots in Brazil," in *Conflict and Competition: The Latin American Church in a Changing* Environment, ed. E. L. Cleary and H. Stewart-Gambino, Boulder, CO: Lynne Rienner Publishers, 1992.

Droogers, A., "Visiones paradójicas sobre una religión paradójica,' in *Algo más que opio: Una lectura antropológica del pentecostalismo latinoamericano y caribeño*, ed. B. Boudewijnse, A. Droogers, and F. Kamsteeg, San José, Costa Rica: DEI, 1991.

Durkheim, E., *The Rules of Sociological Method*, Glencoe, IL: Free Press, 1965.

Dussel, E., *Philosophy of Liberation*, Maryknoll, NY: Orbis, 1985.

"Eurocentrism and Modernity (Introduction to the Frankfurt Lectures)," *Boundary 2* 20, no. 3 (Fall 1993), 65–76.

Economic Intelligence Unit, *Brazil: A Country Profile 1991–92*, London: EIU, 1992.

Eisenstadt, S. N. and L. Roniger, *Patron, Clients and Friends*, Cambridge: Cambridge University Press, 1984.

Ellacuría, I., "Historicidad de la salvación cristiana," in *Mysterium liberationis: Conceptos fundamentales de la teología de la liberación*, vol. 1, ed. I. Ellacuría and J. Sobrino, San Salvador: UCA Editores, 1991.

Escobar, A. and S. Alvarez, eds., *The Making of Social Movements in Latin America: Identity, Strategy and Democracy*, Boulder, CO: Westview Press, 1992.

Evans, P., *Dependent Development. The Alliance of Multinational, State and National Capital*, Princeton: Princeton University Press, 1979.

Falcão, J. F., "A distância da política. Entrevista com Dom José Freire Falcão," interview by Laurentino Gomes, *Veja* (Rio de Janeiro), June 8, 1988, 5–7.

FAPERJ (Foundation for Support and Research in the State of Rio de Janeiro), *Anuário estatístico do Rio de Janeiro*, Rio de Janeiro: FAPERJ, 1981.

Fernandes, R. C., "Santos e agentes – das dificuldades e da possibilidade de uma comunicação entre eles," paper presented in the Colóquio

Franco-Brasileiro em Ciências Sociais, CNRs/CNPq, Paris, 27–30 April 1989.

Folha de São Paulo. Various issues.

Foucault, M., *Discipline and Punish: Birth of the Prison,* trans. A. Sheridan, New York: Vintage Books, 1977.

"What is Enlightenment?" trans. C. Porter in *The Foucault Reader,* ed. Paul Rabinow, New York: Pantheon Books, 1984.

Freire, Paulo, *Pedagogy of the Oppressed,* trans. M. Ramos, New York: Herder and Herder, 1972.

Freston, P., "Pentecostalism in Latin America: Characteristics and Controversies," unpublished manuscript, 1994.

Fry, P. and G. N. Howe. "Duas respostas à aflição: Umbanda e Pentecostalismo," *Debate e Crítica* 6 (1975), 75–94.

Fukuyama, F., "The End of History and the Last Man," *National Interest* 16 (1989), 3–18.

The End of History and the Last Man, New York: FreePress, 1992.

FUNDREM (Foundation for the Development of the Rio de Janeiro Metropolitan Area), *Unidades urbanas intregradas do oeste, plano diretor,* Rio de Janeiro: FUNDREM, 1977.

Gadamer, H.-G. *Truth and Method.* New York: Seabury Press, 1975.

'Gaudium et Spes," in *The Gospel of Peace and Justice: Catholic Social Teaching Since Pope John,* ed. Joseph Gremillion, Maryknoll, NY: Orbis Books, 1976.

García Canclini, N., *Hybrid Cultures: Strategies for Entering and Leaving Modernity,* trans. C. Chiapporic and S. López, Minneapolis: University of Minnesota Press, 1995.

García Delgado, D., "Modernidad y postmodernidad en América Latina: una perspectiva desde la ciencia política,' *Modernidad y postmodernidad en América Latina,* ed. D. J. Michelini, J. San Martín, and F. Lagrave, Cordoba, Argentina: ICALA, 1991.

Gay, R., "Community Organization and Clientelist Politics in Contemporary Brazil: A Case Study in Suburban Rio de Janeiro," *International Journal of Urban and Regional Studies* 14, no. 4 (1990), 648–666.

Gebara, I., "Aborto não é pecado," interview by Kaíke Nanne and Mónica Bergamo, *Veja* (Rio de Janeiro), October 6, 1993, 7–10.

Gebara, I. and M. C. Bingemer, *Mary: Mother of God, Mother of the Poor,* Maryknoll, NY: Orbis Books, 1993.

Geertz, C., "Religion as a Cultural System," in *The Interpretation of Cultures,* New York: Basic Books, 1973.

Geras, N., "Post-Marxism?" *New Left Review* 163 (May/June 1987), 40-82.

Giddens, A., *Central Problems in Social Theory: Action, Structure and Contradiction in Social Analysis,* London: Macmillan, 1979.

The Constitution of Society: Outline of the Theory of Structuration, Berkeley: University of California Press, 1984.

The Consequences of Modernity, Cambridge: Polity Press, 1990

Gill, L., "'Like a Veil to Cover Them': Women and the Pentecostal Movement in La Paz," *American Ethnologist* 17, no. 4 (Nov. 1990), 708–721

Goldenstein, L., "Rambo vem aí," *Novos Estudos CEBRAP*, no. 26 (1990), 39–43.

Gouvêa Mendoça, A., "Um panorama do protestantismo brasileiro atual," in *Sinais dos tempos: tradições religiosas no Brasil*, ed. L. Landim et al., Rio de Janeiro: ISER, 1989.

Gramsci, A., *Selections from the Prison Notebooks*, trans. Q. Hoare and G. N. Smith, New York: International Publishers, 1971.

Gremillion, J., ed., *The Gospel of Peace and Justice: Catholic Social Teaching Since Pope John*, Maryknoll, NY: Orbis Books, 1976.

Gutiérrez, G., "Notes for a Theology of Liberation," *Theological Studies* 31, no. 2 (1970), 243–261.

A Theology of Liberation: History, Politics and Salvation, Maryknoll, NY: Orbis Books, 1973.

The Power of the Poor in History, Maryknoll, NY: Orbis Books, 1983.

On Job: God-Talk and the Suffering of the Innocent, Maryknoll, NY: Orbis Books, 1987.

The Truth Shall Make You Free: Confrontations, Maryknoll, NY: Orbis Books, 1990.

The God of Life, Maryknoll, NY: Orbis Books, 1991.

Habermas, J., *Knowledge and Human Interests*, trans. J. Shapiro, Boston: Beacon Press, 1971.

Legitimation Crisis, trans. T. McCarthy, Boston: Beacon Press, 1975.

"Modernity – An Incomplete Project," in *Postmodern Culture*, ed. H. Foster, London: Pluto Press, 1985.

The Philosophical Discourse of Modernity: Twelve Lectures, trans. F. Lawrence, Cambridge, MA: MIT Press, 1987.

Haddad, S., "Educação popular e cultura popular,' *Tempo e Presença*, no. 220 (1987), 14–16.

Harvey, D., *The Condition of Postmodernity*, Cambridge, MA: Basil Blackwell, 1989.

"Flexibility: Threat or Opportunity?" *Socialist Review* 21, no. 1 (1991), 65–77.

Hegel, G. W. F., *The Phenomenology of Mind*, trans. J. B. Baille, New York: Harper and Row, 1967.

Hennelley, A., ed., *Liberation Theology: A Documentary History*, Maryknoll, NY: Orbis Books, 1990.

Santo Domingo and Beyond: Documents of the Historic Meeting of the Latin American Bishops Conference, Maryknoll, NY: Orbis Books, 1993.

Hewitt, W. E., *Base Communities and Social Change in Brazil*, Lincoln: University of Nebraska Press, 1991.

"Popular Movements, Resource Demobilization, and the Legacy of Vatican Restructuring in the Archidiocese of São Paulo," *Canadian Journal of Latin American and Caribbean Studies* 18, no. 36 (1993), 1–24.

"CEBs and the Progressive Church in Brazil: What Comes Next?" paper presented at the XVIII International Conference of Latin American Studies Association, Atlanta, Georgia, March 10-12, 1994.

Hinkelammert, F., *La fé de Abraham y el edipo occidental*, San José, Costa Rica: DEI, 1989.

Hoffnagel, J., "The Believers: Pentecostalism in a Brazilian City", Ph.D. dissertation, Indiana University, 1978.

Hopenhayn, M., "Postmodernism and Neoliberalism in Latin America," *Boundary 2* 20, no. 3 (Fall 1993), 93–109.

Hortal, J., "Panorama e estatísticas do fenômeno religioso no Brasil," unpublished manuscript, 1990.

IBASE (Brazilian Institute of Social and Economic Analyses), *O mercado de trabalho em Nova Iguaçu*, Rio de Janeiro: IBASE, 1988.

Inter-American Development Bank, *Economic and Social Progress in Latin America: 1991 Report*, Washington, DC: Inter-American Development Bank, 1991.

Ireland, R., "Catholic Base Communities, Spiritist Groups, and the Deepening of Democracy in Brazil," in *The Progressive Church in Latin America*, ed. S. Mainwaring and A. Wilde, Notre Dame: University of Notre Dame Press, 1989.

Kingdoms Come: Religion and Politics in Brazil, Pittsburgh: University of Pittsburgh Press, 1991.

"The Crentes of Campo Alegre and the Religious Construction of Brazilian Politics," in *Rethinking Protestantism in Latin America*, ed. V. Garrard-Burnett and D. Stoll, Philadelphia: Temple University Press, 1993.

"Pentecostalism, Conversions, and Politics in Brazil," *Religion* 25 (1995), 135–145.

Jameson, F., "Postmodernism, or the Cultural Logic of Late Capitalism," *New Left Review*, no. 146 (July-August 1984), 53–92.

John Paul II, "A Pressing Hunger for Bread and Justice," *Origins* 21, no. 21 (October 31, 1991).

"Opening Address to Fourth General Conference of Latin American Episcopate," *Origins* 22, no. 19 (October 22, 1992).

Johnson, P., *Pope John Paul II and the Catholic Restoration*, New York: St. Martin's, 1981.

Johnstone, P. J., *Operation World*, Kent, UK: STL Books and WEC International, 1986.

Jornal da Tarde (São Paulo), various issues.

Jornal do Brasil (Rio de Janeiro), various issues.

Kant, I., "An Answer to the Question: What is Enlightenment?" trans. L. W. Beck, in *Postmodernism: A Reader*, ed. P. Waugh, London: Edward Arnold, 1992.

Kirkpatrick, D., ed., *Faith Born in the Struggle for Life*, Grand Rapids, MI: William Eerdman, 1988.

Kloppenburg, B., "Influjos ideológicos en el concepto teológico de 'pueblo,'" in *Otra Iglesia en la base*, Rio de Janeiro: CELAM, 1984.

"O Marxismo na Igreja. Entrevista com Dom Boaventura Kloppenburg," interview by J. A. Dias Lopes, *Veja* (Rio de Janeiro), January 9, 1985, 3–6.

Kontopoulos, K., *The Logics of Social Structure*, Cambridge: Cambridge University Press, 1994.

Krischke, P. J., "Church Base Communities and Democratic Change in Brazilian Society," *Comparative Political Studies* 24, no. 2 (1991), 186–210.

Laclau, E., "Politics and the Limits of Modernity," in *Postmodernism: A Reader*, ed. T. Docherty, New York: Columbia University Press, 1993.

Laclau, E. and C. Mouffe, *Hegemony and Socialist Strategy*, London: Verso, 1985.

'Lado ocidental," *Veja* (Rio de Janeiro), May 23, 1990, 17–18.

Lalive D'Epinay, C., *El refugio de las masas. Estudio sociológico del protestantismo chileno*, Santiago, Chile: Editorial del Pacífico, 1968.

Lancaster, R., *Thanks to God and the Revolution: Popular Religion and Class Consciousness in the New Nicaragua*, New York: Columbia University Press, 1988.

Life is Hard: Machismo, Danger, and the Intimacy of Power in Nicaragua, Berkeley: University of California Press, 1993.

Lash, S. and J. Urry, *The End of Organized Capitalism*, Madison: University of Wisconsin Press, 1987.

Lechner, N., "A Disenchantment Called Postmodernism," *Boundary 2* 20, no. 3 (1993), 122–139.

Lehmann, D., *Democracy and Development in Latin America: Economics, Politics and Religion in the Post-War Period*, Philadelphia: Temple University Press, 1990.

Lernoux, P., *Cry of the People: The Struggle for Human Rights in Latin America – The Catholic Church in Conflict with U.S. Policy*, New York: Penguin Books, 1980.

The People of God: The Struggle for World Catholicism, New York: Viking, 1989.

Levinas, E., *Totality and Infinity: An Essay on Exteriority*, Pittsburgh: Duquesne University Press, 1969.

Levine, D. H., *Popular Voices in Latin America Catholicism*, Princeton: Princeton University Press, 1992.

Libânio, J. B., *A volta à grande disciplina: Reflexão teológico-pastoral sobre a atual conjuntura da Igreja*, São Paulo: Paulinas, 1984.

López Vigil, M., "Los cristianos y la iglesia ante el colapso del comunismo y la derrota del Sandinismo," *Amanecer*, no. 69 (1990), 32–35.

Löwith, K., *Meaning in History*, Chicago: University of Chicago Press, 1949.

Lukács, G., *History and Class Consciousness*, trans. R. Livingstone, Cambridge, MA: MIT Press, 1971.

Lyotard, J. F., *The Postmodern Condition: A Report on Knowledge*, Minneapolis: University of Minnesota Press, 1984.

Macedo, C. C., "CEBs: Um caminho ao saber popular," *Comunicações do ISER* 9, no. 35 (1990), 23–29.

McFerren, W., "The Politics of Bolivia's Economic Crisis: Survival Strategies of Displaced Tin-Mining Households," in *Unequal Burden: Economic Crises, Persistent Poverty, and Women's Work*, eds. L. Benería and S. Feldman, Boulder, CO: Westview Press, 1992.

McGuire, M. B., "Religion and the Body: Rematerializing the Human Body in the Social Sciences of Religion," *Journal for the Scientific Study of Religion* 29, no. 3 (1990), 283–296.

Maduro, O., *Religion and Social Conflict*, Maryknoll, NY: Orbis Books, 1982.

"A desmistisficação do Marxismo na teologia da libertação," *Comunicações do ISER* 9, no. 39 (1990), 55–72.

Mainwaring, S., *The Catholic Church and Politics in Brazil, 1916–1985*, Stanford: Stanford University Press, 1986.

"Grass-roots Catholic Groups and Politics in Brazil," in *The Progressive Church in Latin America*, ed. S. Mainwaring and A. Wilde, Notre Dame: University of Notre Dame Press, 1989.

"Grassroots Popular Movements and the Struggle for Democracy: Nova Iguaçu," in *Democratizing Brazil*, ed. A. Stepan, New York: Oxford University Press, 1989.

Mandel, E., *Late Capitalism*, London: Verso, 1975.

Mannheim, K., *Ideology and Utopia: An Introduction to the Sociology of Knowledge*, New York: Harcourt, Brace & World, 1936.

Marcom Jr., J., "The Fire Down South," *Forbes*, October 15, 1990, 56–71.

Marcus, G. and M. Fisher, *Anthropology as Cultural Critique*, Chicago: University of Chicago Press, 1986.

Mardones, J. M., *Modernidad y Postmodernidad (I). Posmodernidad y Cristianismo (II). Un Debate Sobre la Sociedad Actual*, Montevideo, Uruguay: CLAEH, 1987.

Marins, J., *Metodologia emergente das comunidades eclesiais de base*, São Paulo: Paulinas, 1980.

Mariz, C. L., "CEBs e pentecostalismo: Novas reformas da religião popular," *Revista Eclesiástica Brasileira* 51, no. 203 (1991), 599–611.

"Religion and Coping with Poverty: A Comparison of Catholic and Pentecostal Communities," *Sociological Analysis* 53 (1992), S63–S70.

Coping with Poverty: Pentecostals and Base Communities in Brazil, Philadelphia: Temple University Press, 1994.

Mariz, C. and L. D. Guerra Sobrinho, "Algumas reflexões sobre a reação conservadora na Igreja Católica," *Comunicações do ISER* 9, no. 30 (1990), 73–78.

Martin, D., *Tongues of Fire: The Explosion of Protestantism in Latin America*, Oxford: Basil Blackwell, 1990.

"Evangelical and Economic Culture in Latin America: An Interim Comment on Research in Progress," *Social Compass* 39, no. 1 (1992), 9–14.

Marx, K., "Contribution to the Critique of Hegel's *Philosophy of Right*: Introduction," in *The Marx-Engels Reader*, ed. R. Tucker, New York: Norton and Company, 1978.

Marx, K. and F. Engels, *The Communist Manifesto*, trans. R. and C. Paul, New York: Russell & Russell, 1963.

Mendes de Almeida, L., interview by Renato Machado, April 17, 1991, TV Program, "Noite e Dia.'

Mesters, C. *Defenseless Flower: A New Reading of the Bible*, Maryknoll, NY: Orbis Books, 1989.

Michelini, D. J., J. San Martín, and F. Lagrave, eds., *Modernidad y Posmodernidad en America Latina*, Cordoba, Argentina: ICALA, 1991.

Mingione, E., *Fragmented Societies: A Sociology of Economic Life Beyond the Market Paradigm*, London: T. J. Press, 1991.

Molineaux, D. J., "Gustavo Gutiérrez: Historical Origins,' *The Ecumenist* 25, no. 5 (1987), 65–69.

Novaes, R., *Os escolhidos de Deus*, Rio de Janeiro: Marco Zero, 1985.

"Nada será como antes, entre urubus e papagaios," unpublished manuscript, 1990.

"O Brasil subterrâneo," *Veja* (Rio de Janeiro), July 12, 1989, 98–105.

O'Brien, D. J., "A Century of Catholic Social Teaching," in *100 Years of Catholic Social Thought: Celebration and Challenge*, ed. J. A. Coleman, Maryknoll, NY: Orbis Books, 1991.

Offe, C., *Disorganized Capitalism*, Oxford: Oxford University Press, 1985.

Oliveira, P. R. de, *Religião e dominação de classe*, Petrópolis: Vozes, 1985.

"Comunidade, igreja e poder – em busca de un conceito sociológico de 'igreja,'" *Religião e Sociedade* 13, no. 3 (1986), 42–62.

"Religiões populares," in *Curso de Verão II*, eds. M. Schwantes et al., São Paulo: Paulinas, 1988.

"A igreja dos pobres e a atividade político-partidária," *Cadernos Fé e Política*, no. 2 (1989), 31–49.

"CEBs: Estrutura ou movimento?" *Revista Eclesiástica Brasileira* 50, no. 200 (1990), 930–940.

"Poder e conflito religioso: Uma abordagem sociológica," *Revista de Cultura Vozes*, no. 85 (1991), 16–25.

Oliveira, J. S. de, *O traço da desigualdade social no Brasil*, Rio de Janeiro: IBGE, 1993.

"O Pesadelo de uma bela cidade," *Veja* (Rio de Janeiro), July 18, 1990, 26–33.

"Outro pito de Roma," *Veja* (Rio de Janeiro), October 26, 1988, 108–109.

Paiva, V., *Paulo Freire e o nacionalismo-desenvolvimentista*, Rio de Janeiro: Ed. Civilização Brasileira, 1980.

Peña, M., "The Sodalitium Vitae Movement in Peru: A Rewriting of Liberation Theology," in *Religion and Democracy in Latin America*, ed. W. H. Swatos, New Brunswick, NJ: Transaction Publishers, 1995.

Perani, C., "Novos rumos da pastoral popular," *Cadernos do CEAS*, no. 107 (1987), 37–46.

"Notas para uma pastoral missiónaria," *Cadernos do CEAS*, no. 127 (1990), 74–83.

Pereira de Queiroz, M., *O messianismo no Brasil e no mundo*, São Paulo: Edusp, 1965.

Peritore, N. P., *Socialism, Communism and Liberation Theology in Brazil: An Opinion Survey Using Q-Methodology*, Athens, OH: Ohio University Center for International Studies, 1990.

Perlman, J. E., *The Myth of Marginality: Urban Poverty and Politics in Rio de Janeiro*, Berkeley: University of California Press, 1976.

Pessar, P., "Unmasking the Politics of Religion: The Case of Brazilian Millenarianism," *Journal of Latin America Lore* 7, no. 2 (1981), 255–278.

Peterson, A. L., "Religious Narratives and Political Protest," *Journal of the American Academy of Religion* 64, no. 1 (1996), 27–44.

Pinto, A., "Naturaleza e implicaciones de la heterogeneidad estructural de la América Latina," *Trimestre Económico*, no. 145 (1970), 83–100.

Poggi, G., *Catholic Action in Italy: The Sociology of a Sponsored Organization*, Stanford: Stanford University Press, 1967.

Prandi, R., "Perto da magia, longe da política," *Novos Estudos CEBRAP*, no. 34 (1992), 81–91.

Przeworski, A., *Capitalism and Social Democracy*, Cambridge: Cambridge University Press, 1985.

Puleo, M., *The Struggle is One: Voices and Visions of Liberation*, Albany, NY: State University of New York Press, 1994.

Ramalho, J. P., "Avanços e questões na caminhada das CEBs (reflexões sobre o VII encontro)," *Revista Eclesiástica Brasileira* 49, no. 195 (1989), 573–577.

Ratzinger, J., *The Ratzinger Report*, San Francisco: Ignatius Press, 1985.

Reiley, D., *História documental do Protestantismo no Brasil*, São Paulo: ASTE, 1984.

Richard, P., *Death of Christendom, Birth of the Church*, Maryknoll, NY: Orbis Books, 1987.

Ricoeur, P., *The Conflict of Interpretations: Essays in Hermeneutics*, Evanston, IL.: Northwestern University Press, 1974.

Ritzer, G., "Micro-Macro Linkage in Sociological Theory: Applying a Metatheoretical Tool," in *Frontiers of Social Theory: New Syntheses*, ed. George Ritzer, New York: Columbia University Press, 1990.

Robertson, R., "The Globalization Paradigm: Thinking Globally," in *Religion and the Social Order: New Developments in Theory and Research*, ed. David Bromley. Greenwich, CT: Jai Press Inc., 1991.

Rolim, F. C., "A propósito do pentecostalismo de forma protestante," *Cadernos do ISER*, no. 6 (1977), 11–20.

Religião e classes populares, Petrópolis: Vozes, 1980.

Pentecostais no Brasil, uma interpretação sócio-religiosa, Petrópolis: Vozes, 1985.

"Neoconservatismo eclesiástico e uma estratégia política,' *Revista Eclesiástica Brasileira* 49, no. 194 (1989), 259–281.

"Pentecôtisme et vision du monde,' *Social Compass* 39, no. 3 (1992), 401–422.

Roof, W. C. ed., *World Order and Religion*, Albany, NY: State University of New York Press, 1991.

Rorty, R., *Philosophy and the Mirror of Nature*, Oxford: Basil Blackwell, 1980.

Rossi, A., "Uma experiência de catequese popular," *Revista Eclesiástica Brasileira* 17, no. 3 (1957), 731–737.

Safa, H. I., "Urbanization, the Informal Economy and State Policy in Latin America," in *The Capitalist City*, ed. P. Smith and J. R. Feagin, Oxford: Basil Blackwell, 1987.

Santa Ana, J. de, "Lecture to the National Team of Advisors to the Popular Pastoral Program," CEDI, Rio de Janeiro, 1991.

Scannone, J. C., "Modernidad, posmodernidad y formas de racionalidad en América Latina," in *Modernidad y Posmodernidad en América Latina*, ed. D. J. Michelini, J. San Martín, and F. Lagrave, Cordoba, Argentina: ICALA, 1991.

Schaull, R., "La Iglesia, crisis y nuevas perspectivas," *Vida y Pensamiento* 15, no. 2 (1995), 8–48.

Scheper-Hughes, N., *Death without Weeping: The Violence of Everyday Life in Brazil*, Berkeley: University of California Press, 1992.

Schultze, Q. J., "Orality and Power in Latin American Pentecostalism," in *Coming of Age: Protestantism in Contemporary Latin America*, ed. D. R. Miller, Lanham, MD: University Press of America, 1994.

Schutte, O., *Cultural Identity and Social Liberation in Latin American Social Thought*, Albany, NY: State University of New York Press, 1993.

Scott, J., *Weapons of the Weak: Everyday Forms of Peasant Resistance*, New Haven: Yale University Press, 1985.

SEAF (State Secretariat for Fiscal and Human Settlement Matters), *Atlas fundiário do Rio de Janeiro*, Rio de Janeiro: SEAF, 1991.

SEDOC (Documentation Service), "V encontro intereclesial das comunidades de base do Brasil," *SEDOC* 16 (October 1983), 265–323.

"Dossiê: Crise na Arquidiocese de Olinda e Recife," *SEDOC* 22, no. 220 (1990), 693–747.

Segundo, J. L., *The Liberation of Theology*, Maryknoll, NY: Orbis Books, 1976.

Sepulveda, J., "Pentecostal Theology in the Context of the Struggle for Life," in *Faith Born in the Struggle for Life*, ed. D. Kirkpatrick, Grand Rapids, MI: William Eerdman, 1988.

Serbin, K., "Brazil Bishops' Vote May Mask Future Power Shift," *National Catholic Reporter*, May 3, 1991, 12.

Smith, J. and I. Wallerstein et al., *Creating and Transforming Households: The Constraints of the World Economy*, Cambridge: Cambridge University Press, 1992.

Sobrino, J., *Jesus in Latin America*, Maryknoll, NY: Orbis Books, 1987.

Soto, H. de, *The Other Path*, London: I.B. Tauris, 1989.

Souza Alves, J. C., "Igreja católica: Opção pelos pobres, política e poder – o caso da paróquia do Pilar," MA thesis, Pontifícia Universidade Católica, Rio de Janeiro, 1991.

Stepan, A. ed., *Authoritarian Brazil*, New Haven: Yale University Press, 1976.

Stoll, D., *Is Latin America Turning Protestant?* Berkeley: University of California Press, 1990.

"Introduction: Rethinking Protestantism in Latin America," in *Rethinking Protestantism in Latin America*, ed. V. Garrard-Burnett and D. Stoll, Philadelphia: Temple University Press, 1993.

Swidler, A., "Culture in Action: Symbols and Strategies," *American Sociological Review* 51 (1986), 273–286.

"Tempestade de Areia," *Veja* (Rio de Janeiro), April 29, 1990, 18–21.

Teixeira, F. L. C., *A gênese das CEBs no Brasil: Elementos explicativos*, São Paulo: Paulinas, 1988.

"CEBs: Recriação evangelizadora," *Tempo e Presença*, no. 234 (1988), 30–32.

"CEBs: cidadania em processo," *Revista Eclesiástica Brasileira* 53 (1993), 596–615.

Thompson, E. P., *The Making of the English Working Class*, New York: Vintage Books, 1963.

"The Poverty of Theory, or an Orrery of Errors," in *The Poverty of Theory and Other Essays*, New York: Monthly Review Press, 1978.

Tillich, P., *The Courage to Be*, New Haven: Yale University Press, 1952.

Toennies, F., *Community and Society*, New York: Harper and Row, 1963.

Touraine, A., *The Post-Industrial Society*, trans. F. X. Mayhew, New York: Random, 1971.

The Return of the Actor: Social Theory in the Postindustrial Society, trans. M. Godzich, Minneapolis: University of Minnesota Press, 1988.

Critique de la modernité, Paris: Fayard, 1991.

Troeltsch, E., *The Social Teaching of the Christian Churches*, Chicago: University of Chicago Press, 1967.

Valle, R. and M. Pitta, *Comunidades eclesiais católicas*, Petrópolis: Vozes, 1994.

Van den Hoogen, L., "Benzedeiras within the Catholic Tradition of Minas Gerais," in *Social Change in Contemporary Brazil*, ed. G. Banck and K. Koonings, Netherlands: CEDLA, 1988.

Van Der Ploeg, R., "As CEBs no nordeste," *CECA* 2, no. 8 (1990), 43–60.

"A Igreja dos pobres no nordeste," *Cadernos do CEAS*, no. 132 (1991), 61–71.

Velez Chaverra, N., "As CEBs nos caminhos do espírito", Ph.D. dissertation, Pontifícia Universidade Católica, Rio de Janeiro, 1985.

Velho, G., "A vitória de Collor: Uma análise antropológica," *Novos Estudos CEBRAP*, no. 26 (1990), 44–47.

Vickers, J., ed., *Women and the World Economic Crisis*, London: Zed Books, 1991.

Vigil, J. M., "O que fica da opção pelos pobres?" *Perspectiva Teológica* 26 (1994), 187–212.

Wagner, H., ed., *Alfred Schutz on Phenomenology and Social Relations*, Chicago: University of Chicago Press, 1970.

Wakefield, N., *Postmodernism: The Twilight of the Real*, London: Pluto Press, 1990.

Wallerstein, I., *The Modern World System*, vols. 1–3, New York: Academic Books, 1974–1989.

"Semi-peripheral Countries and the Contemporary World Crisis," *Theory and Society* 3 (1976), 461–483.

Walton, J., "Debt, Protest, and the State in Latin America," in *Power and Popular Protest: Latin American Social Movements*, ed. Susan Eckstein, Berkeley: University of California Press, 1989.

Wanderlay, L. E., *Educar para transformar, educação popular, Igreja católica e política no movimento de educação de base*, Petrópolis: Vozes, 1984.

Willems, E., *The Followers of the New Faith. Cultural Change and the Rise of Protestantism in Brazil and Chile*, Nashville, TN: Vanderbilt University Press, 1967.

Williams, P. J., "The Tambourines are Banging: The Politics of Evangelical Growth in El Salvador," in *Power, Politics and Pentecostals in Latin America*, ed. Edward Cleary and Hanna Stewart-Gambino, Boulder, Co: Westview Press, 1997.

Williams, R., *Marxism and Literature*, Oxford: Oxford University Press, 1977.

Wright, E. O., "Class Analysis, History and Emancipation," *New Left Review*, no. 202 (1993), 15–35.

Yúdice, G., "Postmodernity and Transnational Capitalism in Latin America," in *On Edge: The Crisis of Contemporary Latin American Culture*, ed. G. Yúdice, J. Franco, and J. Flores, Minneapolis: University of Minnesota Press, 1992.

Index

CAMBRIDGE STUDIES IN IDEOLOGY AND RELIGION

Books in the series